Contemporary British Fiction

Contemporary British Fiction

History and the Present

Edited by

Santosh Gupta

Preeti Bhatt

RAWAT PUBLICATIONS

Jaipur • New Delhi • Bangalore • Mumbai • Hyderabad • Guwahati

ISBN 81-316-0098-X

Published by
Prem Rawat for **Rawat Publications**
Satyam Apts, Sector 3, Jawahar Nagar, Jaipur 302 004 (India)
Phone: 0141 265 1748 / 7006 Fax: 0141 265 1748
E-mail: info@rawatbooks.com
Website: www.rawatbooks.com

New Delhi Office
4858/24, Ansari Road, Daryaganj, New Delhi 110 002
Phone: 011 2326 3290

Also at Bangalore, Mumbai, Hyderabad and Guwahati

Typeset by Rawat Computers, Jaipur
Printed at Chaman Enterprises, New Delhi

Our homage to

Professor R.K. Kaul

Contents

Preface

Contemporary British Fiction: History and the Present has been the outcome of the continued involvement in British Literature of several scholars both inside and outside the Department of English, University of Rajasthan. Several faculty members of the Department have written their doctoral dissertations on British writers and literatures and as supervisors of doctoral work they have encouraged young scholars to pursue British writing. These scholars came together in a national seminar on 'Contemporary British Fiction: Challenges to Theory' held in November 2002, organized by the Department of English. With the exciting discussions and academically sound presentations that were made in the seminar the next step was automatically to get the papers published. However for one reason or the other the actual job of getting the papers published could not be taken up till 2006, when a call was sent once again inviting the papers for publication.

While some of the papers are being published in the form they were first presented, some have been revised, and some written afresh. The insights and readings that have gone into the papers are valuable and we are very thankful to each one of our contributors for their cooperation and their patience in letting us take this time in preparing the volume. Above all we thank the contributors for their intellectual support without which the volume would not have been possible.

Time however waits for none and took in its toll one of our very senior, distinguished and respected teachers, Professor R.K. Kaul, whom we lost in March 2003. He had kept himself well-informed on a large number of literary areas and participated in most of the seminars, conferences and refresher courses organized by the Department of English with keen interest. His paper on John Fowles, included in this volume, was written for the seminar on 'Contemporary British Fiction'. Handing over the paper to me when I requested him, he chuckled and wondered when the paper would be published, for, he said, several other papers given elsewhere had just not seen the light of day. We are happy that we have been able to get the paper and the anthology published and to keep our promise with him.

It gives us great pleasure in dedicating this volume to Professor R.K. Kaul, as a homage to his contribution to English Studies in Rajasthan and his influence on generations of students in the Department of English, University of Rajasthan, and as a token of our deep respect for him.

Jaipur
2007

Santosh Gupta
Preeti Bhatt

Introduction

This collection of 23 essays on recent British fiction and its reflections of socio-cultural changes, of innovative narrative techniques and the impact of new critical theories has been an attempt to review and assess some of the major British writers and their works in the post-imperial period. These essays have grown out of the responses to British fiction's remarkable blend of innovation, tradition and style which continues to attract critical attention as well as general readers' interest. In preparing this volume a focus was made on the British society's engagement with its changing political stature in the post-imperial phase, its impact on the social life and the image of nation and the individual. In the period after the brilliant writers like William Golding, Iris Murdoch and Graham Greene, among others, the fictional form, mode and style changed in a very significant manner, reflecting the cultural, political and social theories, criticism, and, more significantly the changing nature of 'nation'.

The post 1970's period saw the emergence of several extremely talented and imaginative writers whose work looks at the life in Britain from newer, different moorings. Political and historical consciousness took a more radical and an overt standing among writers like Graham Swift, Julian Barnes, A.S. Byatt, Angela Carter, Margaret Drabble, Doris Lessing and Caryll Philips. It was felt that there was a vast range of fiction coming from Britain that was intellectually and aesthetically challenging, inviting new critical readings. These essays take up some of the dominant and subterranean themes and issues in the works selected, examining the cultural contexts as well as the inner dynamics of the texts. Debates about national identity, cultural heterogeneity, pluralistic social fabric currently prevailing within the different parts of Britain and between the minority groups are reflected in the novels, short stories and critical opinions of these writers.

If Britain once seemed to be a well-knit, monocultural nation it has increasingly been perceived and also portrayed as a nation divided amongst the sub-cultures, migrant populations and inner fragments, brought together by a policy of multicultural, multi-ethnic, pluralistic nation. The awareness of the shrinking of the nation within its boundaries in the wake of withdrawal from its colonies all over the world made Britain as much a postcolonial state as its erstwhile colonies. Losing its former position as the supreme political power in the world, the country's image had to be reinvented in the new situation. Reverse movement of migrants from its colonies, and many marginalised people from other parts of the world to the metropolitan city, London, and the other important centres of education, business and cultural events in Britain have made an important impact on the definition of Britain in the second half of the twentieth century, while a debate about the nature and construction of the culture goes on in new critical studies and theories. Critics like Bernard Crick believe that 'Great Britain is, ..., a multinational state' (11). The four contending states England, Wales, Scotland and Ireland form the new federal union of Great Britain. Nations across the seas find their representation through the large diaspora from South Asia, West Indies and the Carribean Islands. In the mingling of such disparate identities, Crick argues that Britain has been "as much a 'melting pot' as was the United States" (11). There has been a history of migration of different ethnic and culturally diverse groups all through history, especially in the nineteenth and twentieth centuries as violence and disruptions occurred all over Europe. Crick is among those scholars who emphasize Britain's pluralistic culture. Susan

Bassnett also expresses the view that there is a need to recognise the pluralistic nature of British 'cultures' as Cultural Studies develop in the Critical sphere (xxiii).

The pluralistic, multicultural social world of Britain contains many new and old voices from the centre as well as margins. Fictions coming from within British borders has never before had so many immigrant writers who have openly interrogated the country's political and social institutions, explored the doubts about history and memory. Having entered the British social world the writers and intellectuals on the margins of the mainstream have stretched out the social borders, contributing richly to the critical and literary world. The migrant intellectuals who have made Britain their home have been articulate about their experiences.

The memories of the past move also the sense of the present as writers explore the aftermath of the Raj and the colonial rule. New readings of history by academics, creative writers and film-makers open up several sensitive spots; they bring to surface the submerged currents of violent suppressions, painful losses and change the perceptions of the past and the present. In this context David Punter feels that as a postcolonial state Britain has had to face its own share of anxieties and uncertainties, pain of loss and withdrawal (72). Several novels and films portray both glamour and pain of the colonial period, but there are many writers like Paul Scott, E.M. Forster, Angus Wilson and A.S. Byatt who look at the underbelly of history, the cultural encounters of both the period during and after colonial rule. David Punter says 'postcolonialism is not a constellation to be held only within the so called Third World; it is a global movement - not in the sense of a political movement, but a movement of collective psyche ...' (72). The 'residues of British imperialism', Punter says, continue to disturb the unconscious levels of the psyche of the nation asking for expression. Many narratives are formed of the disclosure of the suppressed emotions of pain, loss and nostalgia.

The formation of the self through a dialectical, non-conformist questioning of social system, myths and even narrative trends, becomes problematic for women writers who have adopted radical feminist political positions. They use subversive strategies to interrogate male construction of knowledge and hegemonic control of social institutions. Heterotopic dialogues within social practices are seen in women's novels as they examine the family, man-woman relationship, and, the imposition of discriminatory gender roles. Doris Lessing's observations of colonial exploitation, of the suppression of female identity within the liberal western world have brought forth in her fiction severe and critical portrayal. Michèle Roberts, Angela Carter, Margaret Drabble and A.S. Byatt deconstruct the institutions of religion, law, literary canon formation, scientific knowledge as modes of male domination over the making of knowledge systems, and, controlling the less empowered 'others'.

Some of these writers/texts have been the subject of multiple readings, reflecting not only the critical interest they evoke, but also the complex richness of the texts. Dialogic texts that allow the hitherto silenced experiences of women become heterotopic as they disperse women's understanding of the world.

This anthology of twenty-three essays has tried to bring together some of the major issues in the works of a selected few British novelists, mainly of the post 70's period. The creative vibrancy of a high quality is observed in their works which invoke different interpretations. The issues of history, form, patriarchy, feminist theory and genre in these works are examined in these papers. Since films are an integral part of the formation of culture so an essay on films has also been included.

Jasbir Jain's 'Imagining the Past: The Native and Not-So-Native Anchorings' takes up the problems related to the reconstruction of the past through recorded histories, individual and collective memories and the multiple perspectives that subvert notions of 'objective' uniform reality. In novels by Graham Swift, and Julian Barnes history is reviewed, leading to questions of origin, nativeness and belonging that disturb the British people in many ways. Jain analyses the boundaries of space and time, old myths and legends in the works of several writers, who offer new viewpoints.

In P.C. Kar's "Narrative Endings" the significance of the 'ending' to a narrative is related to its ontological and metaphysical implications in narrative fiction, and, art in general. Taking on the modernist vision of 'form' in literature and art, he argues for the opening out of the sense of closure into a continuity. R.K. Kaul examines the defamiliarisation and experimental open-ended structure of John Fowles' major novels in his essay "The Absence of Familiar Landmarks in the Novels of John Fowles."

The predominance of essays on women writers in the anthology reflects the greater interest of readers and scholars in Feminist theory and critical practices. Sudha Rai and Krishna Sharma discuss in their papers two different novels by Michèle Roberts, both focusing on Roberts' questioning of prevalent myths and practices that deny women their due position within society and family. Sudha Rai's "Michèle Roberts' *The Book of Mrs. Noah:* Feminist Rewriting" deals with the biblical myth rewritten from a feminist perspective. Krishna Sharma in "The House and the Church in Michèle Roberts' *Daughters of the House*" examines women's search for space in the religious and family relations, their dissatisfaction with the existing norms, practices and exclusion of female self from the religious structures.

The novels and short stories of Doris Lessing have attracted critical attention from Madhuri Chatterjee, Mini Nanda, Manveer Brar and Supriya Agarwal. Madhuri Chatterjee in "Growing Up in Wilderness: African Short Stories of Doris Lessing" examines Lessing's reconstruction of the colonial experiences of African natives and of young white women growing up in Africa. Mini Nanda, in "Doris Lessing's *The Summer Before the Dark and The Fifth Child*", looks into ways of coping with male gaze and female selfhood in these texts. Doris Lessing's awareness of the racial discrimination in the colonial set-up makes her women characters examine colonialization of women within patriarchy also. Supriya Agarwal's "The Multiple Selves of Kate Brown in Doris Lessing's *The Summer Before the Dark*" analyses the disintegrating self of a woman before she reconstructs it by rejecting the patriarchally imposed femininity. To discover the individual self from within several impositions is an important feminist struggle of the twentieth century. Manveen Brar in " 'The Cages People Live in': The Short Stories of Doris Lessing" treats the entrapment of women within marriage, family and motherhood, separately and combined together, and also examines the suppression of female-identity in the mother's role. She looks into Lessing's radical view of motherhood as an inscription of gender discrimination within the space of family.

Women writers employ several strategies to interrogate, subvert, and revert the phallocentric norms of religion, aesthetics and the construction of knowledge. Santosh Gupta's paper "The Search for Authenticity in A.S. Byatt's *The Biographer's Tale*" discusses Byatt's deconstruction of the genres of biography, autobiography and fiction to review the arbitrary nature of such forms. The novel goes into the dissolution of history's icons – mostly men who were great achievers. Sudha Shastri's "*Nights at the Circus:* Multiple Directions in Narratology" treats the use of humour, parody and magic realism in Angela Carter's novel as a means of destabilizing male authority and power in its multiple forms. Rajul Bhargava discusses patriarchy's agents in forming social, cultural hegemony, in her essay, "Patriarchal Agencies and the Agents of Patriarchy: Re-reading Angela Carter's Feminism." Carter demythologizes the representation of women in myths, utopian visions and androcentric literature. Charu Mathur in "Exuberance as a Strategy in Angela Carter's *Wise Children*" explores the novel through the technique which she calls 'exuberance'. In the *Wise Children*, Mathur looks into heritage as a means of interrogating the social values.

Women are usually projected in romances as passive consumers of male fantasies. These 'romances' are examined in the works of Anita Brookner who employs the figure of women writers as the central characters. These characters in a self-reflexive form interpret their own lives with reference to the romances they write for others. Bandana Chakrabarty in "Anita Brookner: A Reluctant Feminist's Fictional World" views the reluctance of Anita Brookner in admitting her criticism of social values relating to man-woman relationship as a feminist standpoint. Shaila Mahan in "Interrogating the 'Self': An Exploration of Anita Brookner's *Hotel du Lac*" focuses on the manner in which women's novels voice the experiences women have within family while trying to find full growth of their creative talent and the difficult processes of such an articulation.

The evolution of form as a mode of dealing with social complexities has been seen in the works of Muriel Spark, who is another well-established British novelist. Preeti Bhatt explores female self-reflexivity in the novels of Muriel Spark; the complex narrative form that is found in many of Spark's novels is examined in her paper "Subversive Narratives in Muriel Spark's Fiction: A Reading of Two Novels." Urmil Talwar in "The Stories Ghosts Tell: Muriel Spark's Short Stories" examines the unusual, peculiar, unrealistic world in Spark's stories, where the perspective and the location of the narrator plays an important role in shaping the story; again the style destablizes the reader's expectations and value system.

Cultural transformations within the English society are examined by Nidhi Singh, Aruna Pandey and Vijaya Singh. Nidhi Singh in "Multiculturalism in Margaret Drabble's *The Witch of Exmoor*" traces the changes during Margaret Thatcher's governance of Britain in the 1980's, and relates the problems of assimilation and alienation within the English society as different ethnic figures enter into an all English family. Aruna Pandey in "The Role of Epiphany in the Novels of Angus Wilson" examines the shift in the liberal culture of England during the 1970's and 80's and the changing sexual norms as reflected in Wilson's novels. Vijaya Singh in "The Aesthetics of Nostalgia in the Films of Merchant Ivory" perceives the films based on E.M. Forster as another window to British culture and art. She analyses the treatment of Forster's novels in films and their employment of nostalgia to explore lost aura and era through the use of setting, scenes and frames in the films.

The postcolonial experiences of the British is seen by Veena Singh in her paper "The Nowhere People: Paul Scott's *Staying*

On". She analyses the complete reversal experienced by the British at their loss of power and standing in a society which they had commanded and ruled until India became free. Ila Rathore in "Shadows of 'Bloody Past and Uneasy Present': Space in Paul Scott's *The Jewel in the Crown*" explores the use of space in Paul Scott's novel to contrast the ambiguous relationship between the Indians and the British at the national level and at the individual level. In "J.K. Rowling and the World of Harry Potter", Joya Chakravarty looks at popular Harry Potter series for children, into the elements within the narratives that have made the novels so liked by both young and adult and analyses how they relate to the real life as lived in the late twentieth century.

It is hoped that the rich variety of issues, styles and fictional modes which are reflected in these essays present an adequate overview of the vitality and creativity that emerges from a study of contemporary British fiction. This fictional world invites more engagement, more readings and more interpretations, and we hope such readings will come forth.

References

Bassnett, Susan. *Studying British Cultures*. London: Routledge, 1997.

Crick, Bernard. *Crossing Borders: Political Essays*. London, New York: Continuum, 2001.

Punter, David. "Fictional Maps of Britain." *Studying British Cultures*. Ed. Susan Bassnett. London: Routledge, 1997.

1 Imagining the Past

The Native and the Not-So-Native Anchorings

Jasbir Jain

I

Harry, the photographer-hero of Graham Swift's 1988 novel *Out of the World,* describes England in the following words:

> England is green and cool and damp and old and crooked. Look at the map. England is like a little hunched-up old lady at the seaside, her back turned towards the rest of Europe, dipping her toe into the Atlantic Ocean and pulling up her skirt round her shrivelled body. She is sitting down because she is no longer steady on her legs ..... You wouldn't believe that she was once a big, plump, bossy Empress .... England is small .... So it will seem England is only a toy country. (*World* 191-192)

In several ways this passage also outlines the main drift of contemporary British fiction where it is no longer the power of ideology or the conquest of space which is projected but an awareness of shrinking spaces. History, for the British, has turned self-reflexive and has entered a phase of introspection. How is history made and who makes it – men, ideas or events – is the underlying probe in these narratives. The idea of an objective reality has been subverted by the surfacing of multiple perspectives and ideological discourses as the metanarratives of power and progress are put under scrutiny. The engagement with adventure and the Empire has yielded place to frames which revolve round the two world wars, the Falkland whimper and even the Vietnam war. The 'native' British writer (as contrasted with the immigrant) is homing in on England and the writing has entered into a dialogue with the nineteenth century, a dialogue which is not merely an expansion or continuation of a tradition but a questioning and a talking back, an exposure and a disagreement of the way it all happened. Tales of individual experience merge into the experiences of a wider community; the individual character is in the background as the overpowering forces of culture and environment, memory and inheritance take over. There is a recurring engagement with Darwinism, the consequent crisis of faith of which we have enough evidence even in the nineteenth century novel, a close look at the prudery and sexual morality of Victorianism, a disillusionment with the notion of progress and also a rejection of the seemingly 'real'. In this last regard there is a questioning of the nature of reality as well as of realism and a move towards plural perspectives, ambiguity and fabulation.

A.S. Byatt in her essay, "A New Body of Writing: Darwin and Recent British Fiction" has commented upon the 'exciting *mongrel* nature of the new novel' as little Britain crosses Europe, Asia, Africa and America in 'splendidly inventive ways' (Byatt, *New Writing* 4, 441). But this crossing is rendered possible primarily because of the postwar spirit of 'inverse colonialism,' a fact which has been observed by Graham Swift in his novel *Ever After* (62), a spirit which has begulfed and affronted the exhausted folk of the old world, a political reality which has literally brought the periphery to the centre with the overwhelming presence of writers like Salman Rushdie, Ben Okri, David Dabydeen, Caryl Phillips, Hanif Kureishi, Meera Syal and Kazuo Ishiguro constituting now mainstream British writing. Boundaries of both space and genre are crossed and new definitions of art begin to emerge. I take two examples: one from Swift's novel *Out of the World* and the other from Julian Barnes's *History of the World in 10½ Chapters* which is a writing back to H.G. Well's *History of the World* (*The Outline of History*, 1920, and *A Short History of the World,* 1922).

In Swift's novel, the narrator-protagonist Harry, is the son of an armament manufacturer who rejects his parental heritage and becomes a photographer and views photography not merely as the art of seen reality but as an art about 'what you cannot see', which makes the unseen visible as only the eye of the camera can take you there. It thus rules out the role of human cognition as a primary and immediate category working on a merely visual level, and goes on to project it as a process requiring participation and effort which facilitate a conceptual perception. Photography enables you to go beyond the visible.

Barnes on the other hand takes up Gericault's painting 'Scene of a Shipwreck' (Jean Louis Andrè Theodore Gericault, 1771-1824, French painter), the making of which is not an extension of the human eye but involves several other faculties of observation, knowledge, selection and judgment. The artist in the process of his work has left out the anguish and the uncertainty experienced by the survivors on the raft, he has also left out their agitation, conflict, starvation and cannibalism, as well as the flickering between hope and fear as these men waited for an unknown and uncertain future (126). He sacrificed veracity to art, the particularity of the Medusa to the universality of the disaster, he gave up the 'monkey-up-a-stick image' offered by reality for the more solid focus of art (131) and transmuting a catastrophe into a painting (137). What then are the gains of art and of truth? How do they differ from reality and veracity? Barnes writes:

> And there we have it – the moment of supreme agony on the raft, taken up, transformed, justified by art, turned into a sprung and weighted image, then varnished, framed and glazed, hung in a famous art gallery to illuminate our human condition, fixed, final, always there. Is that what we have? Well, no, people die, rafts rot, and works of art are not exempt ..... The masterpiece once complete, does not stop: it continues in motion, downhill (139).

Art has both its limits and strengths; it penetrates the visible world with a superhuman sharpness and even as it captures the known in its defiance of mortality, it goes on to acknowledge change and mutability. Bill Unwin in *Ever After* holds on to poetry which in several ways is superior to visual representation because it uses language. Words carry the possibility of change within their meaning and thus deny the possibility of stability (*Ever After* 235). Joseph Brodsky in his essay "The Keening Muse" has observed 'No one absorbs the past as thoroughly as a poet, if only out of fear of inventing the already invented' (Brodsky 351).

As the various narrators or characters struggle with the definitions of art and reality, move between knowledge and bewilderment, they turn to the past, primarily because the answer to the question 'Who am I?' (*Ever After* 232) lies in the past. The past is not merely a cluster of objective facts, it is not history alone but a whole lot of other things: geography, politics, location, travelling and mobility. The act of knowing the past is a complex one.

You may have noticed that I am wary of using the word 'reconstruct' or 'recover'. The title of my paper stresses the faculty of imagination and that too in the continuous tense. The past has to be brought back, lived again not only through perception, lost documents, records, but through a hermeneutic process of remembering and imagining. The narrative as history differs from history as narrative; the demands of each discipline are different as are their attitudes to human lives and events. History records the dominantly articulated perception of events; it is often the history of successes and conquests though in the postcolonial age it is also a history of revisions. History also looks for causal connections and often works in linear directions. It seeks to validate, justify or denounce the happenings of the past in order to locate the attitudes of the present. Narrative is not necessarily interested in cause and effect, it is also not interested in merely recording events. It is interested in employment, in depths and private motivations. It is also interested in interruptions, disruptions and simultaneities. In the last few decades two different kinds of phenomena have occupied considerable attention. First, the debate about the epistemic or truth-telling character of history and second the shift in literary theory from textual approaches to contextual ones indicated by movements such as Feminism, Marxism, New Historicism, Cultural Materialism and Cultural Poetics.

For the historians, narrative implies an imposition of form (as in Gericault's painting), which events in themselves do not have and cannot have. David Carr in "Getting the Story Straight" expands on this widely-held view and goes on to contest it, developing the arguments put forward by Louis Mink and Martin White that narrative is not mere description but the inherent factor in a structure [in his essay "Narrative and the Real World: An Argument for Continuity" (143)]. Real life is not sequential thus continuity in narrative does not necessitate any linearity. What matters is the interaction between storyteller, audience and character. Stories, David Carr points out, are lived in being told, 'The action and sufferings of life can be viewed as a process of telling ourselves stories, acting them out, living them through' (150). To tell the story of a community, 'is simply to continue the storytelling process through which the community constitutes itself and its actions' (Carr quoted by W.H. Dray "Narrative and Historical Realism" 165). As such the narrative moves outside mere mimesis and mere representation to become an act which produces meaning. Stephen Greenblatt's shift from new historicism to cultural poetics also attempts to signify an engagement not merely with facts and chronicles, but with the meaning which they embody. Memory is no longer simply recollection, recovery of lost documents and accumulation of detail. It functions differently. The common point between history and fiction is the engagement of both with situations which constitute the community. In the process of narrativizing this creative writing moves beyond storytelling and narration to become discourse.

Paul de Man refers to two kinds of memory: *Gedächtnis* and *Errinnerung*. The first reflects the kind of memory which recollects, thinks and remembers while the second is an interiorized memory.[2] It may often be dormant, and may not have any perceptible connection with the outer world. The relationship between *Gedächtnis* and *Errinnerung* need not be a 'dialectical one, but could be one of rupture, heterogeneity and disjunction' (Derrida 56). The act of remembering also has a philosophical dimension as Von Leyden has also observed. Memory has an inbuilt delusiveness and has a subjective element in it, thus no 'genuine' memory is possible. The process of remembering is always fragmentary and ordinarily throws up a collage. It needs to be understood that individual perceptions are bound to differ and destablise the nature of 'reality'. And the act of remembering is more often than not conditioned by some bias located in the present. If one works through these issues, it is possible to see how they subvert the arguments projected by a singular concept of 'tradition' or a sense of the past.

Getting back to Paul de Man's categories of *Gedächtnis* and *Errinnerung,* it would be possible to concede that *Errinnerung* can work in different ways, it can work through language, myths, folk culture and racial memories. Taking this further, I would like to locate *Gedächtnis* in temporality and *Errinnerung* in spatiality. This is where the anchoring of the 'native' and the 'not-so-native' writer differs, where the location of the writer in history, political power structures, in terms of physical landscapes, cultural and social spaces (heterotopias) come to the fore. Individual lives are not lived only in historical sequences, they are lived within social constructs, and like Edward Soja one needs to stress the need to ground social analysis in the intersections of history, biography and society. Historical imagination is "never completely spaceless" (Soja 13-14). In *Postmodern Geographies,* Soja goes on to build on the Foucauldian approach to space which concedes it importance both in communal life as well as in the exercise of power.[3]

With the displacement of western hegemony and the idea of universal structures, space has now opened up in multiple ways resulting in the surfacing of subaltern histories, recovery of lost memories and shifting populations and boundaries. I offer two examples to substantiate my point. The first is a piece by Ursula Owen, a German Jew from Frankfurt, brought to England while still a baby, titled "An Apprenticeship in Assimilation". Owen writes:

> Is it justified to feel an exile in a country to which I came at the age of eighteen months? In fact the odd thing is that I have felt so English for so many years ..... It isn't until I am in my twenties that I really begin to understand I am in an important way a foreigner (Owen 100).

But the public code of behaviour which, in the case of an immigrant, demands abdication of the original 'nativeness' for social discourse and this leads to a split life.

The other piece I wish to refer to is by Joan Michelson's "Reconstructions from a Dutch Childhood", which is an extract from a novel about Jews, their persecution by the Nazis, their sense of homelessness and the Holocaust which are all part of both history and memory and which cannot be driven into oblivion. The Jewish experience has become a metaphor for the oppressed and for the dilemma of not-belonging. Caryl Phillips also uses this for his very intense 1997 novel *The Nature of Blood*.

II

With this long prelude, I now move on to a specific consideration of Graham Swift's *Ever After* (1992), Julian Barnes's *A History of the World in 10½ Chapters* (1989) and Caryl Phillips's *Crossing the River* (1993). Each of the novels makes use of multiple discourses which interject into each other, but the dominant modes they use are different. *Ever After,* as the title itself indicates, takes up its central motif from the genre of the fairy tale and turns the accepted ending 'and lived happily ever after' (78) on its head. It reverses the fairy tale of progress, capitalism, industrialization and romance, and instead resurrects the ghost of Hamlet, the pensive prince (5), a symbol of the melancholy man possessed by a death wish, mourning the death of a father. Swift, in an earlier novel *Waterland,* has already used the structure of a fairy tale and its intersection with history., rooting it in the Charles Kingsleyian world of fabulation[4].

Barnes's *A History of the World* uses a satiric mode and debunks the myth of religion, the idea of a just and a merciful god as well as the professed aims of most human revolutions which hope for a fair and equitable world. Caryl Phillips moves away from both the localized experiences in England, and the religious myth of the Judeo-Christian tradition to focus on the image of the archetypal victim. The concerns with history work at several levels and are grounded in space, cultural memory and a sense of belonging or not belonging.

Barnes's *A History of the World* is a history of a series of disasters, floods, hijackings, holocaust, homelessness, shipwrecks, starvation, life-destroying struggles, obsessions with god and with death. The space he uses are often confined spaces – ships, rafts, cells, aircrafts. And one of his narrators is a woodworm whose identity the reader discovers fairly late in the novel. He is a 'stowaway' in Noah's Ark, an ark built to survive the Flood and to continue life thereafter. This was the very real disaster which struck the Judeo-Christian tradition and which in a way defined all future disasters. Favouritism, partiality, inequality, discrimination, violence with the aim of exterminating others, torture, confinement are all there in the story of Genesis as is the tendency to falsify facts. The description of the stowaway's experiences in the Ark reads like a description of the slaveships and the over-crowded trains of Nazi Germany as the Jews were conveyed to the concentration camps and gas chambers and reminds one of other acts of totalitarian control over others:

> A certain level of security was inevitable, and we accepted double-peg locks, stall inspections, a nightly curfew. But regrettably there were also punishments and isolation cells. Someone at the very top became obsessed with information gathering; and certain travellers agreed to act as stool pigeons. I'm sorry to report that ratting to the authorities was at times widespread. It wasn't a nature reserve, that Ark of ours; at times it was more like a prison ship (4).

The Flood, the rescue operation and the aftermath reflect on the underside of history and the allergorical nature of narratives. Religion, like science, has also been hostile to inner man, pushing him into categories and towards self-alienation. Noah and his tribe are held responsible not only for the extinction of many species, extermination of others but also for establishing power relations. In an oblique way Barnes is also hitting out at the theory of evolution and natural selection because those who survive are more often than not supported by forces other than natural strength. From this initial reworking of the Genesis tale, he moves on to the modern-day Arab-West conflict, the politics of Middle East, the European guilt over the holocaust and a whole series of disasters ending up once again in a world where Heaven and Hell have merged together and Hitler roams freely with the very holy.

What finally is history? – it is 'what historians tell us .... One good story leads to another;' stories which overlap, 'strange links, impertinent connections.... We make up a story to cover the facts we don't know and can't accept .... Our panic and our pain are only eased by soothing fabulation, we call it history' (242).

If Barnes traces the history of disasters, Swift follows the map of England closely as he interweaves personal narratives with scientific discourse. The focus is on England – Cambridge, Devon, Wales, Berkshire, Launceton, Cornwall. There are three discourses embedded in the main narrative. The first is Darwin, his theory of evolution and the crisis of religious faith which beset nineteenth century England, which in its turn is projected through Matthew Pearce's *Notebooks* written between 1854 and 1860; the second is the discourse of development, of bridges being built and railway tracks being laid, the saga of progress and the third is the story of Hamlet. The main story is the loss of the paternal figure and the uncertainty surrounding the fact as to who is Bill's father. The father whose suicide he wishes to avenge by converting Sam Ellison, his stepfather, into Claudius, he learns finally is not his father after all. The honor belongs to an engine driver who had died in the war. Together the various narratives put a huge question mark on all that the nineteenth century had valued, projected and stood for. The Hamletian 'to be or not to be' is a central strand which works through Bill's father's suicide, his own retreat into a university lecturership, his suspicion of Sam, and his own identification with Hamlet:

> the fiction of my life ... may as well serve as the fact. I am my father's son, by whose death my life has been so irreversibly moulded. I am who I am. I am Bill Unwin (there, I declare myself !) I am Hamlet the Dane. (160)

Other intertextualities also work through the whole gamut of British literary tradition and the tales of betrayed love and sacrifice for an ideal – Dryden's *All for Love,* Dido and Aeneas, Launcelot and Tennyson's *Idylls of the King*, Chaucer's *Troilus and Cressida*, all of them surface somewhere or the other.

Caryl Phillips, like Ursula Owen, came to England as a baby of few weeks. His anchorage is not in nineteenth century England or the Christian myth but in the inarticulateness of people on the margins – slaves in *Crossing the River* (1993) and Jews in *The Nature of Blood* (1997). Spanning a period of two and half centuries – from the mid-eighteenth century to the present – it is about the sale and purchase of human beings, about the deprivation which pushed people into it and the greed which rendered it possible, it is about the religious exploitation by missionary societies who used converts to spread their message; and it is also about the manner in which the hypocritical stance of the civilizing mission worked against the very values it professed to uphold. There are four different narratives, interconnected through the repetitive pattern in human relationships and by the impulse for freedom which possesses the exploited. The first narrative is about Nash Williams, the model slave who has been sent to Liberia by the American Colonization Society and who values this return to the land of his ancestors for it is here alone that persons of color can enjoy their freedom (18 Also see 61). The other narratives are about the dispersed family in other lands and times. But the question which are of significance are why does Nash then recede into pagan ways, why does he take four wives and move out of the Christian faith?

Partly because he finds no sustenance from his masters in his new task, and partly because of racial discrimination 'I soon found myself effectively shunned by my fellow Americans'. He is disillusioned because slave factories were opening up within the territory of Liberia matching the white man's hypocrisy with his invasion. In *The Nature of Blood* Phillips works through Jewish aspirations, their struggle and persecution, the self-enforced captivity in attics and basements, identification through the yellow star, the terror of ever present death, break up of families – all which raise questions about belonging and nationhood. The camps are impersonal and inhospitable, crowded with strangers and dead and broken bodies bereft of all human warmth and love.[5] Both the novels present histories of victims and are narratives which reverse the tale of success and progress.

What role does history play in the writing of these writers, what determines the relationship between history and fiction, between event and plot and between understanding and imagination? What sense do the writers wish to make of these events or the meaning they wish to convey?

I am not quite sure whether they are all legitimate questions to ask of literature, but they certainly have a relevance in a larger context. History is not simply their raw material, instead the engagement with history indicates a concern with conditions of the present and its roots in the past. These novels signify a serious attempt to understand the present reality and to move towards a repositioning. Nostalgia has given way to a deep sense of disillusionment as temporal and spatial pluralities work together. Individually they arrive at approximations of individual truths, together they present a statement of human failure and of the failure of the agenda of western civilization. Does this signify the end of meaning or a new realization of truth as the multiple discourses allow the possibility of a humanistic discourse to resurface and new definitions of fictional constructs to emerge? In some ways locations haven't changed as time and again human conditions, feelings, sufferings and responses constitute the staple of our concern but what had changed is the way we reconstruct the past, the way we interpret and relate to reality and the meaning of 'meaning'. Our expectations from art have changed, and the processes that go into its formation have changed as locations, despite increased human mobility, become significant. Graham Swift's anchoring in native England is an significant as Phillips' journeys into the past and his adoption of the metaphor of the eternally dislocated.

Notes

1. See Edward Soja's comments on John Berger's play *A Question of Geography* and his volume of prose and poetry titled *And our faces, my heart, as brief as photos*. Soja goes on to discuss Berger's views on narration (Soja 21-24) and emphasizes the relationship between time and space.
2. Paul de Man "Sign and Symbol in Hegel's Aesthetics," quoted by Jacques Derrida, *Memoires of Paul de Man* 51.
3. Refer Michel Foucault's essay "Of Other Spaces" first published in 1967, an essay which Soja also discusses in his *Postmodern Geographies* (16-19). Soja goes onto discuss the relationship between history and geography – historical geography in short. Space is "fundamental in any form of communal life" just as it is "fundamental in any exercise of power." Location, interstitial spaces, social positionings and discourse all are significant components in the events which go to make history.
4. See Jain "From *Water Babies* to *Waterland*" and also Andrej Gasiorek's *Postwar British Fiction: Realism and After*, 1995. My (Jain's) article differs on several counts from Gasiorek's observations and was written independently of his views. It was presented at a seminar at Chandigarh in early 1995, though published in 1996.
5. The idea of a homeland is important to Phillips and he turns to it in both *The Nature of Blood* and *Crossing the River*. The slave and the Jew both represent the permanently dislocated categories for whom the return to the original home is impossible.

References

Barnes, Julian. *A History of the World in 10½ Chapters* (1989) London: Picador in association with Jonathan Cape, 1990.

Brannigan, John. *New Historicism and Cultural Materialism*. London: Macmillan, 1998.

Brodsky, Joseph. "The Keening Muse". *Literature in the Modern World*. Ed. Dennis Walder. Oxford: Oxford University Press. 1990.

Byatt, A.S. "A New Body of Writing: Darwin and Recent British Fiction". *New Writing* 4. Eds. A.S. Byatt and Alan Hollinghurst. London: Vintage in association with the British Council, 1995.

Carr, David. "Getting the Story Straight" *The History and Narrative Reader*. Ed Geoffrey Roberts. London: Routledge, 2001.

Carr, David. "Narrative and the Real World: An Argument for Continuity". *The History and Narrative Reader*. Ed. Geoffrey Roberts. London: Routledge. 2001.

Derrida, Jacques. *Memoires for Paul de Man*. Translated by Cecile Lindsay, Jonathan Culler, and Eduardo Cadava. New York: Columbia University Press, 1986

Dray, W.H. "Narrative and Historical Realism". *The History and Narrative Reader*. Ed Geoffrey Roberts. London: Routledge, 2001.

Gasiorek, Andrej. *Postwar British Fiction: Realism and After*. London: Edward Arnold, 1995.

Himmelfarb, Gertrude. *Darwin and the Darwinian Revolution*. London: Chatto and Windus, 1959.

Jain, Jasbir. "From the *Water Babies to the Waterland*: Swift's Fairy Tale/History", *Occasional Papers*: Research Journal Punjab University, 1996.

Lerner, Laurence. "History and Fiction" *Literature in the Modern World*. Ed. Dennis Walder. Oxford: Oxford University Press. 1990.

Michelson, Joan. "Reconstructions from a Dutch Childhood". *New Writing 4*. Eds A.S. Byatt and Alan Hollinghurst. London: Vintage in association with the British Council, 1995.

Owen, Ursula. "An Apprenticeship in Assimilation" *New Writing 3*. Eds Andrew Motion and Candice Rodd. London: Minerva in association with the British Council, 1994.

Patterson, Glenn. "Homelands". *New Writing* 4. Eds. A.S. Byatt and Alan Hollinghurst. London: Vintage in association with the British Council, 1995.

Phillips, Caryl. *Crossing the River.* London: Picador, 1993.

Phillips, Caryl. *The Nature of Blood.* London: Faber and Faber, 1997.

Soja, Edward W. *Postmodern Geographies: The Reassertion of Space in Critical Society Theory.* Jaipur: Rawat Publications, 1997.

Swift, Graham. *Ever After.* London: Picador, 1992.

Swift, Graham. *Out of The World.* London: Picador, 1988.

Swift, Graham. *Waterland* (1983) London: Picador in association with William Heinemann. Ltd. (1984) 1992.

Walder, Dennis, ed. *Literature in the Modern World.* Oxford: Oxford University Press, 1990.

White, Hayden. "Introduction to Metahistory". *Literature in the Modern World*. Ed. Dennis Walder.

2 Narrative Endings

Prafulla C. Kar

The topic of my reflection today is the problem of narrative endings. To talk of a novel as if it has a life of its own and, by implication, death, is to address the question of not only the death of the novel as an art-form, as Ronald Sukenick and John Barth have done, but of the notion of fictional closure within the narrow compass of its teleological logic. The word "end" is somewhat complex in its connotations. It is immediately associated with death and its various ancillary effects like completion of a journey, the fulfillment of a desire, the inception of a crisis, and the sudden disruption of a long process not yet completed. So one can see in ending, whether real or fictional, a strange paradox of fulfillment and anticipation. The other implication of the word "end" has something to do with its objective, goals. When someone asks, 'what is the end of life?' he is evidently asking about its expected goals, its philosophical dimension. In other words, he is asking about the desired objective of life lived. This objective has something to do with one's conduct in daily life, which will, cumulatively, result in the final evaluation of his life, either in human or in transcendental terms. So in a similar way, when one is confronted with the problematic of fictional endings, one is, implicitly or explicitly, caught up with these complex questions about closure, dislocation, crisis, fulfillment and anticipation.

This topic has aroused considerable interest among theorists concerned with narrative forms. But it is also a philosophical topic with wide-ranging connotation. In "Four Quartets" T.S. Eliot places it in a complex philosophical debate about what constitutes the epistemic status of the end of a process. Here are the celebrated lines:

> What we call the beginning is often the end
> And to make an end is to make a beginning.
> The end is where we start from.
> ....
> Every phrase and every sentence is an end and a beginning,
> Every poem an epitaph.

Eliot here seems to be conflating the beginnings with endings in order to suggest that history (which is a narrative) is to be understood as 'timeless moments.' He does not define time in temporal terms, but spatially. Time, according to him, is defined in terms of intensity, not range. That is why he says that a beginning can as well be an ending in so far as its experiential depth is concerned; an ending in a similar way may not be taken as the completion of a process, but its renewal. How could one then conceptualize a narrative? Conventionally, a narrative follows a neat pattern of a development from a beginning through middle to an end. This is how Aristotle defined the process of a narrative, and provided a basis for understanding the structure of a work of art.

The Aristotelian notion of a structure corresponds to the classical notion of time as an impending possibility, gradually unfolding toward a moment of finality. It was assumed that it had a fixed origin, although it was not possible to locate it. Thus there was in classical thought a belief in the origin of an event in a transcendent point exterior to human experience. But it was a conceptual invention necessitated by a desire to perceive harmony in the universe. An origin was always thought of as a generative moment; it gave a thrust to an action and pushed it forward to its *telos*. From the vantage point of the *telos* one could look back on the entire process in order to make sense of it. So, the argument goes, a beginning always looked for its ending. The internal logic of the structure of a work of art depended upon this insight. This argument implied that complexity of a system could be understood in terms of the constitutive roles of the parts played in organizing its totality.

Eliot's point in the above lines is a reflection of a debate in the discourse of modern art about the organization of time in a work of art. How would one, for example, correlate the time of the story with the time of the narrative? But that is a topic for another occasion. Here I am interested in discussing the problem of narrative endings and its epistemological implications for the art of storytelling. This problem, however, is not a simple one involving the time and place for ending a work; it concerns the whole range of philosophical attitudes to the notion of eschatology and temporalization of space. A novelist, more than any other artist, is deeply concerned with this problem.

The organization of time in narrative in spatial terms has been the most important concern of the avant-garde writing encouraged and promoted by Modernism. Joseph Frank, in his essay "The Spatial Form in Modern Literature" (1945), speaks about the innovative aspect of the technique of "spatial form" deployed by such writers as Flaubert in the agricultural fair scene in *Madam Bovary* and Djuna Barnes in *Nightwood*. He took his cue from similar use by G. Wilson Knight in his study of Shakespeare's play in *The Wheel of Fire*. Wilson Knight distinguishes between "criticism" and "interpretation" and prefers the latter as a new technique of reading in which a work is perceived to be organized around a few striking images and metaphors spread across it and are connected in space, not necessarily chronologically. It should not, however, be construed that Wilson Knight completely discards the efficacy of sequential reading; on the contrary he feels that both ways of reading are equally valid and need to be understood as mutually complementary. 'One must be prepared,' he suggests, 'to see the whole play [Shakespearean] in space as well as in time' (3). 'A Shakespearean tragedy is set spatially as well as temporally in the mind' (3). Although this kind of approach does not seem as radical as it is later made out to be, it does give a new direction to the act of reading and indicates the saliency of such an approach to the project of modernity in the West.

Wilson Knight develops his interpretive strategy by emphasizing the value of spatial connectivity more than that of development of plot through time. Such a method of reading would enable one to mark the wholeness of a work through the projection of its various constitutive parts on a vast space perceived from a convenient height. Joseph Frank further develops this approach in his well known essay mentioned above, and later engages in a spirited debate with his critics, most notably with Frank Kermode and reiterates the validity of his reading strategy to the study of modem as well as postmodern literature. By comparing a literary text with painting, Frank suggests that no work of art is complete in itself, but is part of extended associations not confined to the immanence of the text in question. In other words, the textuality of a text is not encapsulated within the text but is spread beyond it so that works created by the same author or produced in the same period are connected with one another subliminally and spiritually. The phenomenological critics like Georges Poulet and J. Hillis Miller utilized this perception of the uncanny linkages among texts established through spatial filiations. In his "Phenomenology of Reading" Poulet describes an experience in which he felt intuitively the threads of commonality among several paintings of Tintoretto that he had seen in an exhibit in Venice. His interpretive eye could mark instantly in the various paintings on the wall how they are connected with one another in an ineffable way. This is an example of spatial approach to reading and interpretation taken to its lyrical height. This is also a way of demonstrating that an act of interpretation tends to transform temporality to spatiality so that the scope of its process gets enlarged. Frank outlines in his essay the complex intertwining of language, structure of the narrative and the perception of the reader in the act of interpretation. But the perception of the reader seems to get the upper hand in the process, because it is the reader who always perceives the wholeness of a work of art: from its disparate parts through what he calls his 'reflexive reference.'

The theoretical and practical implications of the spatial mode of interpretation are far-reaching. As I have suggested earlier, this approach was made at the height of Modernism in order to justify the relevance of the narrative style of avant-garde writing and to undermine the teleological logic of mimesis. This critique of the mimetic mode of representation was perhaps necessitated to celebrate the decline of the imperious mode of fiction developed self-consciously to support the hegemony of the imperial power. The disenchantment with realism and the corresponding emphasis on the aesthetics of inner experience highlighted by Modernism brought about a significant change in the outlook of both the creative writers and critics, which resulted in various kinds of technical innovations including the attempt to slow down the pace of the narrative in order to achieve higher density of psychological effect. The novel tried to achieve the same kind of concentration as the painting without closing itself off at the end of its story. Gerard Genette, the French structuralist critic has built an elaborate theory on the structure of narrative in the light of 'ut figura poeisis.'

The reason why I began my talk on narrative endings via a detour of Joseph Frank's notion of spatiality is to situate the debate on endings on the controversial domain of space as a substitute for temporality in the framework of a novel. It is generally assumed that, with the emergence of Modernism on the literary scene, the old notion of time as sequence determining the plot of a narrative was made obsolete. The classical notion of mimesis had provided the basis for realism and naturalism in fiction, but the linkage between the world and the text began to be disrupted in the beginning of the twentieth century with the world war and subsequently with other catastrophic events. As the artist began to rely upon his inner resources and on the self-referentiality of language his links with the world began to be snapped. So the work he produced as an artifice of pure imagination needed a new way of conceptualization. Frank's notion of spatiality did serve such a purpose and was a timely product.

Let us examine a little more closely this notion and its implications for studying narratives. By replacing temporality of plot with spatiality of structure Frank brought about a new orientation in thinking about the nature of narrative. In the older notion of plot the emphasis was on progression of character and plot through complications toward a point of resolution at the end. Thus the story seemed to move on predictable lines toward its closure. The closure was more a psychological condition than a mechanical ending. The beginning was the generating force which propelled the action to its ending. Thus one could say that the beginning was proleptic and the ending was analeptic. The entire plot of the novel was encapsulated within this closed form. With the end of the novel the expectation of the reader seemed to have come to an end.

By turning from this kind of mode of linear narrative to a painterly spatial canvas Frank and his associates have expanded the logic of the narrative beyond its graphic boundary to the circumambient space outside. History and time are not negated, but are re-configured in the changed perspective. The past incidents return to the canvas as streaks of memory overlapping the present and intermingle with the contingent experiences in dialectic interplay of association. In other words, time is transformed into space, or, to put it more concretely, the fragments of time are sprinkled across the range of space and lose their sequential demarcations. The experience of epiphany, which is used by Joyce and Proust, is one such mode of transformation. The language games that the authors play in the new narrative become continuous exercises of combinations and permutations and transcend the designated boundaries of the work. By freezing time and activating space these writers have suggested that a narrative is an endless possibility.

Frank's justification for the spatial approach to narrative involves his penchant for turning fiction into myth. The earlier mode of temporality was part of the fictional paradigm, with beginning, middle and end; the new mode is mythical in the sense of its totality of representation through the simultaneous assemblage of constituent parts. But the word "myth" employed by Frank has become the point of controversy among critics. Frank's notion of spatial form is a way of turning the timely aspect of history into the timeless world of myth. He says that the characteristic quality of modern literature is its 'transformation of historical imagination into myth – an imagination... which sees actions and events of a particular time only as the bodying forth of eternal prototypes.' In his sharp reaction to Frank's notion of myth as the core aspect of spatiality Frank Kermode distinguishes between fiction and myth and calls the latter an ossified idea divorced from the living reality of everyday experience. Fiction, for him, is a necessary act through which a writer or a critic comes to terms with his crisis, whether it is apocalyptic or otherwise. Echoing Wallace Stevens, he says that a man all the time creates fictions in order to make his life worth-living in the face of a crisis: 'So the prisoner invents a clock, the shadow cast by a gable on a wall which he can see through the fretted glass of his high window. Time cannot be faced as course and actual, as a repository of the contingent; one humanizes it by fictions of orderly succession and end' (160). The key expression here is, 'one humanizes it [time] by fictions.' This is what Lear tells Cordelia: 'Let's sing like birds in the cage, and mock the gilded butterfly.' Kermode believes that time should not be reified into a myth and turned into a frozen metaphor; it should be humanized through supreme fictions of order and pattern and be harmonized into the everyday experience. He finds fault with the notion of spatiality on the ground that it tries to kill time by arresting its flow and submerges the contingent into the abstraction of the eternal. To him this amounts to be a form of totalitarianism.

One of the ways, according to Kermode, to 'humanize' time and to make it a living part of one's experience is to create fictions of beginnings and endings and thereby to avoid the oppressive monotony of successivity. He gives the example of clock's "tick tock" to suggest that the two sounds here are ways of psychologically responding to the progression of an event. Between the beginning and ending one seems to create a little room for order and lives by it. This is a human need and is satisfied by creating little rooms in fiction. That is the reason why both Judaism and Christianity created fictions of the End, Apocalypse and Deluge so that we know that our end is not very far. The utopias and dystopias serve this purpose too through futuristic projections of prophecy. It is not the end, but the "sense of an ending" that makes life worth living. The fluidity of time needs to be appreciated and utilized for shaping human desire and hope, but should not be arrested. There is both a religious and psychological justification for this, and Kermode bases his argument in his *The Sense of an Ending* on this premise. In a highly lyrical passage Kermode celebrates the notion of eschatology as both a religious and secular need:

> End is a fact of life and a fact of the imagination, working out from the middle, the human crisis... We need ends and *kairoi* and the *pleroma*, even now when the history of the world has so terribly and so untidily expanded its endless successiveness. We re-create the horizons we have abolished, the structures that have collapsed; and we do so in terms of the old patterns, adapting them to our new worlds. Ends, for example, become a matter of images, figures for what does not exist except humanly. Our stories must recognize mere successiveness but not be merely successive; *Ulysses*, for example, may be said to unite the irreducible *chronos* of Dublin with the irreducible *kairoi* of Homer. In the middle, we look for a fullness of time, for beginning, middle, and end, in concord (60).

Kermode pits chronicity of clock time with *kairoi* of psychological time in order to create a dialogue between them so that they get interlaced with each other and shed their oppositional stances. In the myth celebrated by Joseph Frank time is transformed into the timeless and becomes a fixed abstraction. Kermode employs the Thomist expression of *aevum* (time of the angels) to suggest that even the so-called timeless beings as angels recognize the effect and need of time. Fiction as a mode of representation of reality brings together the chronicity of human beings with the *kairos* of angels and participates in the living process of experience without attempting to transcend it. That is why beginnings and endings are desirable fabrications, supreme fictions by which life becomes meaningful. Kent's poignant question in *King Lear* 'Is It the

Promised End?' seems to sound familiar and happily resonant in the context of our eschatological reflections.

But the end that we imagine and construct in fiction remains an elusive phenomenon, never fully realized. It only remains a wishful fantasy in its tantalizing possibility. In his essay "The Problematic Ending in Narrative" J. Hillis Miller seems to confront both Frank and Kermode on the question of narrative endings and argues that however one may wish to reach the end of a novel in the psychological sense, one will not succeed, as the ending continues to remain chimerical. By invoking Aristotle he says that the notion of "complication" in a narrative problematizes the whole notion of beginnings and endings. 'The tying/untying, the turning point, is diffused throughout the whole action. Any point the spectator focuses on is a turning, which ties and unties. This is another way of saying that no narrative can show either its beginning or its ending. It always begins and ends still *in medias res*, presupposing as a future anterior some part of itself outside itself' (4).

Miller sees the ending as problematic because the narrative does not close off there but creates a fresh condition for a beginning. What seems to him as unraveling of a story at the end of complications turns out to be another complication:

> The word ravel already means unravel....To ravel up a story or to unravel it comes to the same thing....In a similar way, no novel can be unequivocally finished, or for that matter unequivocally unfinished. Attempts to characterize the fiction of a given period by its commitment to closure or to open-endedness are blocked from the beginning by the impossibility of ever demonstrating whether a given narrative is closed or open. Analysis of endings lead always, if carried far enough, to the paralysis of this inability to decide (7).

Here Miller has raised an epistemological question about how one comes to know that the ending has arrived. The ending of a work of art should not be confused with the point where the book literally closes with the printed word 'end.' Although there is a mechanical need to stop the work at some point, the narrative, however, may continue in the mind of the author or the reader, or at least the expectation for a new beginning is generated in the mind of the reader. When Huck Finn leaves the charge of the rescue of Jim with Tom and 'lights out the territory ahead of you' he seems to be tempting the reader to expect a new story interlocked to the old. Despite Kermode's argument for an expected ending of a narrative in consonance with the desire of the reader, the ending actually never occurs in the true sense of the term. But Kermode does not seem to be dogmatic in his notion about ending and implies that ending is not a fixed attribute in the mind of the reader but acquires its character and shape in response to the contingencies of experience. This idea seems to be similar to Miller, although to Miller ending is more elusive than it appears to be. To Kermode, ending has some substantiality, but to Miller it is an aporia caught up in the perpetual enigma of dispersal and possibility.

Thus I want to conclude here with a rather tentative note suggesting that the notion of narrative closure is more a structural myth necessitated by a desire for an epistemic fulfillment rather than a condition for an ontological logic of the text. Both Kermode and J. Hillis Miller seem right in their suggestion that ending is a possibility and a chimera respectively. Thus at one level a narrative seems to close off; at another level its so-called closure is in fact a new beginning and thereby its proliferation.

References

Frank, Joseph. "Spatial Form in Modern Literature." *Sewanee Review* 53 (Spring, Summer, Autumn 1945).

Frank, Kermode. *The Sense of an Ending: Studies in the Theory of Fiction.* London: Oxford University Press, 1966.

Knight, G. Wilson. *The Wheel of Fire: Interpretations of Shakespearian Tragedy.* London: Methuen, 1949.

Miller, J. Hillis. "The Problematic Ending in Narrative." *Nineteenth Century Fiction*, Vol. 33, No. 1 (June 1978), pp. 3-7.

3 *The Book of Mrs. Noah*
Theory and Practice in Feminist Rewriting

Sudha Rai

The opening up of discourses of knowledge motivated by postcolonial, feminist or poststructural enterprises is an important development for the academic fields of history, sociology, and literature. Feminists amongst other marginalised groups and races have been at the forefront of such enterprises, interrogating the master narratives of creation or the homogenized and closed patriarchal knowledge systems hitherto accepted uncritically. An interesting and powerful literary experiment in challenging the nexus between religion and patriarchy supporting the Judeo-Christian world is Michèle Roberts' feminist rewriting of the biblical story of Noah and his ark. Her novel *The Book of Mrs. Noah* voices a counter discourse to the portrayal of the relationships in the Biblical story, questioning the representation of a benevolent God, the father, who saves Noah and a few chosen others from the Flood.

My paper shows firstly, how *The Book of Mrs. Noah* by the contemporary British woman writer, Michèle Roberts, is a feminist rewriting of Genesis in amplifying the suppressed female voices in the original narrative, according them the power to contest knowledge and truth. Male protagonists are deflated to unheroic dimensions or exposed in their anxieties and weaknesses.

Secondly, I enquire into the ways in which Roberts' novel invokes the feminist ideology of Virginia Woolf's canonical text, *A Room of One's Own*, and then rewrites its ideological and aesthetic resolution of 'androgyny' especially for women writers. The paper illustrates the convergence of theories drawn from oral narratives, Western feminist theory and the formation of Lacan's hypothesis of the value of the 'mother' to the formation of the authentic 'self', and its reworking in feminist theory. Finally, I offer some observations on the problematic of feminist rewriting in the postmodernist genre, as the insistence of the former on battling 'difference' in terms of 'masculine' and 'feminine' offers a challenge to the thrust of postmodernist writing on destabilizing meaning.

A few comments on the Noah story in its other versions as oral narratives, prior to the Old Testament version, are pertinent here. The biblical Noah and the flood story are now shown by current researches in the area to be a reworking of an older story or stories, with variants that are culture-specific. Thousands of years before this ark was built, we are told, for instance, that an ark was built by the Sumerian Ziusudra. In Babylon he was called Uta-napishtim, the only mortal to become immortal. In Greece he was called Deucalian who repopulated the earth after the waters subsided, with the help of his wife Pyrrha and the great goddess of the waters, Themis.

'Prepatriarchal religion acknowledged the female presence in every part of the cosmos,' as Adrienne Rich states in her discussions on "The Primacy of the Mother," (Rich: 1986). The supremacy of the female mother in the earlier story cycles is evident, as it is the Great Mother, who for causing the destruction of humanity punishes the god who causes the flood. However the reference to the great mother is erased in the biblical version: God the father, who is supreme, enters into a covenant with Noah who faithfully executes god's instructions for building the ark and endures the phases of waiting that lead up to their being saved. Another important aspect in the older story cycles affirming the primacy of the mother is the symbolic representation of the birth of a New World. The Indo-European peoples accepted the idea that: 'a watery chaos would swallow up the world at the end of its cycle, out of which a new world would be reborn in the womb of the formless mother. The ark and its occupants represented for them therefore the seeds of life passing through the period of Chaos from the destruction of one universe to the birth of the next.' (Still: http://2think.org)

I

By inventing a full-fledged persona for Mrs. Noah, rather than the skeletal reference to her in the Genesis, Michèle Roberts situates another perspective on the flood and the nature and existence of God, supporting Mrs. Noah's interrogation (67) of the representation of god the father in Genesis: "God the Father wanted Order. So he invented heterosexuality, monogamy and the family." Roberts suggests through the rewritten context of the events, which precedes god's injunction to Noah, that Mrs. Noah's version of the story is perhaps more convincing than the biblical version. Roberts' sketches the gendering of Mrs. Noah as a girl, her submission to her husband, Jack, and her private religious communion with a non-threatening, non-punitive god through a sensuous openness to nature. Unlike Noah, Mrs. Noah, who is intuitive, understands the implications of the Flood in its positive and life-affirming interpretations, as the renewal of a new world and not as a disaster visited on humankind by a punitive god.

Roberts also fleshes out the character of Noah's daughter-in-law, Sara who conceives, and carries through her pregnancy to term while they are confined to the ark. The conversations between the two women build in the dimensions of female relationship and female psychology in the context of Sara's pregnancy. 'Sara is someone I can really talk to', says Mrs. Noah. The rewritten content of the Noah story attempts not only to rewrite history by situating women as participants within it – (though the Bible's validity as a historical document is unresolved to date) – but also, to question the absolutes of an autocratic, punitive and limited male leadership which endorses gendering and excludes women from the fight to think, imagine and express themselves.

Roberts chooses the modern-day protagonists of her novel, a couple, whom she names Noah. Repetition of names suggests continuity from the ancient to the modern Everyman and Everywoman, and all the gender issues that surround male-female relationship in marriage. Noah, a busy executive in a pharmaceutical company, works at his research and takes his wife for granted. Mrs. Noah, a librarian, who accompanies her husband to a conference in Venice, is faced with the tedious prospect of engaging herself for two months while her husband attends the conference, and later, pursues his research in Italy. Her crying need to have a child – unvoiced to her husband for the last two years (and her fears about the unknown perils of motherhood) trouble her, as she knows Noah is resistant to becoming a father and will not take on responsibilities or give up his individual life for the child.

Mrs. Noah, the librarian, therefore engages herself with a fantasy: 'I need work to do. I need books. I'll invent a library' (18) she decides. She invents an Ark, renames herself as its arkivist, and sends out a letter of invitation telepathically to five sibyls, whom she also invents. The sibyls are separate from the well-known sibyls of classical mythology of ancient times. Mrs. Noah's sibyls are named as the Re-vision sibyl, the Deftly sibyl, the Babble-on sibyl, the Correct sibyl and the Forsaken sibyl. Each sibyl is an aspiring writer, in crisis because of the roles she is playing out as a result of marriage, divorce, motherhood, or single parenthood, with divergent attitudes to the roles that she is required to play as a woman. The social contexts of the novel belong to contemporary Western society and confront the dis-ease with the feminist issues of female sexuality and trapped creativity, along with the grassroots problems of the economic needs of women and their need for security. The sibyls on the ark have all their needs taken care of. Free to write once again, the only condition for them on the ark is that each of them will tell stories. 'Can one of you tell us a story about a mother?' asks one female persona (141).

The satire on masculinity is built up by Roberts, when a male character called the Gaffer, turns up uninvited in Mrs. Noah's ark.

He is in a crisis since he has written nothing after the Bible and wants to glean some tricks of the trade from the women writers. The Gaffer, whom Roberts clearly indicates to be a persona for god, as also a symbol for the male writer in general, in his exchange with the women writers opens up many issues pertaining to the new feminist awakening which has left the male with a crisis of identity. The gender issues of masculinity and femininity of the 1980s in Britain are thrown up by Roberts, and are shown to be confusing and irreconcilable.

II

It is necessary to consider in the context of a feminist rewriting, the other important intertextual frame in Roberts' novel -Virginia Woolf's 1927 work, *A Room of One's Own* – and the theory that informs it. Problematising the issues of women's economic need, dependency, need for private space and recognition of selfhood obliterated by patriarchal consent, Virginia Woolf singled out the specific contribution of women writers. She saw this as being the ability to portray women in an expanded manner against the portrayals by men that were limited and distorted. Further, she had asserted the woman writer's capacity to present features of men that men are unable to see for themselves. A third advantage was their ability to depict relationships between women for, as Woolf points out, men have virtually portrayed women only in relation to men. Accepting Woolf's dictum that women writers can capture 'those unsaid or half-said words which form themselves when women are alone', Michèle Roberts constructs a postmodernist feminist metafiction that deploys the language of the Unconscious as a feminist discourse of the self. A room of one's own is resituated as an ark of one's own, a refuge and an enabling space for a community of women who want to be wanderers, a dream-fantasy space that can work out the transition to a new world through the action of writing, replacing the 'thinking process' in Virginia Woolf's text with dream as a form of thought.

Theorising 'fantasy,' Rosemary Jackson (1981) states 'An understanding of the subversive function of fantastic literature emerges from *structuralist* rather than from merely *thematic* readings of texts. It has been seen that many fantasies from the late eighteenth century onwards attempt to undermine dominant philosophical and epistemological orders. They 'subvert and interrogate' (175) nominal unities of time, space and character as well as 'questioning the possibility, or honesty of re-presentation of those unities' (176). The function of fantasies in Jackson's thesis is 'to set up an opposition to the capitalist and patriarchal order which has been dominant in western society over the last two years.' Fantasy also aligns itself with all those forces, which threaten to disrupt a tradition of rationality.

Employing the mode of a feminist fantasy then, Michèle Roberts' Mrs. Noah depicts the struggle of the woman writer to find the environment or make one, (in Virginia Woolf's terms), conducive to the genius who seeks expression. The five sibyls emphasize in the stories they tell that despite a certain success as women writers, their anxieties continue to resolve around securing their own inviolate space, away from the madding world of men and children, and, the countless claims on their bodies. The feminist consciousness and the intertextual frame of *A Room of One's Own* are used as a refrain to signal the text's ideology that it is women who can best interpret themselves – not men. The ideal of androgyny theorized in *A Room of One's Own* for the woman writer, ('poetry ought to have a mother as well as a father') is cast aside and the ideal desired psychological state is that of child-mother bonding, the pre-oedipal merging of self, theorized by Freud and reinterpreted by Lacan.

III

The Book of Mrs. Noah is a slithery and slippery text, literally and metaphorically. The process of discovery of selfhood for Mrs. Noah, especially, is worked out through the agency of water. Plunging into the waters at Venice, she takes a dream journey on the ark, returning with the narrative of her past. The dammed-up reservoir of a woman' s unconscious breaks through in the stream of consciousness narrative of the five sibyls and Mrs. Noah, pouring out the sedimentation of their oppression and grief, desire, a longing for love, creativity, and an erotic pleasure, as the serpentine narrative, suspended between dream and reality unfolds. Many women's lives are narrated and within each woman there exists a multiplicity of selves. The text is a choral expression of the diverse possibilities representing the onward flowing current of these women's lives.

The reality of dreams frames *The Book of Mrs. Noah* and all attempts at writing by women writers. The dream sequences in the novel are significant feminist texts read even on their own and dreams are read as 'a form of unconscious communication with oneself'. Ignes Sodre and A.S. Byatt in their conversation on 'Dreams and Fictions' (Swift 1995), distinguish between 'mythic dreams', which have both 'universal and perhaps a private significance,' and " another kind of dream [in which] the dreamer is wrestling with family, relationships or relationships amongst people known, or half-known. The latter variety of dreams that are almost like, 'hypotheses, or explorations of hidden feelings or judgements' (231) say 'if I said this to them what would they do?' The novel opens with a dream dreamt by Mrs. Noah, in which Noah is struck down by lightning. In a parodic rejoinder to Christian belief that Eve was created out of Adam's rib, Mrs. Noah dreams that Noah is ripped out of her side, and she is free of the coupling that denies her selfhood. The dream in its sub-textual interpretation calls upon Mrs. Noah to separate herself from the masculine controls of her husband. Alas, however, the dream is but a dream. Noah is not dead and the novel that slides in and out of the biblical Noah story and that of the modern-day develops an allegory of the afflicted relationship between men as lawgivers and women as their subordinated selves. The potential appeal of Venice as a romantic landscape which excites passion, is aborted with Noah's controlling presence, so that Mrs. Noah who would like to explore the city in her own terms comments: 'I lose all sense of direction. Venice loses me' (10).

Michèle Roberts rewrites another dream for the biblical Mrs. Noah, a dream that inscribes metaphorically the procreative dimensions of a woman's body on the future of the world. The earth is depicted as a woman in labor and the breaking of her waters is the alternative explanation provided for the Flood. Whereas Jack (a name given to the biblical Noah) had interpreted the same dream as a portent of disaster saying, 'god has warned me that he is about to destroy the world,' other interrogations of the master narratives of Creation follow.

The modern Mrs. Noah's ark is fitted out like a modern luxury liner – with a library, a kitchen and vast spaces where each sibyl can fulfill her desire to write. Food, a material reality which Virginia Woolf critically examines in *A Room of One's Own* in order to build up her thesis of women's poverty and men's wealth, is related by the Re-vision sibyl to a new context – language: 'Language is as changeable and delicious as food, coming from outside to her inside.'

While the biblical Mrs. Noah had cooperated with Noah's and god's plan by boarding the ark, Roberts shows how the modern Noah refuses to do likewise when *she* makes a plan to take a journey on the ark: 'I argue that it is time to board the ark, to make the voyage. Noah promised to accompany me. Now he says that he has changed his mind. It is too soon. He is not ready. He is not sure he'll ever want to come with me,' (7) summing up the masculine fear, and the masculine resistance to women's choices and the initiative taken by them.

The narrator is catapulted into her journey of self by a glimpse of her grandmother in a third dream sequence. She runs frantically after her. She is led to an ark moored in the lagoon and aborts (as we are led to think at this stage in the narrative) – her husband's attempt to stall this important transition in her life, by jumping into the waters of the canal. 'If I have my grandmother's blessing I can leave for the ark without too much fear,' she says... 'I need my ancestor at my back' (14). Specific matrilineal guidance comes to the narrator from her grandmother: 'Get on with you, you story teller. Become a journey woman. Build your ark. Sail off in it. Get going...' 'You've got to invent your own life. Its up to you' (14).

As a postmodernist text, the alternative matrilineal tradition is again destabilized, as another grandmother figure, or another type of grandmother, this time a cold and discouraging one is also posited by the author as another distinct possibility. Mrs. Noah self-reflexively comments, 'It could also happen like this.' The journey into the depths of her unconscious is enacted as the process of going down in a lift. 'I take the lift down inside myself, pressing the button marked Help. I drop past floor after floor of memory, down past death, down to the bottom floor of the unconscious,' Mrs. Noah writes. Roberts also incites the reader into exploring a variety of alternative images and symbolic meanings in the ark. 'What kind of ark do I want?' Mrs. Noah asks herself, replying – 'I'll invent a library' (18), designating herself Arkivist of the ark. The Ark is an all-women's library. 'Every woman who has ever lived has deposited here her book'(20). It also has a chapel. 'The ark is not only an archive: it is a rest home that swims, a workshop that floats, a bubble of temporary retreat for women who need time to write away from their families and domestic cares.' The reversal of the hegemonic appropriation of space by the male canon is wittily stated, Men's books are of course available on inter-library loan (20).

The alterations that have come up in women's history is suggested in the varied lives the sibyls lead .The Deftly sibyl wants to leave her husband as 'living with George, in George' s space, at George's rhythm, it is impossible to concentrate properly on her writing.' The Re-vision sibyl, a writer of short stories for women's magazines is a divorced woman with a daughter, getting maintenance from her husband, currently in a lesbian relationship with her lover. She switches creative modes, from writing to cooking. The Babble-on sibyl would rather write than go to church on a Sunday morning, resorting to subterfuges to achieve this end. Churches frighten her since her baby died and she has constant dreams of death.

The Forsaken sibyl has been rejected by her lesbian lover Julia and is plunging herself in work, confronting loss. The fifth sibyl, the Correct sibyl, a journalist dealing with the issues of women and violence, a disciplined writer, churning out a thousand words a morning is now confronting a drying up of her creativity. She knows however that in the modern, capitalist industrialized scenario 'she must stay on the production line, produce the season's new variety, special offer' (30).

Do women write differently from men? The entry of the Gaffer, an uninvited male guest aboard the women's ark is Roberts' strategy for considering the question of gender, sex and its relationship to writing. While the Gaffer refers to himself as the speaker of the word of god, author of the Bible, the women dismiss this self-styled designation, but permit him to stay aboard. As the Re-vision sibyl says: 'So why not let a man in, as an experiment? It might be interesting to match our writing against his, and to see to what extent they're different' (51).

For Mrs. Noah the ark becomes a space for finding the unity of her self, 'Here in my arkive on the ark, mind and body are not split' (210). The ark of the present and the story cycles of the past come together as receptacles which bear the seeds of a new life – a new self for Mrs. Noah, of a burst of renewed creativity for the writers who occupy that space. The depictions of women writers and their ambitions, offer a suitable rejoinder to the distorted perception of that male student who in the past had taunted Mrs. Noah saying, 'You cold virgin sitting cooped up in the library reading mediaeval love songs, how can you understand them when you know nothing of sex' (210).

The Book of Mrs. Noah rewrites feminism by working in poststructuralist theories of uncertainty of meaning and postmodern metafictional positions on authorship and narrative endings. An important chapter of the novel describes the conversation between the sibyls, Mrs. Noah and the Gaffer about the tensions in man-woman relationships cast in the register of postmodernism. 'I want to be the author of my own story' says the Forsaken sibyl, 'and of my own life...yet if I become a narrator and tell a story I'm talking about something that's over, something that ends. I can't bear endings' (217). Asks the Babble-on sibyl: 'What will I have to break in order to change my situation? Will I break too?' (218). The Gaffer raises issues for the menfolk, asking 'What about the men who love women but are rejected by them?' The Gaffer serves as a symbol for the uncomprehending male, unwilling to surrender a power that he feels is being rapidly appropriated from him 'These days he broods, male writers don't stand a chance.' The existential crisis of god the father in the figure of the gaffer is sounded out 'Terror pokes him in the back of his knees. Where did I come from? How did I begin?' he asks (239).

The writer figures in the novel are advocates of the psychoanalytic theories of Freud and Lacan especially, and there are acknowledgements of the major intellectual upheavals of the twentieth century, from Marxism to Deconstructionism, alongside the intertextuality of Feminist theories, whose seams of ideas and debates have made a break with the old world in one sense.. Despite these movements which analyze the exploitation of the marginalised however, patriarchal controls persist in most societies.

IV

A new formation for recovering the mother is constituted in the act of feminist rewriting combining the perspectives of oral narrative, specific cultural and historical positions, psychoanalysis and feminist theory. Michèle Roberts endorses the values of bonding with the mother symbiotically, and in our dream states. 'My first ark is the woman's body,' as one woman character says. Michèle Roberts connects the Freudian-Lacanian thesis of the father as Law who disrupts the pleasure of the infant-mother bonding, applying Lacan's thesis to the imaging of the patriarchal father – both God and Noah. Writing too is your mother, for through it you give birth to yourself, as Mrs. Noah discovers. *The Book of Mrs. Noah* is an agonized search for a unification of self, coming from women who long to situate themselves within their bodies and their language, discovering a deconstructed women's sub-text in language that confers selfhood and thwarts the Lacanian sense of alienation where the self is ultimately a fiction. Rejecting Woolf's agenda of androgyny – for Roberts erases the masculine in women – *The Book of Mrs. Noah* is a representation of the search for creativity and mother bonding within traditions of female spaces. While language and reality may not enjoy a synchronous relationship as signifier and signified in the conscious mind, in the unrepressed, ungendered depths of the unconscious mind and in dream there lies a way out of the alienation of the self.

A feminist rewriting employs personifications that serve women, such as the sibyls. The lives narrated show us the huge gap between the actual and desired status for women in society and rejects thereby the idealistic philosophies circulated in society. The attempt is to rectify knowledge frameworks from their very root.

Women's fantasies are a form of dialogue with the repressed self – they constitute a form of imaginative action which strengthens the self. The woman is both the speaker and the listener in these fantasies (rewritings) – unlike other social communicative spaces where she is silenced – as she structures her self to combat denial in any form. 'I want to tell a woman's story. I want to create a woman's voice' (192-93) says one of writers in *The Book of Mrs Noah*. 'Meditating on the Old Testament, then discarding it, she will write a new text with herself as the subject that speaks.' (214). While Noah, the conference man, compiles his statistics, his wife writes herself into a fantasy. Choosing water as the channel for a woman 's rebirth, the novel intertextualises the ideas and issues of plural feminisms, written from the perspective of and in the context of British feminism, in issues relating to the 'contemporary' such as shared parental care or alternative sexual orientation.

Feminist rewriting marks a power shift observable in the conferring of a separate, strong identity on Mrs. Noah who is no longer an extension of Noah. The text analyses the condition of the female subject trapped within family structures. It erases patriarchal values and rewrites the lineage of the mother in values and beliefs. However, British women novelists reflect the fragmentation of the woman's movement in 1980s with disquiet. The 1980s is a period in the U.K. when 'women's rights are under attack and suffering increasing erosion...the abolition of the universal maternity grant (replaced by a means tested payment);

the unsuccessful anti-abortion bill introduced by David Alton; and clause 28 of the local govt. act which, effectively making discrimination against lesbians and homosexuals, seeks to prevent the public funding of their organizations, thus endangering the survival of the lesbian help-lines and support groups...' (*The Guardian*, 6 April 1987, quoted in Pauline Palmer).

V

Finally, some observations on the mutations effected on the postmodernist novel through the genre of feminist rewriting. Postructuralist approaches to language, in one sense, aid and abet the feminist agenda by emphasizing the constructed nature of reality, patriarchal reality included. The rewriting of history critiques and expands the homogenized symbol of *woman* into a multiplicity of realities, approving the diverse routes a woman wishes to explore for her fulfillment. Pauline Palmer refers to 'the radical shift in theorization of motherhood and mothering in feminist thought.'

The theme of motherhood is approached from perspectives ranging from rejection of motherhood because of its burdensome aspects, to viewing the mother as the tool of patriarchy in socializing children into traditional roles, to a reappraisal of motherhood, viewing it as a privileged woman's territory that must not be surrendered.

In the feminist theory propounded by the French school represented by Hélène Cixous, and Julia Kristeva there is a theorization of 'the connections between writing, femininity, and pr-oedipal states problematising the *ecriture feminine* – writing with inspiration in the body originating from the mother's voice' (Pauline Palmer 1989). Eagleton (1996) in his analysis of Kristeva's theoretical positioning writes: 'It is important to see that the semiotic is not an *alternative* to the symbolic order, a language one could speak instead of 'normal' discourse; it is rather a process within our conventional sign-systems, which questions and transgresses their limits.' Fantasy and dream can serve as forms of experience emancipated from rational modes of thought that are seen as essentially male.

The Book of Mrs. Noah finds its center in the conviction that the reality of women can be recorded best by them, only through acts of self-interpretation, denying phallocratic structures the power of representation over them. The narrator dumps once and for all the master narrative of creation, and places herself at the helm of creation. She writes in her diary, 'I was taught that art is supposed to last, to be preserved in libraries and museums, to defy rotting and perishing, to contain eternal meanings that transcend history, that survive the time-span of the body. My art won't be like that. The creation of the world happened in seven days and seven nights. Writing in this diary won't be like that. My creation will be as daily as dusting, or dreaming' (288).

The act of feminist rewriting affirms that the structuralist notion of difference, existing in the terms of gender – 'masculine' and 'feminine' – continues to remain firmly etched and cannot be dissolved even in poststructuralist texts. It is in this sense that feminist texts such as *The Book of Mrs. Noah*, pose a challenge to poststructural theory's denial of mutually exclusive terms or categories. If men cannot see the difference, women will rewrite it.

References

Eagleton, Terry, *Literary Theory*. Oxford: Blackwell Publishers Ltd., 1996.

Jackson, Rosemary, *Fantasy*. London and New York, Methuen, 1981

Palmer, Paulina: *Contemporary Women's Fiction*. New York: Harvester Wheatsheaf, 1989.

Rich, Adrienne. *Of Woman Born: Motherhood as Experience and Institution*. 1976. London; W.W. Norton & Company, 1986.

Roberts, Michèle. *The Book of Mrs. Noah*. London: Methuen, 1988.

Still, James. "Biblical flood," from Barbara Walker *The Women's Encyclopaedia of Myths and Secrets*, http://2think.org.

Swift, Rebecca ed. *Imagining Characters*. London: Chatto & Windus, 1995

Woolf, Virginia. *A Room of One's Own*. 1929. U.K. Penguin Books Ltd, 2002.

4 John Fowles
Two Novels

R.K. Kaul

I regret that there are no challenges to theory in the paper that I am about to present. It is because I am suspicious of the word 'Theory', which I consider to be neither literary criticism nor philosophy. I still recall the sterility of the presentation of Gayatri Spivak, during the Seminar on what was called "Locating-Dislocating Post Colony".

I cannot help remarking that Fowles is only a year or two older than I am. He belongs to my generation. I spent five years of my life in his country, three of them at the same University and yet could not find a single landmark in the novels which reminded me of England. In fact Fowles lives in Lyme Regis, a sea port on the southern tip of Dorset i.e. the Hardy Countryside which I have actually visited.

The reason for the absence of familiar landmarks is not far to seek. Only one major novel i.e. *The French Lieutenant's Woman* (1969) is set in England, the very place in Dorset where he lives; all the other novels, [I have not read *The Aristos* (1965) and *Daniel Martin* (1977)], are allegorical or mythical and have as little relation to contemporary England as Shakespeare's *As You Like It* or *Twelfth Night* had to their time. Indeed one critic relates *The Magus* to the Romance tradition.[1] Another critic points out that Magus is a card in the Tarot pack. Like *The Magus, The Ebony Tower* (1974) which includes *Eliduc* and *Poor Koko, Mantissa* (1982) and *A Maggot* (1985) are all remote from contemporary reality. If *The Ebony Tower* and *The Magus* belongs to the world of romance, *A Maggot* recreates the early eighteenth century with its Quakers, its Dissenters, witchcraft and so on. *Mantissa* is about a patient who suffers from amnesia. His doctor and nurse, both female, practically rape him to awaken his memory. And yet at the end we are left in doubt whether these incidents actually took place inside or outside his mind.

I am happy to say that although I have read around twenty articles and reviews pertaining to Fowles's works I have not come across a single reference to Derrida, Lacan or Lyotard. It was idle to expect that postmodernist jargon would not invade the criticism of Fowels's works but the editor of *MFS,* William Palmer, has dismissed Conradi's book on Fowles because it is riddled with theoretical jargon e.g. "aporetic backwash", "metalepsis", "autarky", "anagnorisis" etc. (*MFS* 8).[2]

I shall focus on only two of the novels, viz. *The French Lieutenant's Woman* and *The Magus.* These happen also to be the most popular. The absence of any familiar landmarks in the former is easily accounted for. It is a pastiche, a conscientious but very readable attempt to recreate the Victorian novel.

The author has put in a lot of research into this re-creation. He tells us that fires were stoked in the kitchen i.e. the fuel used was coal because there was no electricity and hence no cinema, let alone television. The chief source of lighting were candles and gas lamps. There were bathing machines on the beach as in Smollett's time. The modes of transport were trains, trams and landaus. The automobile had not yet been invented. There were no flushing lavatories whose use began in 1900. He even tells us that sheaths made of sausage skins were already in use; hence pre-marital intercourse was the rule rather the exception. The chief pastimes were the game of whist and the organization of balls and concerts. Sun tan had not yet come into fashion. Dandies had given place to snobs. Thackeray is there to confirm that. In the matter of ladies, fashions, there was a revolt against the crinoline and large bonnets.

The author takes great pains to recreate the intellectual milieu of the mid-Victorian period. Many of the Victorian assumptions were being challenged. Marx's *Capital* was to appear in 1867. But revolutionary social ideas were already in the air. The Oxford Movement (1833-45) made a considerable impact on the religious temper of the age. Charles Lyell's *Principles of Geology* (1830-3) proposed that the earth's features had been shaped over a long period of time by natural forces, thus clearing the way for Darwin's theory of Evolution.

Darwin's *Origin of Species* was published in 1859. In this novel there are heated arguments over Darwin between Dr. Grogan and Charles, the protagonist. Apart from such well-known sources of intellectual history, the author also throws light on the social history of the period by quoting from a Commission on child abuse.

To supplement our familiarity with the period, Fowles quotes epigraphs from G.M. Young, the social historian, Tennyson, Leslie Stephen, Marx, Matthew Arnold and the poems of Hardy and A.H. Clough who gave expression to religious scepticism. The word "agnostic" incidentally was coined by T.H. Huxley in 1869. The author tells us that Charles, the protagonist, was an agnostic at heart.

The story itself is the story of the eternal triangle. Charles, the gentleman of leisure whose hobby is paleontology (a hobby shared by the author) is engaged to be married to Ernestina. She is the daughter of a draper while Charles is blue-blooded. Charles is also expected to inherit his uncle's property. Unfortunately the uncle remarries. Ernestina is a mere doll. She has no talent except for spending a great deal of money over dresses. She is completely devoid of any intellectual capacity or aesthetic taste.

We get some idea of the affluence of the upper middle class in the heyday of the British Empire from the fact that Mrs. Poulteney has 13 servants. The reference to Mrs. Poulteney provides the opportunity for introducing the heroine of the novel, Sarah Woodruff who has been employed on compassionate grounds by Mrs. Poulteney.

With the entry of Sarah complications begin. Her character is that of a typical coquette but she is possessed of both intelligence and a wide knowledge of literature. She also has a command of French. She rebuffs Charles the first time he offers to accompany her to the dairy. But she knows that Charles cannot escape from her clutches. On the pretext of a palaeontological expedition Charles goes to the Lyme in the hope of meeting Sarah. This time she is more communicative.

Sarah has, however, concocted a fictitious account of her past. She gives out that she is married to a French lieutenant whose return she expects everyday. In fact her excuse for visiting the harbour every day is that she might find him. She is determined to confess her imaginary past to Charles against his wishes. She even names her seducer.

The next time Charles meets her he succumbs to her charm, lifts her and kisses her. His involvement with Sarah makes him indifferent to Ernestina. He does not even notice her "elaborately seductive dress". Charles hands over his purse to Sarah for financial help and advises her to leave Lyme Regis.

At this point the narrator devises an innovative strategy. He brings the story to a happy end. He informs us that Charles takes up his father-in-law's business and settles down with Ernestina. But then the author changes his mind. He is not satisfied with this ending.

Instead of living happily ever after in wedlock, Charles stops for the night at Exeter, meets Sarah and finally has intercourse with her. Incidentally it is Sarah who contrives on a false pretext to lure Charles. Charles discovers that she is a virgin. The story of her betrayal by the French lieutenant was a fabrication. Charles breaks off his engagement to Ernestina, thus losing the respect he commands in local society.

The author gives another twist to the tale. It appears that Sarah has left Exeter without leaving any address behind. Charles goes as far as Boston in search of Sarah but discovers at last that Sarah has changed her name to Mrs. Roughwood and turned into a New

Woman. In fact she has become a part of the Rossetti household. She has no further use for Charles. On this disappointing note the novel ends. The other novels also end inconclusively. Apart from the author's success in recreating the Victorian ethos his success lies in giving an unexpected twist to the story at every turn. He keeps the reader under his spell – a rare achievement for a modern novelist.

I now turn to *The Magus* (1966), Fowles's most ambitious work. It has also turned out to be popular with the readers like *The French Lieutenant's Woman.*

This novel, unlike the other allegorical fiction of Fowles, is difficult to interpret. The author has given us a confusing variety of clues. It is impossible to follow all of them. He warns us that the novel's alternative title is *The God Game* and adds 'I did intend Conchis to exhibit a series of masks representing human notions of God in ... a series of illusions about something that does not exist in fact, absolute knowledge and absolute power' (10). It is not clear whether human notions are mistaken or such a God does not in fact exist. This metaphysical or theological question will be taken up towards the end of the paper.

Repeatedly he compares Conchis to Shakespeare's Prospero. Prospero too controls the destinies of all the characters in the play. He even casts a spell on the sea and captures his usurping brother and his companions. He begins by colonizing the island and enslaving its original inhabitants, Caliban and his mother Sycorax. He contrives to save Ferdinand from amongst the passengers on the boat which he captures so that his daughter can find a suitable mate. In Shakespeare's world, however, it is understood that Prospero is only playing god and at the conclusion he drowns his book of magic into the sea. Life returns to normal. Besides he practices what is called White Magic. There is no transaction with Mephistopheles as in *Doctor Faustus*.

In Fowles's novel too Conchis is playing at being a god but we are not sure that the belief in God is not itself an illusion. We are warned at the very beginning that an omniscient and omnipotent God does not exist. The key word for an understanding of the author's philosophy is 'hazard' (129). There is no plan behind the universe. Even the word 'universe' is a misnomer. It is in fact a chaos. The question of such a vast mess having been 'created' does not arise. The word 'created' implies a Creator but how could anybody in his senses have created such a mess?

Who then is Conchis? He is a magician who uses both magic and money to play with the destinies of his victims for his own diversion.

From the narrative point of view the story begins with the protagonist Nicholas Urfe migrating to Greece. He gets a job at the Lord Byron School in Phraxos, an island in Greece. He soon discovers an earthly paradise close by in a village called Bourani which is ruled over by Conchis the Magus.

During the war, we are told, Conchis betrayed his country by collaborating with the Nazis. He also ordered various acts of wanton cruelty. It should be mentioned that Marquis de Sade's shadow is cast on the whole novel. There are numerous epigraphs from his works.

Not all the cruelty consists in mutilating human bodies wantonly. Even in human relations there is complete ruthlessness. The characters are narcissistic; they are disillusioned cynics and their professed existentialism is nihilistic.

Although Conchis is called 'The Magus' or the magician he does not use Dr. Faustus's methods of exercising his magical power. He does not need the help of Mephistopheles to carry out his wishes. Instead he uses hypnosis and hypothermic syringes. Thus he arranges sexual affairs between Nicholas and Lily, who is inter-changeable with Julie and June. We know that there are two young and beautiful girls who flirt with him. Nicholas is charmed by the idyllic surrounding and the girls who are willing to play love games with him. They make him forget the Australian girl Alison to whom he had made love before coming to his island. She repeatedly reminds him of her existence.

But once he comes under the spell of Conchis he is subjected to various forms of sadism. What is more, he is invited to view the sadistic games which Conchis organizes for his entertainment. After Nicholas has been fully enslaved by Conchis, and infatuated with Julie, he is cast out to fend for himself. He tries to go back to his first love Alison though he knows she was also in the service of Conchis and had been playing the role assigned to her.

Still he engages in a prolonged search for her, thus reminding us of Charles's search for Sara. The conclusion is similar. Finally when he finds her, she is inaccessible like a priestess from the temple of Demeter. They part. He is left to drift along, like Charles.

The author's emphasis on the word 'hazard' suggests that Fowles, like Lucretius, considers the world to be a product of fortuitous concourse of atoms. There is no purpose or design, no creator, no future to look forward to, no heaven or hell waiting for us.

But beyond the belief in scientific atomism which is morally neutral as science should be, there is an explicit emphasis on sadism and wanton cruelty. From this I extrapolate the author's belief in the malignity of some supernatural force, which is theological in its nature. If God is both omniscient and omnipotent where does the pain and evil in this world come from? Christianity, Hinduism, Buddhism and Islam have all found ingenious but unconvincing explanations for the evil and pain in this world. Only the Zoroastrians recognize that there are two independent sources of good and evil. The Persian and Urdu poets talk of the malignity of the sky and stars. Fowles is not encumbered by any such metaphysical belief. He believes that cruelty is inbuilt in man, without speculating on what its source could be.

Note

1. See J.E. Lewis and B.N. Olshen, "John Fowles and the Medieval Romance Tradition", *MFS*, Spring 1985, 15-30.
2. Ibid. p. 8.

References

Fowles, John. *The French Lieutenant's Women*. London: Janathan Cape, 1969.

—. *The Magus*. 1965.

Lewis, J.E. and B.N. Olsher. "John Fowles and the Medieval Romance Tradition", *MFS*, Spring, 1985, 15-30.

5 The Search for Authenticity in *The Biographer's Tale*

Santosh Gupta

Antonia S. Byatt's novels are elegant entertainments where 'romance' is woven with pastiche, parody and scholarship. Alex Clark in his review of *The Biographer's Tale* (2000) considers the earlier novels like *The Virgin in the Garden* (1978), *Possession: A Romance* (1990), *Angels and Insects* (1992), *Babel Tower* (1996) along with *The Biographer's Tale* as he comments that her novels are full of 'complicated ideas, network of references and endlessly proliferating interrelated symbols and images'. She is recognized as one of the most talented of the present day British novelists as each one of her novels opens up a brilliant world of fabulation and modern sensibility.

Possession: A Romance, her Booker Prize winning novel and *The Biographer's Tale* share an interest in biography's accuracy and reliability. These novels are built upon the interconnections between the observing eye of the biographer and the 'subject' of a biography, between facts, fictions and myths that are constructed and circulate around a person and inevitably enter a biography.

The problems that one faces in the process of re/constructing the persona of someone no longer alive are dramatized in these novels and Byatt uses these interconnections to satirize the rise of the biography industry and the machinations used by academe to exploit the popularity of the form. The elevation of biography from a literary form to an authentic history of a person claiming the objectivity of scientific writing is deconstructed, through an exploration of its traditional devices and inherent uncertainties.

Alongwith a critique of the boundaries of literary genres Byatt also looks into another aspect of modern cultural practices. In most of her novels an important subtext is the making of human knowledge through the methods of scientific observation and the claims of history as a genre to greater authenticity than the other forms of modern discourse. As a literary artist, keenly aware of modern scientific researches, Byatt brings to her novels an involvement with the claims of scientific method, and its dialectics with imagination as a means of knowing the reality.

This dialectic is important for Byatt primarily as she also looks for the ways of knowing the 'other'. The most valuable pursuit for her characters is that of learning about human character. Richard Todd feels that Byatt's engagement with the 'real' world and people 'raises a larger point that has informed Byatt's novel writing from the very beginning which is that (like Iris Murdoch) Byatt explores the battle between 'real people' and 'images' in ways that involve intense scrutiny of the either/or readings of symbolic language' (72).

The danger of real persons becoming only symbols or images when they are seen through diaries, letters and their writings is realized by the two researchers, Roland Michell and Maud Bailey, in the novel *Possession*. They are involved in studying separately, the poems of two Victorian poets, Randolph Ash and Christabel LaMotte. A correspondence between Randolph and Christabel is discovered by these two twentieth century scholars who then begin to see the poets in their human and personal dimensions. This probing into the relationship of the past figures casts its enchantment over Randolph and Maud as they come closer to one another in their own lives. The past figures merge, to some extent, with their personalities and cast a shadow over them. *Possession* playfully depicts the interface between the past and the present, observed and the observer, the text of the letters as a reality and as a literary object. The novel raises issues of the autonomy of the text and the reader's role in recreating it.

With *The Biographer's Tale* Byatt presents in a more challenging manner the reader's role in constructing the text of a 'person'. An erudite writer herself, she uses a lot of material from scientific research on subjects like eugenics, animals in different parts of the world, and phrenology to build up convincing scientific figures. How the world becomes a material for a text, and how it is through 'texts' that we know the world are some of the queries raised as a young man, Phineas G. Nanson in the novel decides to give up a Postgraduate Course in Critical Theory and write a biography.

Phineas gives up the course on critical theory for he finds them too vague, abstract, and repetitive. A simple statement about Shakespeare's play would, in the poststructuralist jargon, result in 'page after page of citations from Foucault (or Lacan or Derrida or Bakhtin)' (4), he observes. He much prefers the simplicity and directness of the language of earlier critics, for he wants 'things' and 'facts' in his life. In the desire to deal with facts, he turns to study a biography and his tutor, Ormerod Goode, assigns him the project of writing a biography.

Phineas starts off on the project by reading a celebrated biography of Elmer Bole, a very well-known scientist, who besides being an explorer, has several other talents and achievements. The author of this biography is Scholes Destry-Scholes who had died a few years ago. Impressed by this biography, Phineas decides to write a biography of the biographer, Destry-Scholes. As Phineas pursues this project the novel *The Biographer's Tale* becomes a palimpsest, using diverse kinds of texts, diaries and details of the material being prepared for new biographies Scholes was planning to write. There is also the material about Scholes' life that Phineas Nanson collects from different sources. These texts within the main text give it a divergence and disjunctedness in which several forms come together: illustrations of bees, flowers, photographs of some of the persons Scholes was writing on – C. Linnaeus, a taxonomist, Galton, a statistician, and H. Ibsen, the playwright, and pieces of Scholes' writings on these persons.

Byatt researches well on the subjects that she selects for any one of her novels, whether it is the language of law, evidence in court and property rights in the *Babel Tower,* the life of Queen Elizabeth I and poets of that period in *The Virgin in the Garden*, and taxonomy, eugenics, writings of Ibsen and the mating habits of bees, beetles and other animals, in *The Biographer's Tale*. The research mixes with other subjects, many voices speak through these subjects, creating a metaficational text, about the writing and readings of literary texts, biographies and other discourses. The novel deconstructs the manners of biographical writing, acts of reading and interpretation through the several biographies that the novel presents.

Phineas Nanson reads first the three volumes of Elmer Bole's biography written by Destry-Scholes. He learns about the manner of material collection, and the method adopted by Destry-Scholes in the composition of the biography. Destry-Scholes had once delivered a lecture on "The Art of Biography" at the Department where Nanson was presently studying. He gets a copy of the lecture from Ormerod Goode, his tutor, and finds the traditional, well-established approach, emphasizing facts, actual events, restraint on the part of the biographer (5). Scholes very clearly forbids the biographer from going beyond the data that he has, for he believes that the biographer should confine himself to the verifiable facts only. Nanson plunges himself into the task and sets off to collect details about Scholes from people who may have known him personally.

Phineas Nanson enters into the pursuit of scholarship, to study the subjects studied by Scholes, and by his subjects – Linnaeus, Galton and Ibsen. The task becomes extremely challenging and confusing, and howsoever much he tries to give shape to the material available to him, he finds himself stuck by doubts about the veracity of his interpretations.

The gradual deconstruction of the art of writing biography raises doubts about the reliability of any biography as such, for Nanson discovers, that, contrary to the claims made by writers, any biographical text requires and contains inevitably some elements of fictionalizing, and also, interpretation in the selection and organization of material. Biography had been elevated to the level of science in its supposed objectivity of the writer and reliance on 'facts'. Biography was one of the most revered forms of writing in the eighteenth and nineteenth centuries deriving its prominence and respectability from philosophy of Enlightenment. In the age that upheld the individual's strength of character as an important mark of a successful man, the biography of a great/successful man became an uplifting text. In the famous biographies details of the struggle against adverse circumstances by the subject (of the biography) were given, actual words spoken by the person were used to provide inspiration to the readers, the classic example being that of Dr. Samuel Johnson's biography written by Boswell. The biographer tried to take down the words spoken by Johnson in his discussions on various subjects and carefully checked the details about his great man's life to write an authentic biography. Boswell has been an important model biographer for later writers. The nineteenth century, being an age of multifaceted explorers, scientists and scholars, became all the more fertile ground for writing the lives of these great persons.

The respect for biography as a means of moral and liberal education was implicitly based on the truthfulness of the text – that all the information and details were true to life. The popularity of the *bildungsroman* in fiction and arts was similarly due to the interest in the growth, development and achievement of an individual as a result of the person's character – character being destiny.

These forms of writing were also based on the idea of a stable, unified personality, a recognizable and stable character. The philosophical concept of commonly shared human sentiments further reinforced the portrayal of the life of a person, outstanding, for any reason so that the readers could emulate and draw inspiration from that personality.

Phineas begins his pursuit of the details about the work and life of Destry-Scholes with a similar belief in the value of biography and the traditional method. He goes to the British Museum, to read the very books Scholes had read, to occupy the chair he had used. He collects his notes and half prepared texts, and sets down to look for the figure of Scholes in all this material. It is when Phineas gets into the act of writing that the process reveals its problems. Writing about another person amounts to recreating him/her from the data, which in itself lacks order, meaning and connectedness. Faced with this Phineas asks the question: 'How one may ask does such a man set about constructing another human being, in some sense *ex nihilo*, an individual who was not there before and now exists, but whose very identity must leave space for the creative puppet mastery of a director ...' (84). The writer as the director controls and gives shapes to the 'other' who has been reduced to the form of a puppet.

Phineas' doubts reflect the postmodernist, and poststructuralist views about the ever shifting and eluding nature of human personality and the textual nature of any re/construction of a personality. Through the gradual loss of faith in the writer's objectivity and image's factuality, the ambition of Phineas begins to get bogged in epistemological doubts. He is not certain that whatever he wrote about Destry-Scholes, would have any reliable degree of objectivity. At this point he recognises the elements of fiction and narrativization that enter into every biography.

Phineas' loss of faith in the historical truthfulness of biography is further aggravated as his research reveals to him the 'lies' that are incorporated into Elmer Bole's life story, and Scholes' own story of his life. He finds that 'the biographer had quite deliberately woven lies and inventions into the dense texture of collected facts.' Was this (he wonders) 'a wry comment on the hopeless nature of the project of biographical accuracy, or was it just a wild and whimsical kicking over of the traces?' (236)

Not only are facts invented by the writer and some of the 'facts' are unreliable, there is an unavoidable element of imposition of the writer's view point in the arrangement of the material. Phineas finds two shoe boxes full of index cards of Scholes, haphazardly arranged, containing the material on the lives he was working on. Phineas arranges the cards differently only to find a new meaning, new life emerge (247). It becomes clear to him that such an arbitrariness could be dangerous, for the image or life that would emerge would be a fictional construction by Phineas, the raw material losing its autonomy and independence.

In the process of shuffling the cards and arranging them (the material on the lives of Linnaeus, Galton and Ibsen that D. Scholes had collected), Phineas wonders which of the orders D. Scholes would have preferred. He begins to see that the material gives rise to different images of these persons; that is, the images came from the material – it was not contained in any external object. Each new version and textual formation would construct a 'new Ibsen, a new Galton'.

The disillusionment of Phineas makes him reluctant to really write a biography for his initial responses to Scholes' claims to facts have now changed. He had been writing about his project – all the details of the quest, obstacles and the gradual disappointment. Another serious doubt about the biographer's objectivity comes to him as he looks at the material about Scholes and fails to catch hold of an authentic image of Scholes. He tries to see the man in the photographs that Vera, Scholes' niece has given him. But he is disappointed at not finding a clear image of Scholes in any of them. Photographs, another material produced by technology and respected for faithfully reproducing the reality, also fail him, for here too he finds the important role played by the observing 'eye'. He reads the various cards, and tries to arrange them, 'the threads of connection' he says 'are my own' (227). As Phineas reads carefully the notes of Scholes on the scientists, especially Galton, he has fleeting visions of the image of Galton or somebody in that material. Phineas can not be sure whose image it was that he saw in the material – was it of the man who was being studied, or of the observer himself? He is caught in the maze of the images that begin to reflect one another – becoming a kind of maze of mirrors. At a later stage, Phineas finds his own image also superimposed on the others. He asks another disturbing question: is it a composite portrait of the 'subject' Galton, the first researcher, Scholes, and the second researcher Phineas (236). Such doubts subvert the faith in the objectivity of biography as a history of one person.

In the questions Phineas raises over the whole project, the postmodernist dismissal of the heroism of adventurers and explorers can also be seen. Phineas voices this rejection when he speaks for his age: 'We don't believe ... in great men and we like to see human beings as parts of large social structures whose mechanisms and inter-relations we can uncover and describe' (236). Phineas voices his loss of enthusiasm in hero worship of adventurers and explorers, distancing himself from the love of cataloguing, naming, classifying the 'other worlds' outside England and Europe that was carried out in the imperial phase of West's history. Europe in the modern age expanded its hold over the world, conquered it through the process of naming it, its animals, people and spaces. Men like Elmer Bole, C. Linnaeus and Galton, travelled far and wide, noting down each detail of tribal people, the flora and the fauna of the area, and made their observations the basis of many unscientific, unfounded generalizations. Byatt gives remarks by Galton where he compares the behaviour of the ox with that of human beings (66-67) generalizing about the shared habits of gregariousness in cattle and human beings. Such studies given confidently also supported racist and sexist discrimination. Eugenics and phrenology became important but false masters for a whole generation, subsiding into oblivion after the mess of the world wars.

Byatt incorporates some scientific writings mainly to parody the excessive zeal of their authors, the scientists and their over-confident assumptions. Through pastiche and parody she mocks their excesses and failures. The postmodern distrust of a 'master' mind building up a grand scientific treatise/narrative is also reflected through these pseudo-scientific writings. Byatt invents a lot of the material, mocking the style and tone of these great men, exposing their human weaknesses. Byatt creates through these passages 'a "space of interrogation" which asks whose reliability is to be represented through this process of naming' (Marshall 3). Postmodernism opens out the appropriating and power-giving projects that the western scientists became party to. Phineas's inquiry of the intentions and reliability of such knowledge making makes important subversion of the claims of such adventurers.

The Biographer's Tale is a fragmented and disrupted text, with hybrid material woven along the story of the biographer caught in serious aesthetic debate within himself. It is a metafictional text, drawing attention to the illusory and provisional nature of the biography's claims of realism and factuality. Patricia Waugh discusses the theory and practice of metafictional art and says that 'Metafiction sets up an opposition, not to ostensibly 'objective' facts in the 'real' world but to the language of the realistic novel which has sustained and endorsed such a view of reality' (6). Byatt critiques the biography as a literary genre from the standpoint of its claims to a possibility of knowing and re-presenting a person without any mediation by the writer's personality, style or ideologies. Such an unmediated transmission is not now possible to believe in. In Patricia Waugh's words 'metafiction shows us how the reality we live by/in, is similarly 'written', reminding us that 'we no longer inhabit a world of eternal verities but a series of constructions, artifices impermanent structures' (6).

Similar doubt about the absolute truthfulness to real lives are also dramatised by Muriel Spark in her novel *Loitering With Intent.* Lord Quentin not only re-writes the 'Lives' of the friends as he commissions a set of writers to write their biographies; he also uses the inventions to mould and run their lives. Fiction and facts merge into one another, depicting the textual nature of our lives.

Phineas' recognition of the mixture of fiction, facts and the writer's point of view in the writing of a biography is a part of the postmodernist sensibility that he displays through out this exploration; if he does not acknowledge this sensibility initially, his inability to make up his mind to write the life of Destry Schoes is a movement in that direction.

The Biographer's Tale then acquires a dialogic disjointedness, as the narrative movement and character's views take different directions. Phineas keeps disclaiming any belief in postmodern and poststructuralist theories; he insists on living his life spontaneously, and, passionately. But the text emerges as a carefully elaborated metafictional and postmodernist tale, raising doubts about the claims of scientific objectivity of biography and emphasizing its narrative elements.

Hayden White has argued in his *Metahistory: The Historical Imagination* in *Nineteenth Century Europe* (1973) how history is always constructed with the elements of narrative – plot, design, point of view, playing a determining role. Byatt shows in the context of biography the unavoidable role of imagination, interpretation (subjective elements) and of making up, mixing of facts and fiction in writing a biography. Rejecting the plan to write or biography, Phineas goes on writing – about his life, with the two women, Vera Alphage and Fulla Biefeld, he became friendly with during the search for Scholes' material. He wants to love both of them, and the text goes on to describe the two holidays with them taken separately in two consecutive years. From a man devoted to writing a biography, he becomes a writer of an autobiography.

The differences in the intention of the character and the author create interesting dialectics of meaning. The novel's style and tone change once Phineas makes up his mind to abandon the project of writing – the biography; instead, he goes on to write about 'himself' – his career as a writer, a lover, and, a traveller. The novel uses 'theory' as such to play with its usefulness, yet also subverts its overwhelming presence. Despite conscious intents to be free of theory the character and the novel are however deeply involved with the contemporary theories.

The different kinds of discourses that are integrated in the novel give it a density of texture and meaning. It becomes a 'multi-dimensional text' in the way Roland Barthes defines a 'text' as 'a multidimensional space in which variety of writings, none of them original, blend and clash. The text is a licence of quotations, drawn from the innumerable centres of culture' (32). Byatt uses several linguistic varieties, art objects and poems depicting the limited nature of each form, the element of human intervention that is required to represent reality. Using parallels, analogies in the intertextual material, Byatt makes them a complex web of connections, meanings and suggestions. It may be a challenging reading but *The Biographer's Tale* pays one richly in aesthetic pleasure for taking up the challenge.

References

Barthes, Roland. *Image, Music, Text*. New York, 1977.

Byatt, A.S. *Possession*. London: 1990, Chatto & Windus, 1990.

Byatt, A.S. *The Biographer's Tale*. London: Chatto & Windus, 2000.

Clark, Alex. 'Mischief Maker'. *The Guardian*, Internet 3 June 2000. http:/books, guardian.co.uk/

Marshall, Brenda. *Teaching the Postmodern: Fiction and Theory*. New York: Routledge, 1992.

Todd, Richard. *A.S. Byatt*. U.K.: Northcote House, 1997.

Waugh, Patricia. *Metafiction: The Theory and Practice of Self-conscious Fiction*. London: Methuen, 1984.

6 Interrogating the 'Self'

An Exploration of Anita Brookner's *Hotel du Lac*

Shaila Mahan

Literature has traditionally been regarded as a reflection of the cultural and social dimensions of society which holds a mirror to the values that have dominated the course of human evolution. But as feminists have argued, in most societies literature has generally been tuned to the male viewpoint; women in contrast, have been 'marginalised', 'repressed' or 'silenced' in literary works. Fortunately, in the past few decades, writings by and on women have gradually evolved and acquired a validity and significance of their own. At one level, they question values and structures earlier taken for granted and the established definitions of freedom and creativity.

Besides being sensitive portrayals of societal dynamics, fictional writings also provide insight into the individuals who create them, for writers often use their creations to explore their own deepest personal, social and psychological dilemmas. This is particularly true of women authors [whether poets or prose writers], and in this context, it is hardly surprising that women's writings have in recent decades thrown up all kinds of questions related to the oppression, exploitation and colonization of their gender. While women's writing cannot be treated as a monolithic structure and all women's writing is not necessarily feminist, the genre certainly has its own characteristics and qualities. In her quest for artistic self-expression within a dominantly patriarchal set-up, the woman writer gives a voice, visibility and validity to aspects of female experience that were earlier ignored or simply submerged by male writers. Women's writings in recent decades have helped to probe, reach and express the female 'self' as has probably never been done before in human history.

It seems pertinent to examine here what exactly is meant by the term 'feminine'. Just as we should not confuse female and feminists, it would also be erroneous to presume that anything and everything written by women, will be 'feminine'. As Toril Moi remarks: 'It has long been an established practice among most feminists to use 'feminine' (and masculine) to represent *social constructs* and to reserve 'female' and 'male' for the purely biological aspects of sexual difference' (Moi 65). Moreover, there's a huge difference between literature, which happens to be simply authored by a woman and what we may call women's literature. For example, the novels of Iris Murdoch and Ayn Rand are written by women, but they cannot be labelled as women's novels. The latter category actually consists of only those writings of women which are written *from a 'female' point of view*, where the authors write and articulate specifically women's emotions and experiences boldly and candidly.

Virginia Woolf in this context says, 'there is the obvious and enormous difference of experience in the first place, but the essential difference lies in the fact, not that men describe battles and women the birth of children but *that each sex describes itself*' (emphasis added. 26). In other words, women's writing offers the possibility of a focus on women, through an understanding from within. Many contemporary writings by women can be fully appreciated only in the light of theoretical formulations of feminist literary critics which have virtually redefined the nature, role and status of women in society. Virginia Woolf's *A Room of One's Own* (1929) enquires into the socio-cultural situation of women in a historical perspective and highlights the control of all political, economic and social power by men. Simone de Beauvoir's *The*

Second Sex and Kate Millet's *Sexual Politics*, emphasize sex as a biologically-determined entity and gender as a socio-cultural construct. Beauvoir points out how men see woman as the 'other': 'She is the incidental, the inessential as opposed to the essential. He is the subject, he is the Absolute. She is the other' (*Beauvoir* 16).

Feminist critiques have expanded the scope of literary studies to now include an analysis of sexual, social and political issues and their body of work has emphasised the need to study the writings of women as a means to understand the hitherto hidden feminine 'self'. This paper attempts to trace the 'self', the autobiographical threads in the writings of Anita Brookner, one of the most outstanding British novelists of the past two decades. While most of her fictional creations contain elements of the author's 'self', this paper restricts itself to a study of Brookner's most celebrated novel *Hotel du Lac* which is considered the most autobiographical of her works, and also brought her the Booker Prize in 1984. Edith Hope, the central protagonist of the novel, is perhaps the creation closest to the author's own self and the paper strives to draw some broad parallels between the novelist's life and the story of Edith in a bid to understand the restrained self-exploration that Brookner undertakes in *Hotel du Lac*. This is followed by a brief study of some of the other prominent women characters of the novel in so far as they highlight the crucial issues and dilemmas of women that seem to be a special concern for Brookner. The entire exercise is aimed at delving into the psyche of the novelist – creator and the exploration hopes to reveal, at least partially, the extent to which Anita Brookner's 'hidden self' is reflected through her most famous creation.

I

In the past two decades, Anita Brookner has been one of the most prolific novelists in the English language. She began her professional career as an Art Historian at the Courtland Institute of Art in London where she also took her PhD. Brookner's teaching career included lecturing at the University of Reading from 1959 to 1988 and serving as the first woman Slade Professor at Cambridge in

1967-68. Finally, she secured a Readership at the Courtland Institute from where she retired in 1987. But Brookner began her writing career only in 1981 with her debut novel, *A Start in Life* and since then she has been producing a novel almost every year. By now she has written a total of twenty one novels of which *The Next Big Thing* has been published in 2002. The large majority of Brookner's creations focus primarily on women protagonists who are generally single, middle-aged and financially independent but usually prove to be losers in love. Her impressive body of work has by now secured Brookner a distinct reputation as a novelist with fine moral discriminations and careful aesthetic distinctions that place her 'in the front ranks of contemporary English fiction writers' (*Moritz* 70).

While Brookner's professional career is an open book, little is known about her personal life, its ups and downs. Biographical information on her is strictly limited as Brookner is reticent about giving exact personal details of her life. In an interview with Valerie Grove, Brookner remarks: 'I have no private papers. I shall leave no trace. That's the ideal' (Grove 14). But a broad outline can be gleaned from her various interviews which provide invaluable insights into her private persona. The only child of a businessman and a retired professional singer, Brookner grew up in a middle-class London suburb. Her Polish-Jewish parents were immigrants and despite their reasonable professional successes, Brookner has described them as an 'ill-matched couple' who were 'silent, stoical... and very unhappy'. Schooling permitted the young Brookner a welcome and much-needed escape from the claustrophobia of her home and her education at a leading school in London was followed by graduate studies at the famous King's College in London. While she pursued her academic interests and followed it with several years of teaching and research, Brookner remained single and nursed her elderly parents till their death in the late 1960s.

In all her interviews, Brookner is discreet about divulging any information about the facts of her life, especially as they relate to other people. Nevertheless, she is generally candid about her own views, desires, needs and disappointments and has acknowledged that her autobiographical 'self' permeates much of her fiction. When asked whether her novels speak of her own condition, Brookner responded: 'The particulars are all invented, but they speak of states of mind which forced me to do something about those states of mind' (Haffenden 1985, 59). In the same interview; she has also described her novels as 'transcripts' from her own 'passage through life, and a rather unsuccessful passage' (Haffenden 1985, 70). Clearly, the recurring focus of her fiction on virtuous and self-restrained women who despite their economic independence remain haunted by conventional patterns of behaviour and aspiration, has its basis in Brookner's own life and moral dilemmas. So while she is a strictly private person, her literary creations are a distinct echo of her inner personality.

Given this brief background, it seems pertinent now to trace Brookner's most celebrated creation in some detail. Of her twenty one novels, *Hotel du Lac* is probably the one which gives maximum insight into the novelist's mind. In a nutshell *Hotel* tells us the story of Edith Hope, a middle-aged British spinster who is packed off by her friends to *Hotel Du Lac* in Switzerland so that she can regroup after a horrible social disgrace, which is not immediately revealed to us. Ms Hope, it turns out, is a romance novelist who spends her days at the Hotel working on her new novel, interacting with her fellow guests and looking back at the chain of events which brought her to this place. She reminiscences and introspects about her past life, writing undelivered letters to her married lover David; and as she works on sections of her new novel, Edith meets Neville, a man she initially thinks will transform her life. But eventually, the spinster-novelist rejects the 'practical' option of getting married and makes the distinctly 'feminist' choice of remaining single; instead of a life of pragmatic arrangements, Edith returns to her life of romantic fictions in London.

The novel opens in a deserted Swiss Hotel with grim and bleak details '.....it was late September, out of season; the tourists had gone, the rates were reduced' (*Hotel* 7). The 'unfortunate lapse' for which Edith is exiled to this hotel is revealed in the course of the narrative as backing out of a marriage at the last moment. The 'brief exile' is imposed on Edith for embarrassing herself and her friends so that she comes out 'wiser and properly apologetic' through the experience. The secret of the mistake is disclosed through prolonged reminiscences where Edith recounts how she had jilted Geoffery, the man she had planned to marry, leaving him [literally!] standing as a waiting bridegroom on the very steps of the marriage Registry Office, as she 'saw in a flash, but for all time, the totality of his mouse like seemliness' (*H* 129) and ordered the taxi-driver to simply drive past him.

The fiasco with Geoffrey is treated in a semi-comic manner and the wry undertones of the narrative voice indicate his unsuitability for Edith from the start. Geoffrey is shown to be 'lonely since his mother died" (*H* 118) and is introduced to Edith as a potential husband. Edith falls into the trap of accepting the proposal because she feels that she is getting too old to attract a marriage alliance based on love and she thinks this might be her last chance for a 'safe and sensible future.' (*H* 119) but soon comprehends that the proposal really offers 'little to arouse her enthusiasm' (*H* 122) and realises that she may be exchanging the small joys of her independent life and her own flat for an 'airless world' (*H* 122). That Geoffery is hardly a compatible match is clear from his reaction when Edith finally jilts him: 'I am only grateful that my poor mother did not live to see this day' (*H* 131). The author drives home this point even further when soon after the episode Edith sees Geoffrey 'emerging from Penelope's house...looking decidedly more cheerful' (*H* 133).

Essentially, *Hotel* reconstructs the mental journey of Edith as she recognizes the self-deception inherent in the romantic myth which has a powerful hold on her mind: the tortoise and hare motif derived from Aesop's fable. The widely-held belief that the virtuous would be rewarded and the tortoise would always emerge victorious in the end, is ultimately demolished in Edith's eyes. Though Brookner makes a tortoise her central focus, she does so without any distortion of truth in her favour. Rather, Edith as an author of romance novels of the Mills & Boon variety, serves as a successful device to present a contrast between the 'happily-ever-after' fantasies that she churns out for her women readers and the unsatisfactory nature of her own interaction with the three men who enter her life in the novel. Eventually, it dawns upon Edith that unlike the fable, the prize in reality goes to the hares of the world and almost never to the tortoise. As Edith points out to her agent: 'The tortoise wins every time. This is a lie, of course, ... In real life ... it is the hare who wins. Every time. Look around you.... Hares have no time to read, they are too busy winning the game.' (*H* 27-28). Edith's perception that it's the hare who wins invariably in contemporary times is clearly based on Brookner's own vision which is re-created in many of her other fictional creations also.

There are several striking similarities between Anita Brookner and the heroine she creates in *Hotel*. Edith is a thirty nine year old woman who writes under the pseudonym of Venessa Wilde and has five published novels to her credit. Like Brookner, Edith is a novelist from the beginning of *Hotel*; and both write about women's issues and attempt a self-appraisal through their writings. Interestingly, like Brookner, Edith is the single offspring of her parents and achieves enviable professional success. Moreover, Edith is not just single, middle-aged and financially independent but also a lonely and introverted woman, and like her creator she is essentially self-reflective and given to frequent bouts of brooding self-exploration. No wonder, Brookner acknowledges a close relationship between her protagonist and her own self: 'It's a personal story and I meant every word' (Kenyon 1988, 154).

Edith, like Brookner, has an immigrant background. We find the words 'exile', 'homelessness' and 'loneliness' being used throughout the novel, a subtle but strong reflection perhaps of Brookner's own sense of alienation and loneliness. Many of the characters of *Hotel*, especially Edith, are subject to a deep sense of doubt, despondency and dislocation. Edith's mother is shown to be from Vienna and her childhood memories are suffused with eccentric, misfit relatives who seem quite out of place in England. Besides *Hotel*, many of Brookner's striking characters in her other novels are also shown to have 'a sad European past' and they all seem to share an outsiders' perspective of life in mainstream London.

Most scholars attribute this alienation to Brookner's Jewish background: she has often called herself 'a sort of Jewish exile' (Smith 67). Her parents were Polish Jews; though born in England, her mother belonged to an immigrant family of Polish Jews while her father too was a Polish Jew. Brookner as a result seems to consider herself foreign and rather alien in England and she is quite uncomfortable with her Jewish background: 'I think my parents' lives were blighted – and in some sense mine is too – largely by the fact... of being strangers in England, not quite understanding what was happening and being done to them' (Haffenden, 1984). 'You're never really free of your own history, are you?' (Bailey B.B.C. Interview). 'I have never learned the custom of the country, because we were Jews, tribal and alien' (Kenyon, 1988).

Brookner, however, prefers discretion to disclosure on these aspects in her fiction. But what she has on occasion said of Jane Austen, could well be applied to Brookner's own writing: 'I think she made a tremendous far-reaching decision to leave certain things out.' The words "Jew" or "Jewish" rarely occur in Brookner's writing, and perhaps not even once in *Hotel*, but this silence is an unconscious pointer that she is quintessentially an Anglo-Jewish writer. The chronic sense of dislocation, loneliness and alienation that Edith suffers from, makes her aware, like Brookner, 'of what it is like to be lonely, perceptive, an observer' (Mayne, Radio Interview). No wonder, sensitive scholars like Schechner describe this condition as 'ghetto cosmopolitanism', and 'a frame of mind which gives rise to moods or tonalities... seen as particularly Jewish, an ambivalence towards oneself and others'. Although Brookner does not wish to be 'ghettoized', and deplores any 'Jewish eagerness to reclaim lost souls', [in fact she prefers to be known as an 'English' writer, and has indeed achieved much recognition as one of the most accomplished writers of English fiction], her novels mirror the deep-rooted alienation that is latent in her psyche and can be traced to her Jewish background. It may not be an overstatement to assert that the trauma and angst of the

European Jewish past runs almost like a connective tissue through Brookner's fiction and though at a conscious level she strives to keep this hidden, the delineation of her characters unwittingly reveals the subconscious state of their creator.

Another commonality between Edith and Brookner is their difficult childhood; Edith is shown to have undergone a traumatic childhood and whatever is known of Brookner's personal life also suggests a rather troubled childhood. Brookner admits that her parents were 'hopeless as guides' and that it is from literature that she tried to learn about life. In an interview, Brookner remarks regretfully: 'Mine was a dreary Victorian story. I nursed my parents till they died' (Kenyon 1989, 12).

In particular, there is considerable overlap in the portrayal of Edith's relationship with her mother and what her creator probably experienced in her own life. The deep bonding between mother and child is missing in both the cases for Brookner has often referred to herself as a 'grown up orphan' (Haffenden 1985, 63). During her stay at the Hotel, Edith recalls in one of her pensive moments the 'painful memories' of her childhood: 'Her strange mother Rosa, that harsh disappointed woman' who had little compunction in mocking her 'pale silent daughter' and constantly made Edith run around on errands like "bringing cups of coffee which her mother deliberately spilled (*H* 48). In sharp contrast, Edith meets the much-attached mother-daughter duo of the Puseys – Iris, the mother and Jennifer, the daughter – who are also guests at the Hotel. She cannot help noticing how both share a comfortable, cosy intimacy 'none of which she herself (Edith) had ever known' (*H* 48). The spectacle of the mother and daughter staying together in harmony leads Edith to recall uneasily about her own mother and she reflects sadly how she had always felt bereft in terms of love and never experienced closeness with her. It is important that her perception of the relationship between the Puseys changes considerably when she sees that in reality this is just an exaggerated affectation while in reality the two are far from being as inseparable as they strive to project.

Edith's love-hate relationship with her mother seems to be an extension of the ambivalent relationship that Brookner seems to have shared with her mother. Though her mother had scorned Edith while alive, as Edith tries to sympathetically understand her mother, she is able to realise the pathos and disappointment underlying her mother's outer harshness. Edith reminisces: '....when she raised her eyes from her book, her eyes too were faded from blue to grey, and full of dreams, longings, disenchantments' (*H* 104). She pinpoints the reasons for not reaching out to other women with affection and understanding: 'I am harsh because I remember Mother and her unkindness, and because I am continually on the alert for more. But women are not all like Mother, and it is really stupid of me to imagine that they are' (*H* 88). All this is a clear reflection of the emotional scars left by Edith's childhood through which Brookner appears to be wanting to come to grips with her own difficult upbringing in a home where she was not just a lonely-only child but also her parents, as the author confesses, were distinctly 'ill matched'. Despite the broad parallels noted above, Edith is by no means a biographical replica of Brookner. Instead, she serves as the medium through which Brookner not only spells out her views on various issues but also explores moral puzzles and traumas that confront most women. In Edith's life, the most crucial role is played by David Simmonds, her married lover, whom she considers her precious 'breath of life'. Brookner unfolds this relationship gradually and with finesse through Edith's reminiscences and her letters which in turn contribute to her 'self'-scrutiny. We come to know how she met David at a party, arranged by her friend Penelope Grandison. David is an auctioneer married to a strikingly beautiful woman, Priscilla, whom Edith regards as a 'hare', sure of her worth and keenly holding on to what she has.

While Edith knows about the tempestuous relationship between David and his wife, she is also aware that he will never leave his wife. Edith, however, is conscious that she herself fulfills some basic urge in her lover, satisfying 'his delightful and constant appetite' (*H* 60). She remembers 'those lovely meals that she cooked for David' and his loving response 'I never get this stuff at home', (*H* 29) which seems pregnant with deeper meaning. But this mutually satisfying physical relationship is only suggested but never really explored at length by Brookner.

Instead, what is examined in detail is Edith's deep and growing attachment to David which leads her to practise a virtuous fidelity towards him. His infrequent visits cause Edith tremendous agony but what keeps the relationship moving is that 'sooner or later, he had come back' (*H* 30): 'Perfectly composed, tending her garden, writing, her face closed against pity, sympathy, curiosity, Edith kept silent and yearned for David' (*H* 84). But having inherited rather Victorian ideals of suitable 'womanly' behaviour, she lies to all who think there's no romantic angle in her life. Indeed, even with David himself, Brookner's heroine hides her 'self' behind a veil of cheerful, uncomplaining exterior: 'She prided herself on not giving anything away, so that he never knew of her empty Sundays, the long eventless evenings, the holidays cancelled at the last minute' (*H* 61). Even when David seeks her after long, unexplained gaps, Edith never asserts herself or questions him regarding her own needs/desires though she does seem to realise the 'tortoise existence' that she is leading.

It is her letters which serve as an outlet for revealing her deepest feelings for David, as Edith is unable to directly express her emotions to her lover. In one of these letters, there's a moving confession of her sentiments: 'My dear darling, you cannot know how much I think of you and long for you '(*H* 50) and the third person narrative fills the rest, 'This she blotted carefully and laid aside.' What the third person narrative unveils through these uninterrupted letters is the contradiction within Edith. While her emotional attachment to David is clear from the letters and she also appears quite conscious of the lack of an equally strong emotional bond from his side, Edith's emotional inability to accept the reality of her relationship pushes her to seek a psychological release through the fantasies depicted in her novels. The inherent pathos of her delicate situation is not just conveyed but also mitigated by the irony contained in the narrative voice. This narrative irony is greatly intensified when we learn at the end of the novel that Edith never posted even one of the five letters she wrote during her stay at the *Hotel*. The letters are a means of introspection for Edith helping her to recognise her 'self'. They are a clever flashback device through which the reader is told about all that has happened in the past.

Edith's hopes and convictions regarding the relationship of happiness to love are expressed most clearly during her conversations with Phillip Neville. A rich, worldly and successful man, Neville is the only male guest in the predominantly women-dominated *Hotel* and proposes marriage to Edith. She is flattered by his attention and interest and a little overcome by his being 'furiously intelligent' (*H* 97). He takes her out for walks, entertains her in his lightly humorous manner and is able to guess that she is bored, lonely and has a secret love life, which is causing her distress. After numerous walks and conversations with him, she begins to think of him as 'a companion of really unusual character and perception' (*H* 162).

Neville's views about marriage, life and love, however, are diametrically opposed to those of Edith and she humorously refers to him as 'a devil's advocate' (*H* 97). Outwardly, he seems an eminently suitable match for any woman: he has the characteristics of the hero of the nineteenth century romantic fiction; he is 'good looking', 'fine', 'reticent', 'courtly' and 'conducts himself altogether gracefully' (*H* 97). But Edith's witty statement is also loaded with Brookner's irony in the light of her limited perception about Neville, who is simultaneously developing a physical relationship with Jennifer, about which she comes to know later. Brookner's light narrative irony exposes Edith's mistaken notion that she has perhaps met the kind of intelligent hero who knows what is good for the heroine. In the kind of popular novels that Edith writes, such a man is often projected as the dream hero. But in *Hotel,* Brookner has not only examined the subconscious attraction for the myth of the masterful, all knowing male on Edith's mind, she has also subverted the need for attachment to such a myth, in a light parody of it, in the semi-humorous conversations between Neville and Edith.

Neville has some partial similarities with the Jane Austen hero who is usually instrumental in educating the heroine in some essential social values. Neville also takes upon himself the task to instruct Edith. He acknowledges Edith as an 'excellent woman' (*H* 101) and a 'lady' but also asserts that "modesty and merit are very poor cards to hold" (*H* 166) in the contemporary world and are rarely rewarded. He advises Edith to adopt a stance of enlightened selfishness and to have relationships, without investing emotionally in them; and he claims that disappointment is inevitable if she continues to regard love as essential to a satisfying relationship.

As a seemingly rational alternative, Neville offers Edith a relief from her single status and the concomitant psychological exile, by suggesting that she should marry him and acquire a position of social eminence. In this, he appears to he the perfect suitor, offering traditional courtship and marriage, but the manner in which he proposes presents a parody of the very offer. Edith is partially taken in and consents to the match because be cloaks his offer of marriage among faultless arguments for her betterment and what he calls, her 'true self interest' (*H* 166). He suggests that marriage would enable her to face the people who have not sufficiently respected her, because of being a single woman. Although he talks of a union based on 'shared interests', 'truthful discourse' and 'companionship' (*H* 167), a closer look at the kind of marriage he is suggesting reveals to Edith that it is to be merely an 'arrangement'. He calls it "a partnership of the most enlightened kind" (*H* 166), in which the main factor is to be that each partner would be free to take lovers and pursue their own affairs, as they like. In, response, Edith asks Neville a relevant question: 'Why me' and his reply is quite revealing: 'perhaps because you are harder to catch than the others' (*H* 170). At face value, this seems a compliment for Edith's virtuously led life. Ironically, what Neville really implies by the remark is that although he advocates the case for mutual freedom but judging her for what she is, he does not really expect her to pursue her own love affairs. He tells Edith about his previous wife who ran away with another man and made him a laughing stock; he sees her (Edith) as a part of his possessions, a vindication against his betrayal by his previous wife. But clearly, he has little intention to love and cherish her as a person; rather he considers it convenient to parade her as his wife, while he pursues his sexual pleasures elsewhere.

While Neville professes to be in tune with contemporary, 'modern' morals, the marriage offer is really a mockery of the kind of 'home' Edith ardently desires. She can see that he is offering a marriage just in name and not himself. When Neville argues with Edith that she is wrong to think that she cannot live without love, it triggers a self-analysis within Edith and leads her to finally assert her most deeply felt beliefs about the relationship of happiness to love: 'I mean that I cannot live well without it. I cannot think or act or speak or write or even dream with any kind of energy in the absence of love. I feel excluded from the living world ..... My idea of absolute happiness is to sit in a hot garden all day, reading or writing, utterly safe in the knowledge that the person I love will come home to me in the evening' (*H* 98).

Edith makes the important distinction that what she seeks is not romantic love but a 'home' and domestic happiness, based on love, trust companionship and sharing. To quote Edith 'I am not a romantic. I am a domestic animal. I do not sigh and yearn for extravagant displays of passion, for the grand affair, the world well lost for love.' What Edith yearns for is the emotional gratification that can be attained from the love of a mutually bound couple.

The narrative irony directed at Edith's illusion about the implications of a marriage with Neville reaches a climax when she accidentally sees him emerging from Jennifer's bedroom in the early hours of the morning. Actually, Edith is going down on her way to post her letter to David, informing him about her decision to marry Neville. She is now confronted with a typical Brooknerian 'moral puzzle,' that makes her realize the heavy emotional and psychological cost that such a 'loveless marriage' would extract from her.

Soon after this incident, Edith tears up her last letter to David which she was about to post; instead she sends him a telegram. In this telegram, she first writes 'Coming home' but after some reflection, feels that the wording is inaccurate and crosses it out, to write simply 'Returning'. Brookner's own interpretation of this ending is helpful. To quote Brookner: "'Coming home' would be coming back to domestic propriety: 'home' implies husband, children, order, regular meals, but 'Returning' is her more honest view of the situation. To that extent she does break through to a clearer vision' (Haffenden, 1985, 71). This 'sad yet dignified ending,' emphasises Edith's continued state of inner homelessness. Nevertheless, it shows an affirmative action on Edith's part, in the context of the inner journey and appraisal of 'self' that she has gone through, in the course of the novel.

In its total effect, *Hotel* is most unlike the romances that its protagonist, Edith is shown to write. Yet, it is interspersed with some romantic elements, in the sense that it identifies Edith's longing for the ideal of love. Out of the 'exile of one sort or another' (*H* 165), which had been predicted for her, she chooses the 'exile' of being on her own, where she is at home with and can freely pursue the choice of her own values and still hoping. Merle Rubin has rightly pointed out that Brookner's theme in *Hotel*, is "more powerful perhaps for the extent to which it is submerged, in the great Romantic theme of hope in the face of despair' (Rubin B3).

At one level, one can almost read *Hotel* simply as a story of Edith's unsuccessful attempt at achieving a sense of belonging, through the conventions of marriage and family. Edith's quest for happiness through love is essentially a search for 'home'. 'Home' is a recurrent metaphor in Brookner's fiction. It denotes not only her protagonists' craving for fulfillment and commitment through family and marriage but also perhaps her own. Edith fails to secure any lasting heterosexual relationship and is disappointed in her persistent quest for fulfillment in life through love, a failure she shares with Brookner herself.

In the novel, Edith constantly faces the huge moral choice of marriage versus singlehood, a dilemma Brookner was herself confronted with through all her adult life. While she has achieved remarkable professional success, both as an academician and as a novelist, Brookner has on several occasions regretted her inability to create a family of her own and regards it as a major gap in her personal life. In an interview given almost two decades ago, Brookner admitted: 'I wanted to get married. As it is, I've never really left school. That's my sad story' (Barber 27) It's a sentiment that Brookner echoes even in her most recent interviews. Answering Boyd Tonkins' query on whether she really wanted to get married, she responds: 'Of course. All the time. I wanted children.' Surely, its not impertinent to submit that Edith's constant introspection on staying single or getting married is a dialogue haunting Brookner's own mind and aims at resolving a critical issue confronting the author's inner self.

Besides Edith, Brookner uses other women characters to explore her psychological dilemmas and resolves the complex issues raised through them in her own way. She even employs these characters as a means to tackle the multiple concerns that are crucial to the lives of most women. She explores the images of women in *Hotel* in her quest for understanding other women and herself. There is, for instance, Penelope Milne, a typical example of a 'modern' woman who uses her sexual freedom as a sense of achievement rather than for improvement of the quality of the relationships between the sexes: for Penelope 'men were conquests,' 'She spread about her a propaganda of rapid affairs, rapidly consummated, with a laughing lack of commitment on both sides'(*H* 57).

But once she reaches the Hotel, Edith is initially fascinated by the glamour of the Puseys, the colourful mother-daughter combination. Soon Edith comes to know that their main reason of coming there is for shopping and following their example she too is tempted to indulge herself. But she soon gets bored with this self-indulgence and gradually starts viewing the Puseys in the right perspective. She finds their elaborate dressing up on Mrs Pusey's birthday party 'bizarre'. Iris Puseys' attitude enables Brookner to examine the romantic myth, that a woman truly loved is the one who is successful in making a man worship her. In a conversation with Edith, Iris discloses, 'A woman should be able to make a man worship her... perhaps I've been fortunate...My husband worshipped me' (*H* 74). But Mr Pusey is given no name, profession, character or title and is just called 'my husband'. This throws light on the insensitivity of Mrs Pusey towards her husband and her narcissism. The same narcissistic attitude is also reflected in her relationship with her daughter whom she doesn't allow to grow and mature and who in turn keeps on having clandestine affairs.

In her attempt to define herself as a woman, Edith can find no single, acceptable image of a modern, fulfilled, liberated woman whom she can admire and emulate. She starts empathising with some of the other women characters like Mrs Bonnevil and Monica, who feel a sense of homelessness and exile, like herself.

The image of the lonely, old widow Mme de Bonnevil and her exile at the Hotel, offers a sad comment on the undervaluing of an aged woman, by her only child. Her son has sent her away to the Hotel because of the inconvenience of having her with him. Edith notices how she accepts the imposed homelessness with a cultivated cheerfulness for the sake of her son, whom she loves dearly. His brief, token visits to her are still the most eagerly awaited moments for herself. Being old, she has lost her looks and capacity to nurture, the two qualities associated with desirable 'feminity' by patriarchal standards. Brookner deals with the agony of aging and the problems faced by elderly women through the portrayal of Mme de Bonnevil.

Edith's insightful understanding of the predicaments of the women around her and her analytical reflections about them enable her to enlarge her own sensibility and be more responsive towards them. She matures enough to see through the superficial vanities and game playing of women like Penelope, Jennifer and Mrs Pusey. Brookner's utilizes Edith's experiences and interaction with other women guests at the hotel to trigger a self-appraisal in

Edith. Edith seeks an answer to the critical question of 'what behaviour most becomes a woman' (*H* 40). Clearly, the reflections of her central protagonist and the variety of women characters she comes across, provide Brookner with a platform to explore several concerns and questions raised prominently by feminist thinkers in recent years and her discussion of these tricky but critical queries enables us to get an invaluable insight into the workings of her 'inner self'.

Another striking feature of *Hotel* is the deft interweaving of various narrative strands. Besides the omnipresent narrator–author herself telling us of all incidents in third person, there is an additional narrative strand: the chain of letters written by Edith to David, her lover in England. The third person narration, directly reports the events and conversations of the characters and even delves into Edith's thought processes; but the unposted letters offer a mode for deeper scrutiny of Edith's state of mind by providing a comparative subtext. The process of letter writing is used as a flashback strategy which provides a device for recollecting the past incidents by Edith. These narrative devices, besides providing links about Edith's life to fill up the missing gaps are a form of self reflection. They play a major role in giving revealing glimpses into her childhood, the nature of her relationship with her parents and the three men who play significant roles in Edith's life. Like some of Brookner's other heroines, Edith is shown to fall in love with the wrong men. However, unlike the heroines of novels like *A Start in Life,* and *Providence* who are left disappointed at the end, Edith is finally able to analyse her 'self' in her relationship with her lover.

II

Elaine Showalter, the leading American feminist critic, has worked on the growth and evolution of the female tradition. In her well-known work, A *Literature of Their Own,* she traces the literary history of English women novelists and demonstrates that the development of this tradition is similar to the growth of any literary subculture. She identifies three historical phases of women's literary development the 'feminine', the 'feminist' and the 'female' and defines them as phases of 'imitation', 'protest' and of 'self discovery' – three major phases of historical development common to all literary movements. "First, there is a prolonged phase of imitation of the prevailing modes of the dominant tradition,... Second, there is a phase of protest against these standards and values...And finally there is *a phase of self-discovery*' (Showalter 13 emphasis added). In this broad survey of a continuously evolving female tradition, our study clearly suggests that Brookner belongs to the final phase, the phase of self-discovery; her fiction seems to be, almost deliberately designed, to search her own elusive 'self'.

As mentioned earlier, Brookner is strictly private about the details about her personal life but she is fairly candid about her views on women's issues. When questioned whether she had any objections to being described as a 'woman's novelist', Brookner responds, 'Not in the least; women have devoted themselves to a certain kind of story-telling, which is extremely valid and extremely absorbing, mainly to other women, but to men as well, I think. It's a quite different genre. It does limit itself, but it tends to go deeper' (Kenyon 1989, 22). Brookner not only accepts that she writes women's fiction but also emphasizes the relevance of this specific 'genre'.

Brookner, however, is by no means overtly feminist; in fact she resists the 'feminist' label. In her reviews and interviews she has often been quite outspoken in her criticism of feminists and feminism. In an interview with Shusha Guppy she makes it clear: 'As for the radical feminism of today, the rejection of the male, I find it absurd. It leads to sterility' (Guppy 16). In another interview with Haffenden she categorically maintains that she does not take the extreme stand of denouncing males: 'I do not believe in all-men-are-swine programme' (Haffenden 1985, 70).

The foregoing study of *Hotel* inevitably leads to some broad conclusions which seem applicable to several women protagonists in Brookner's fiction. While her novels are not consciously feminine texts, they habitually analyse sexual politics. Moreover, the female protagonists in her novels reveal the social construction of a 'feminine' consciousness. Through the spotlight on the nuances of human relationships, as experienced and felt by sensitive female characters, her novels deal with a range of concerns and issues that are pertinent for all women. As her fiction works to create self-awareness in her protagonists' minds, she also offers an implicit female resistance to indifferent and dehumanizing forces in the patriarchal set-up. Her exploration of contemporary male and female attitudes towards each other, in relation to the familiar issues of sexuality, marriage, motherhood and economic independence is informed by an underlying 'feminist' concern for a healthier interaction between the sexes.

A prominent strain in *Hotel* is the inexorable revelation of the author's autobiographical 'self'. The novel is certainly not autobiographical in the sense of describing her entire life but incorporates her scrutiny of the feminine self. Sheila Hale's observation that Brookner's novels are not 'crudely autobiographical; they are far more devastatingly self-analytical' (Hale 36) appears to be particularly relevant for the manner in which Brookner explores her personal puzzles and moral tribulations through the fictional creation of Edith Hope. As she remarks about her novels, Brookner's basic effort is to make her writing 'as objective as possible, no self pity and no self justification' (Guppy 150). By the end of the novel, Edith begins to understand her inner self which yearns for love and affection and she realises that she is presenting an agreeable exterior in her relationship with David simply to win and hold onto him. Edith in this regard is like other Brooknerian heroines who all undertake their own types of story telling and the purpose of this exercise, as Brookner affirms, is to go through a special kind of 'moral examination, a self examination' (Haffenden 1985, 72).

Brookner clearly displays a 'feminine' sensibility and provides perceptive insights into the workings of women's psyche, and she achieves this remarkable feat by providing subtle nuances in her chosen area through a detailed and seemingly inane depiction of the 'trivia' of everyday existence. Brookner's self merges with the characters she creates. Many of the women she creates indulge in brooding self-analysis and as Brookner creates careful, clever, individual portraits of them, she maps the territory of their hearts with an extra-sensitive sensibility.

References

Bailey, Paul. Interview on BBC Radio. 1988 from fitzroydearborn.com/ London.

Barber, Michael. "Bluestocking blues." *Books and Bookmen,* Mar. 1983:26-27.

Beauvoir, Simone de. *The Second Sex.* 1949. Harmondsworth: Penguin, 1982.

Brookner, Anita. *A Start in Life.* London: Triad Grafton, 1982.

Brookner, Anita. *Hotel du Lac.* 1984. London: Penguin, 1993.

Brookner, Anita. *Providence:* London: Triad Grafton, 1983.

Grove, Valerie. " 'Hell would be quiz night at The Bull in Ambridge.'" *Times* 16 June 1995: 14.

Guppy, Shusha. "The Art of Fiction: Anita Brookner." *Paris Review*, (Fall 1987): 147-69.

Haffenden, John. Interview with Anita Brookner, *Literary Review.* (September 1984).

—. "Anita Brookner: *Novelists in Interview.* London and New York: Methuen, 1985. 57-75.

Hale, Sheila. "Self Reflecting." *Saturday Review* May/June 1985:35-38.

Kenyon, Olga. *Women Novelists Today: A Survey of English Writing in the Seventies and Eighties.* Brighton: Harvester Press, 1988.

—. "Anita Brookner." *Women Writers Talk: Interviews With 10 Women Writers.* Oxford: Lennard, 1989. 8-24.

Mayne, Richard. Interview on Radio 4, Oct. 1984 from fitzroydearborn.com/london.

Millet, Kate. *Sexual Politics.* London: Virago, 1970.

Moi, Toril. *Sexual/Textual Politics: Feminist Literary Theory.* 1985. London: Routledge, 1989.

Moritz, Charles, ed. *Current Biography Yearbook 1989.* New York: H.W. Wilson Company, 1989. 70-73.

Pykett, Lyn. "Anita Brookner", *Contemporary Novelists,* Ed. Lesley Henderson. 5th ed. Chicago: St. James Press. 1991. 147-48.

Rubin, Merle. "Anita Brookner's Novels: Old Moral Choices without the Old Rhetoric." Rev. of *Hotel du Lac. Christian Science Monitor.* 1 Mar. 1985: B3

—. 'Casting Moral Puzzles: A Novelist on her Craft." *Christian Science Monitor.* 1 Mar. 1985: B 3.

Schechner, Mark. *The Conversion of the Jews and Other Essays.* London: Macmillan, and New York: St Martin's Press. 1990

Showalter, Elaine. *A Literature of Their Own: British Women Novelists from Bronte to Lessing.* 1977. London: Virago, 1978.

Smith, Amanada. "PW Interviews: Anita Brookner". *Publishers Weekly*, 6 Sept 1985; 67-8.

Tonkin, Boyd. Interview with Anita Brookner. 'You should play Russian Roulette with Your Life'. June 29, 2002. from Independent.co.uk

Woolf, Virginia. *A Room of One's Own.* 1929. London: Penguin, 1945.

—. *Contemporary Writers.* London: Hogarth, 1965.

7 Exuberance as a Strategy in Angela Carter's *Wise Children*

Charu Mathur

'All art is political and so is mine. I want readers to understand what it is that I mean by my stories', says Angela Carter (Personal Interview: 1985). This does not imply a tendency to urge a particular course of action. To argue, in Carter's view, is to explore rather than persuade and exploring ideas, she says is 'the same thing as telling stories, since for me, a narrative is an argument stated in fictional terms' (1985: 13). As a postmodern novelist her novels reveal an implicit desire to provoke questions rather than to provide answers and engage with contradictions without seeking necessarily to solve them. In an attempt to jolt the reader out of customary associations and habits of thought, she continuously reinvents herself as a writer. In her later novels she employs a profligate narrative style to decolonise the thought process. *The Infernal Desire Machine of Dr. Hoffman* (1972) is fabulistic in form. In *The Passion of New Eve*(1977) there is a rejection of one kind of mythical language only to substitute it by another, while *The Nights at the Circus*(1984) has an allegoric approach to narrative. This technique of decolonization, however, is most pervasive in her last novel, *Wise Children* (1991), where she looks into the possibility of resorting to exuberance as a strategy to manoeuvre the contradictory and undermining forces of life, to an advantage. The violence in the events depicted in the earlier novels of the 1960s and 1970s (the rapes, the physical and marital abuse of women) and the aggression implicit in the representations is replaced by a violent exuberance that reaffirms the narrative logic by forceful fabulist enactment.

A woman storyteller who tells tales that do not quite fit into the social order of things; Carter nevertheless, avoids portraying women as occupants of the oppressed camp. This is, as Merja Makinen argues, perhaps because 'exuberance sells better than discomfort' (Makinen 27). The mellowing down of textual aggression is an attempt to engage in a dialogue with the reader, which is also Carter's idea of 'narrative utopia' (Sage 50). A reader-friendly text is created by way of transference of ecstasy from the narrator to the reader. The writer does not assume an opposition between politics and pleasure. Instead, there is a subtle employment of the tools of dramatic performance like masquerade, carnival, burlesque, parody, travesty and spectacle to create a pervasive textual irony without sacrificing the novel's character as an entertainer. The novel can be read on as many levels as the reader can comfortably cope with. Combining political enlightenment with genial pleasure is a difficult act to pull off. Yet Carter's vibrant style enables her to simultaneously be 'in the demythologizing business' (Haffenden 91) without adversely affecting her position 'in the entertainment business' (Haffenden 82). Her rapturous representations blur the edges of realism, dissolving the rigours of plot and characterization, which result in a radical disruption of expectations. By deconstructing the social fictions that regulate our lives she wittily presents the relationship between cultural institutions and human agency as dynamic and malleable.

The depiction of elasticity between the inter-relationships of an individual with the family, class, culture and society has been effectively achieved in *Wise Children*. The first person narrative mingles empirical fact with fictional elements to assume a baroque style of voice that radically rewrites the moral code in an epicurean direction to expose the orgies of binary conditioning. The novel tells the tale of 'the imperial Hazard dynasty that bestrode the British theatre like a colossus for a century and a half' and its bastard progeny, Dora and Nora Chance, identical twins who are illegitimate twice over: by birth because their father denies his paternity of them time after time, and by profession, where, as a novelty act, they danced the boards in music hall, appear briefly as extras in an ill-fated Hollywood musical, and finally undress (though never beyond the G-string) in seedy post war strip shows (*Wise Children* 10).

The story is told by Dora who spills out more than a century of family romance and history, though the action of the novel takes place in just one day. A special day however, it is the anniversary of Shakespeare's birthday which happens also to be Dora's and Nora's own – this year their seventy fifth. It is birthday and centenary, too, of another set of twins, Melchior and Peregrine Hazard: father and uncle (but which is which) of these performing sisters, 'the Lucky Chances' (98). The grotesque abundance of twins and the exaggerated coincidence of the day of birth in the legitimate as well as illegitimate line anticipate the future spilling out of skeletons from the closet. The double faced Hazard/Chance family is served up to the reader as a model for Britain and Britishness, obsessively dividing itself into upper and working class, high and low culture. And just as Dora proves these strict lines of demarcation to be false within her own family, so too her story shows the reader how badly these compartments fit the complexity and hybridity of British society and culture.

The dislocation of binary oppositions in hegemonic representations in society is achieved through a bouncy narrative that sustains a buoyancy of mood all through the novel undermining the logic of rigid social ideology. The cockney comedy of *Wise Children* can be read in terms of evolutionary metaphors that not only challenge legitimacy but also celebrate the vitality that hails from the 'wrong side of the blanket' (8). The legitimate and illegitimate worlds, as Kate Webb interprets, 'rely upon one another's mirror image of difference through which to define themselves, such a celebration of illegitimacy necessarily implies a valorization of the system which produces outcasts' (1995: 194). One of the vital questions that Carter poses in the novel is – what should a wise child do? Should she revel in the wrong-sidedness of her position and therefore take advantage of the system that produces it, or should she reject the culture of dualism altogether and therefore erase her underprivileged position? The Chance sisters manage to have their cake and eat it too. They revel in their wrong-sidedness to sustain their opposition to authority. At the same time they show that the culture and society they inhabit is not one of rigid demarcation but has always been mixed up and hybrid. In portraying the twins as bubbly fun-loving beings, Carter consciously avoids the precarious idealisation of the passive victim. The Chance sisters are no glassy fragile forms but exemplary postmodern heroines who take control of their own performances and manipulate their self-stagings for their own advantage. Dora's story is not one of martyrdom or victimhood. She knows that as outsiders she and her sister Nora enjoy freedoms that their legitimate twin sisters, Imogen and Saskia, could never hope for.

Nevertheless, the stance they assume is not an assertive feministic one but a stratagem of convenience. At seventy-five, they are still full of robust enthusiasm, 'We're stuck in the period at which we peaked. All women do . . . . We paint an inch thick. We put on our faces before we come down to breakfast . . . . the habit of applying war paint outlasts the battle', says Dora (5-6). The sisters abound in high spirits and refuse to be drawn into despair even when they are informed about the death of their cherished godchild, Tiffany. 'Life must go on', says Nora with an existential acceptance of the facts of life and death (52). 'Hope for the best, expect the worst," a maxim learned from 'grandmother' works for them and it is with resilience that they negotiate the dualistic structures of class and gender' (33). The exuberance of Dora's personality comes from a special kind of resourcefulness. As Webb puts it

> She seemed like Shakespeare's bastard Edmund, determined not to let the Dionysian wheel of fate settle her life, but to find in the 'Chance' of her wrong sidedness neither shame,

> nor restrain, but opportunity. . . . Maybe one of the meanings of the twins is the idea that one need not be afraid of one's image, but should embrace it, love it instead. Like the autoerotic Dora and Nora, one can 'feast' on oneself (1995:201).

This fanatic self-love is a feat they inherit from the Hazard family who consider themselves custodians of the Shakespearean culture and therefore of the legitimate theatre he symbolizes. The Hazards' excessive enthusiasm in the 'mission' approaches madness. Rudolph's evangelical zeal for spreading the word of Shakespeare was so great that he "crossed, crisscrossed" the globe, and travelled 'to the ends of the Empire' in his efforts to sell the religion of Shakespeare and the English values he represented (17). Rudolph's mania results in a 'Shakespearian funeral pyre' when he decides to play *Othello* on Broadway (20). In a burlesque imitation the margins between drama and real life dissolve when old Rudolph kills both Cassius Booth who played Iago and his own wife Estella who played Desdemona, before killing himself. There is no bubble burst however, as one of the twin sons Melchoir picks up the threads with zealous commitment and continues to dominate the stage as a legendary Shakespearean actor. The ancestral 'King Lear crown' that is salvaged from the burnt down house in Hollywood is a symbol of the legacy that is preserved with equal fervor. By showing Shakespeare at the heart of modern culture, Carter is arguing that plurality and hybridity are not simply conditions of modernity, products of its wreckage, but have always existed and are products of life itself. The Chance sisters who belong to the music hall, the illegitimate and unacknowledged child of the Shakespearean stage also revel in the ecstasy of their profession. 'What a joy it is to dance and sing!' is Dora's refrain (5). However, as Webb observes, 'she is aware of the effect that enthusiasm and self-absorption of carnival can have upon others: aware too of the ways in which this power can be harnessed by a dominant group and brought to bear upon a weaker one' (1995: 196). So she celebrates this craziness yet deftly shows how intimately connected are Shakespeare's cultural dominations and British imperialism.

The fall of the Hazard dynasty parodies the fall of British Empire. Dora's refrain, a Miltonic phrase, 'Lo, how the mighty have fallen', is both a silly semantic joke and a serious intimation of the world she inhabits (10). Carter, unlike many modernist writers sees in the decline of the Empire, not the death of bad old things, but the birth of good new ones. And she uses laughter as a means to herald the new world – laughter that defies dogmatism, authoritarianism or any narrow-minded seriousness. Moreover, laughter in the novel is linked with transgression. All along we witness 'fathers' and 'daughters' transgressing their roles. Runulph shoots himself leaving his twin sons fatherless. Melchior also, rejects his role as a father to the Chance sisters and in a funny ironical twist; it is revealed how he did not father his so-called, 'legitimate' daughters. Even Perigrine who is a deviant in the Hazard family never openly acknowledges his relationship with his daughters Imogen and Saskia. 'Having never experienced fatherly feelings', states Webb, 'they often confuse them with sexual ones. Hence the tradition of Lears marrying their Cordelias. In the same way absent fathers are mysterious fathers which is why these enigmatic creatures become for their daughters the object of such longing and romance' (1995: 207). Perigrine who becomes 'a sugar daddy' to the Chance sisters is also a paradoxical presence for it is in him that Dora sees all her lovers pass by as she and he make love at Melchior's tumultuous birthday party (34). It is this errant behaviour of 'fathers' and 'daughters' that creates among the Hazards and Chances so much opportunity for the breakdown of order, for transgression. Besides, the Chances as orphaned children are free children – free from the prescribed authority of the parents; a situation which allows them a little more space in which to fashion themselves.

This Bakhtinian idea of carnival is central to *Wise Children*. All through the novel, Carter plays out ideas about relationships to the carnivalesque transgression of order that is, according to Bakhtin, at once both sanctioned and illegitimate. The focus is on the social nature of dialogue and the idea of struggle inherent in it. The transgressive use of language becomes a means by which transgressive ideologies get articulated. The celebration of the music hall culture asserts that popular cultural forms designated as 'low' culture by the self-legitimizing authorities of the official 'high' culture, draw upon traditions of grotesque realism to deploy laughter, irony and satire to oppose the 'high' culture and its established authority, a deployment whose chief source is the folk tradition of grotesque realism.

Similarly, the transgressive depiction of Melchior's birthday party presents Bakhtin's 'world of topsy-turvy, of heteroglot exuberance, of ceaseless overrunning and excess where all is mixed, hybrid, ritually degraded and defiled' highlighting its revolutionary potential (8). The flamboyant attitude of the Chance sisters asserts liberation from the established order and marks a suspension of all hierarchical rank privileges, norms and prohibitions that makes possible a special type of communication normally not possible and hails a period of change and renewal. The Rabelaisian boundary-buster Perigrine also embodies the carnivalesque spirit. He is a multiple man, and his multiplicity makes him elusive. Hence, Dora and Nora observe 'He gave us all his histories, we could choose which one we wanted – but they kept on changing, so. That was the trouble' (31). His elusiveness questions the very nature of reality and holds it up for introspection just as the whimsical personality of Perigrine's mother, Estella poses a challenge to convention and the accepted order. She becomes a symbol of the carnival idiom filled with the pathos of transformation and regeneration and a sense of gained relativity of prevailing truths and authorities. Carter describes her as a woman whose 'hair was always coming undone . . . tumbling down her back, spraying out hairpins in all directions, her stockings at half-mast, her petticoat would come adrift in the middle of the street, her drawers start drooping. She was marvel and she was a mess' (12). Her comic gust of energy disturbs the old order of Runulph who is known for his 'gift of gravitas' and hence the collapse, for the binaries of the comic and the tragic involve the binaries of class as well (12). 'Tragedy, eternally more class than comedy', sighs Dora meaning both that it has a classier pedigree than comedy and is associated with the classes than the masses (58).

In the figure of Gorgeous George, Carter displays a diffusion of these dualistic structures. 'George was not a comic at all but an enormous statement', observes Dora (66). Clowns and fools, characteristic of the medieval culture of humour were the constant accredited representatives of the carnival spirit in everyday life out of the carnival season. Thus licensed, George's jokes mock ideas of strength and purity. His comedy is parodic and perfectly timed while his punch line, when it is finally delivered, is a withering attack on archetypal representations and highlights the plurality of British culture. Twining humour with irony, Carter shows this plurality not as a postmodernist deletion of value but an insistence on contradictions and difference arising as a consequence of the inevitable process of cultural dialogics. Historically, these have always existed underneath the traditional myth of order and continue to co-exist and negotiate with the powerful. The focus is on mocking and exploding the constrictive stereotypes and in celebrating the sheer ability of the Chance sisters to survive, unscathed by dualistic ideologies. Their unscrupulous manipulations tell us that the world of absolutes is fading and now we live in, what Webb describes as, 'a world of endless refraction. The days when a looking glass reflected just one wicked witch, one absolute image of otherness, are gone. Now we have . . . . a glasshouse of perpetual reproduction. Our relationship to these multiple, often contradictory reflections, especially for women, is as important and as determining as our relationship to other people' (1995: 201). The images we relate to now are variable and shifting and need to be addressed with a corresponding flexibility. Contradictions are a sign of hope and differences have to be negotiated rather than fought over.

This strategy of rewriting social ideology has however, become all too familiar in recent years, but Angela Carter is significant because of the awareness with which she walks the tight rope between carnivalesque exuberance and rational critique. In *Wise Children* the music hall comes to represent the carnivalesque deflator of the bombast of 'high culture' epitomized in the myth of Shakespeare's genius as national treasure. But the novel ends up reinforcing the myth, notably in the scene at the end of the novel, in which Dora and Nora achieve their heart's desire when they are publicly reconciled with Melchior Hazard. As Britzolakis states, 'a self-conscious and camp sentimentality licenses a reconstitution of the family under the sign of Shakespeare' (187). Feeling victorious, Dora exclaims, 'Nora and I were well content. We'd finally wormed our way into the heart of the family we'd always wanted to be a part of. They'd asked us on stage and let us join in, legit. at last' (226). This assimilation was effected not by confrontation but by the defiance that grotesque humour and linguistic exuberance affords. Nevertheless, Carter is also aware of the limits to the power of laughter. The carnival cannot rewrite history but it can be a means of adapting to the present situation and does offer the tantalizing promise of how things might be in the future, if we altered the conditions which tie us down.

References

Bakhtin, Michail., *Rabelias and His World*. (1968). Trans. H. Iswolsky. Bloomington: IN, 1984.

Britzolakis, Christina. "Angela Carter's Fetishism". *New Casebooks: Angela Carter.*, Ed. Alison Easton. London: Macmillan, 2000.

Carter, Angela. *Come Unto These Yellow Sands: Four Radio Plays.* New Castle – Upon – Tyne, 1985.

Carter, Angela. "Notes from Frontline." *On Gender and Writing*. Ed. Michelene Wandor. London, 1983.

Carter, Angela. *Wise Children*. London: Vintage, 1991.

Haffendon, John. "Angela Carter", *Novelists in Interview*. London, 1985.

Makinen, Merja. "Angela Carter's *The Bloody Chamber* and the Decolonisation of Feminine Sexuality." *New Casebooks: Angela Carter.* Ed. Alison Easton. London: Macmillan, 1995.

Sage, Lorna. *Angela Carter.* Plymouth, 1994.

Webb, Kate. Personal interview 18 December, 1985.

Webb, Kate. "Seriously Funny: *Wise Children*". *New Casebooks: Angela Carter*. Ed. Alison Easton. London: Macmillan, 1995.

8 Subversive Narratives in Muriel Spark's Fiction

A Reading of Two Novels

Preeti Bhatt

Muriel Spark (1918-2006) is one of the major contemporary British writers whose fiction reflects her understanding of narrative technique as a means to communicate profound ideas. Spark evinces a serious and sustained engagement with the socio-cultural situations around her. Her novels convey through the fictional mode her concern for the social, political and cultural problems existing in the present world. This concern is embedded in the subtext of the narrative, and is reflected through the narrative strategies. In her fiction Spark presents her perceptions of the emotional dilemmas experienced by individuals – dilemmas that have originated from societal relationships and conflicts.

Spark has consistently disturbed conventional reader-expectations through her innovative narrative strategies. She has moved ahead of the experiments done by modernist writers and by using subversive techniques of narration, has questioned the idea of reality as a unified whole. Many of her novels undermine conventional narrative practices to subvert traditional ways of thinking and of looking at the world. She has examined contemporary epistemological issues, as the complex relationship between fiction and reality, between man and God, and between the self and the other. Spark is often described as a postmodernist writer due to her experimentation with narrative technique to convey the contemporary understanding of reality and existence.

The present paper focuses on two of Muriel Spark's later novels, *The Driver's Seat* (1970) and *Loitering With Intent* (1981) with a view to examine her search for a narrative form which reflects the contemporary reality. In both these novels Spark discards the traditional narrative form with its linear, mimetic and conclusive representations of reality. Through the use of postmodernist narrative technique in these novels, Spark subverts the mode of writing which insists upon a direct, simple reproduction of external reality, based on an epistemological questioning of the process of knowing the world. Through her fiction Spark conveys the idea that knowledge is a relative concept, which changes with the change in perspective.

The realistic mode of narration used extensively in the eighteenth and nineteenth centuries presented an empirical perspective. Neo-classicism believed that art imposed order on life, which is disordered and chaotic, and represented a linear chronological view of life. Alice R. Kaminsky in *The Theory of the Novel* (1974) comments that the realists attempted to imitate the unidimensional quality of human life, their 'rationale being that since individual life has the order of a beginning, middle and end, the novel should reflect such order' (225). By faithfully imitating the real external world in the novel, the author represented man's anxiety to dominate and control the world. Ronald Sukenick in the essay "Twelve Digressions toward a Study of Composition" (1974-75) states that the realistic novel 'whispers assurance that the world is not mysterious, that it is predictable – if not to the characters then to the author…' (429).

In the early twentieth century, modernist writers like Virginia Woolf, James Joyce, T.S. Eliot and others experimented with narrative technique as they questioned the conventions associated with realism. They focused on the flowing human consciousness, on the resources of myth, symbol and language, to give form and meaning to the disintegrated world of their time. During the 1950s, the novels expressed a persistent concern with the difficulty of confronting the changed landscape of the postwar social life. The two world wars had had a devastating impact on the imagination of the writers, and the subjectivism in modernist writing was thought to be incapable of dealing with social issues. The trauma of the wars included not only impending death and destruction, but also fear and despair at the worldwide fragmentation, the constant process of mutation and the fragmentation and formation of new countries. To present the changing reality of the changing world, new narrative techniques were required and created by several writers.

Alain Robbe-Grillet in the essays contained in the volume titled *For a New Novel* (1963) discussed the idea of the *nouveau roman* or the anti-novel. Robbe Grillet's novel *La Jalousie* (1957), Michel Butor's *La Modification* (1957) and Nathalie Sarraute's *Le Planetarium* (1959) were some of the novels of this kind. The traditional elements in the narrative like a causally and chronologically ordered plot, or the analysis of the states of mind of the characters, were conspicuously absent in these novels. In the *nouveau roman*, the focus, argued Robbe-Grillet, was on a neutral description of objects rather than on character studies. He criticized the use of the pathetic fallacy in the traditional novel. He contended that a writer who invested human attributes in a lifeless object was guilty of believing that the physical world is man's domain, while in reality this is not so (Weightman 232). In "A Future for the Novel" (1956), Robbe-Grillet stated, 'Let it be first of all by their *presence* that objects and gestures establish themselves,' and continued further, 'and let this presence continue to prevail over whatever explanatory theory that may try to enclose them in a system of reference, whether emotional, sociological, Freudian or metaphysical' (75). Hence the numerous descriptive passages in his novels, in which precise definitions of shapes, sizes and colours of objects are offered.

The French experimental novel raises basic questions about the relation between the narrative voice within the text, the author and the reader's role in reading and interpreting. Alin Robbe-Grillet's novel *La Jalousie* effectively conveys this idea through its narrative technique. The omniscient, omnipresent narrator of the realistic novels is replaced in Robbe-Grillet's novel by the limited perceptions of a man through whose eyes mainly most of the action is shown. The objective narrator of the traditional novel thus becomes his own subject in the *nouveau roman*. This man is engaged in an obsessive activity, and the truth of his description cannot be presumed, for at some points in the novel his imagination takes charge, and produces false impressions, the products of his delirious mind. Muriel Spark's concern with narrative modes and techniques was reflected this widespread thinking about fiction, storytelling and narratology. The influence of the *nouveau roman* was apparent in some of Spark's novels, especially on *The Driver's Seat*.

Muriel Spark was keenly interested in poetry and imaginative writing of all kinds since her childhood. She appreciated the tightly constructed and condensed form of poetry and also stated in her autobiography *Curriculum Vitae* (1992), 'any good novel, or indeed any composition which called for a constructional sense, was essentially an extension of poetry' (206). Before beginning her career as a novelist, Spark wrote a number of critical treatises and biographies mostly on nineteenth-century writers – *Child of Light: A Reassessment of Many Wollstonecraft Shelley* (1951), *A Selection of Poems by Emily Brontë* (1952), and *The Brontë Letters* (1953), all three of them edited with an introduction by Muriel Spark. Later that year Spark produced two more books on Emily Brontë and Mary Shelley, *Emily Brontë Her Life and Work* (1953), and *My Best Mary: Selected Letters of Mary Shelley* (1953), both edited in collaboration with Derek Stanford.

Spark's first novel, *The Comforters* (1957) has a highly experimental form in which the writer plays with the idea of writing fiction. The author, the narrator and the characters, all at their own levels, weave elaborate tales so that different kinds of fictions coexist in the narrative. Through these fictional stories Spark underlines the constructed nature of the text, and makes the whole novel an elaborate, sustained game of artifice. Spark, in all her novels, continues the innovations and experimentation, which she had begun since her very first novel. *The Driver's Seat* (1970) can be taken to be the culmination of the experimentation in the first phase of Spark's career as a novelist. This novel contrasts with all the earlier novels of Spark in its highly economical narrative style, the dry, terse tone, and the lack of specificities in the narrative.

The Driver's Seat is a succinct account of the last thirty-six hours in the life of Lise, a thirty-four year old woman, who plots the events of her own murder which, eventually, is committed at Lise's own invitation by a rehabilitated criminal. Characterization in this novel is minimal and the narrative is highly controlled by a sense of impending doom. In a major part of the narrative Lise's activities are recounted in minute detail in the present tense: 'Lise breathes as if sleeping, deeply tired, but her eye-slits open from time to time. Her hand moves to her brown leather bag on the lamp-shelf and she raises herself, pulling the bag towards her' (15). This creates the impression that the story is unfolding in front of the reader's eyes. The narration in the present tense continues throughout the novel, 'Lise walks up to the great windows of the Pavilion and presses close to look inside, while he follows her. Then she walks round the back and over to the hedge' (105). This narrative mode carries within it the possibility of surprise and contrasts with the smug and secure narration in the past tense of the realistic novel. Glen Cavaliero calls it 'the historic present: this is a *fiction*, a portrayal of the way things happen' (205).

As in the novels of existentialist writers, the personal details about Lise's family and background, her complete name, her place of residence, the destination of her air-journey is completely absent. With specific details about the locale of action and time missing, Lise becomes a solitary, alienated woman in a wide world, rootless due to the lack of a significant past. William McBrien in *Twentieth Century Women Novelists* (1985) comments that 'the setting and its citizenry seem abstract, Kafka-like, artificial, impersonal' (169) with nothing to console or to hold on to as a means of support.

In the postmodernist novels, the focus is not on the flow of the characters' thoughts to explore their inner reality. Instead these novels present the surface behaviour of the characters, focusing only on the external action to suggest the opacity of the minds of individuals. This is the recognition of the impenetrability of one person's mind by another as the realist concept of a stable unified character gave way to new psychoanalytical and philosophical approaches. Iris Murdoch, a contemporary of Muriel Spark, also, in her novels, attempts to portray the impenetrability of the human psyche. In an essay "Against Dryness: A Polemical Sketch" (1961), Murdoch describes human beings as 'benighted creatures sunk in a reality whose nature we are constantly and overwhelmingly tempted to deform by fantasy' (17). In many of her novels she demonstrates the problems created by the limited understanding of individuals about the 'other' and the human tendency to impose one's presumptions upon the real self of the 'other'.

Spark, in *The Driver's Seat*, emphasizes the difference and the distance between the reader and the character through the narrator's unwillingness to probe into Lise's mind. The narrative remains directed only on the surface and presents 'an entirely external focalization on one character' (Roberts 58). Lise's psychological depth is not shared with the reader at any point in the narrative. Malcolm Bradbury observes that Spark's characters 'have will and style but no psychologically established motives, real history, or conditioning milieu' (251). Though this remark cannot be applied to all her novels, it is quite correct of the heroine in *The Driver's Seat*. The narrative voice reports Lise's actions in an uninvolved manner as if from a distance, 'She puts the bunch of keys in her handbag, picks up the paperback book and goes out ... Who knows her thoughts? Who can tell?' (50). This lack of narratorial comment on the protagonist serves to estrange her from the reader, who finds it hard to empathize with Lise.

In Spark's novel, the linear narrative of realism is subverted by repeated references to Lise's tragic end. The opening sentence of Third Chapter states, 'She will be found tomorrow morning dead from multiple stab-wounds, her wrists bound with a silk scarf and her ankles bound with a man's necktie...' (25). Such flash-forwards decrease considerably the element of suspense, and the focus is directed on how things happen rather than on what happens in the novel. Jago Morrison in *Contemporary Fiction* (2003) comments on the time scheme in contemporary fiction that 'the comforting, coherent, linear-historical frames characteristic of realist fiction have often been replaced by more fractured and unsettling narrative forms...' (34-35). The intrusion of the scene of Lise's gruesome murder disturbs the reader, while indicating the deterministic nature of events in the narrative. The repeated shifts to the future underline the omniscience of the narrator and simultaneously point to the novel as a created text in which the reader finds it impossible to get involved.

In *The Driver's Seat*, Spark parodies the conventional detective novel through the plot structure. Frank Kermode in "Novel and Narrative" (1974) describes a detective story as one which is told in such a way that 'the principal object of the reader is to discover, by an interpretation of clues, the answer to a problem posed at the outset'. Kermode points out that in a murder-mystery the crime 'precedes the narrative which bears the clues' (159). The clues may be simple and straightforward, or misleading and enigmatic. But these clues form critical links in the sequence of events preceding the crime and enable the investigator in the story, and the reader herself to solve the mystery by reconstructing the entire episode.

In this novel the crime actually occurs at the end of the novel, and the narrative describes, using the point of view of an eyewitness narrator, how the victim Lise herself selects, pursues and forces the killer to perform the crime. Her earlier actions indicate her aim to create a public sensation, and simultaneously, to leave a series of clues for the police (and also for the reader), before she dies a violent death. In a traditional mystery story, these clues would be painstakingly located and analysed by the investigator. As Ian Rankin states in "Surface and Structure: Reading Muriel Spark's *The Driver's Seat*" (1985), the clues are present here from the very beginning, 'but to fit them all together on a first reading, blind as it were, is impossible' (146).

Lise, from the beginning of the novel behaves abnormally, drawing attention to herself all the while. She buys a garish, eye-catching dress, which she wears during her plane journey and is rude, irritable and impatient with the people she encounters. Lise seems to be pursuing two ends through her strange dress and behaviour. She, through her choice of extraordinary, attention-seeking clothes, 'fabricates a non-identity, throws away all evidence of a real self' (Hart 32). Lise successfully obliterates her old identity and invents a new persona, one that is bizarre and therefore memorable. Judy Little in *The British and Irish Novel Since 1960* (1991) suggests that Lise turns out her holiday trip into 'a plot to erase what little self she has. Instead of defining a self, she is undefining it as efficiently as possible' (10).

It is only after Lise has been murdered at the end of the novel that the reader realizes that throughout the narrative, Lise was driven by a sense of violent destruction as her impending destiny. *The Driver's Seat* becomes the story of a lonely character, pursuing and challenging her fate while seeking her killer, who is also her lover. Bryan Cheyette in *Muriel Spark* (2000) observes, 'there are no reasons given for Lise's actions other than her need to overcome her sense of rootlessness and, as a spinster, her loneliness' (77). Lise's obsessively self-destructive behaviour reflects the tragic mental state of the individual in a society, which has lost all sense of hope and happiness due to its materialistic concerns.

Towards the end of the novel Lise once gives vent to her emotions and weeps, saying, 'It makes me sad ... I want to go back home and feel all that lonely grief again. I miss it so much already' (96). Lise, an unknown, unloved person finds no meaning in existence in which there are no moral or religious concerns to lend purpose to her life. George Lukács's description in *The Meaning of Contemporary Realism* (1963) of the hero in modernist literature is applicable to her – 'without personal history', 'thrown-into-the-world meaninglessly, unfathomably,' one who 'does not develop through contact with the world' (21). It is through her carefully plotted death, that Lise ensures that she will receive due recognition, something for which she probably yearned in life.

Spark in *The Driver's Seat* creates a myth about the plight of the modern woman in the contemporary world. Lise's uncanny foreknowledge about her horrifying end is in fact an awareness of the tragic destiny of 'every woman' like her, who is independent, unescorted and alienated and therefore prone to the carnal desires of perverted men. She is a typical woman of the present society who is unable to enter into stable relationships with men due to the patriarchal setup of the world, which curbs her independence, and exploits her as an object. Her solitude and desolation becomes an ill omen of the end that awaits her – which is usually rape and murder.

Man-made objects find repeated reference in Spark's novel, and, at times, are described with meticulous detail. Lise's immaculately organized flat contains pinewood furniture which is 'all fixed, adaptable to various uses, and stackable' (14). The meal served to Lise during her plane journey is described in precise terms: 'silver wrapped processed cheese', 'biscuits wrapped in cellophane', 'empty plastic coffee cup' (31). Spark appears to be influenced by the *nouveau roman* in this novel, for she dispassionately presents descriptions of the external world to emphasize their 'otherness', their detachment from human emotion. Alain Robbe-Grillet states in his critique of the new novel: 'It is matter itself which is both solid and unstable, both present and imagined, alien to man and constantly being invented in man's mind' (*For a New Novel* 148).

The writer in this novel emphasizes the decline of the concept of individualism and the increasing hold of consumerism on the modern society. Much of the action in the narrative takes place in public buildings – airport terminals, hotels, bars, and departmental stores, where human individuality is of no import and where everyone is merely a consumer. These open public buildings indicate a loss of private personal space for the individual. The world portrayed outside is buzzing with people – policemen, porters, waiters, salesgirls, student mobs, yet, as Norman Page in *Muriel Spark* (1990) points out, it is 'a world without attachments, loyalties, or stable relationships' (73). The overcrowded world outside heightens the irony of the situation, that in the present society people are indifferent to the emotional needs of others, and for an individual like Lise, death is the only means of establishing contact with others.

Through the character of Lise Spark demonstrates the human condition in the modern world – the helplessness and perplexity of human beings as they face an irrational, absurd universe. The meaninglessness of human existence forces Lise to seek her end, an end that is predetermined for her in the present pleasure-seeking callous society. The impact of Lise's shocking murder is especially achieved through the device of subverting the plot structure and by defamiliarizing the story and the characters. The form of the novel – deceptively simple, yet highly sophisticated, strikingly brings out the metaphysical connotations implicit in the narrative. The sudden end that Lise meets at the end of the novel underlines the uncertainty of human existence and the lacuna in human knowledge and understanding. Human life, however rationally lived, becomes devoid of meaning when one dies. Lise's life and death baffle all explanations.

In *Loitering With Intent* (1981), the structure of a novel-within-the novel explores the enigmatic relationship between fiction and reality. The characters in this novel are constructed by the writer as involved in their struggle to understand the world outside and also one's self as an artist, and as a human being. In this novel Muriel Spark uses the protagonist, Fleur Talbot as a surrogate figure to look back at the time when Spark herself had begun her career as a novelist. Liam McIlvanney in "The Politics of Narrative in the Post-war Scottish Novel" (2002) states for Spark's more closely autobiographical novels like this one, 'It is here that Spark's baleful puritan economy, in which everything must be working to an orchestrated purpose, is relaxed, and the writing follows only the random pull of memory' (195). The narrator, Fleur, is a successful novelist who describes the genesis of her first novel, *Warrender Chase*. In the course of the narrative Fleur comments on the art of writing fiction and some of her views are, as Ruth Whittaker has said, 'echoes, almost word for word, of statements made by Mrs. Spark herself in interviews' (121). These critical comments make *Loitering With Intent* a self-reflexive, self-begetting novel where the process of writing itself becomes the subject of writing.

Spark's novel becomes a means to create the 'self' of the protagonist while tracing her development and maturity as a fiction-writer. Steven G. Kellman in *The Self-Begetting Novel* (1980) points out that such a novel 'recounts the creation of a work very much like itself, but it is also the portrait of a fictive artist being born' (7). The novel gives Fleur, the narrator and the central character an identity and an existence. It is through this novel that Fleur becomes alive and acquires a personality, a 'self' and a name.

Muriel Spark's self-conscious protagonist is evaluating the novel she is writing, and her experiences during that period in her life form the focus of the present novel. Spark has used the fictional mode to re-examine the metaphysical, conceptual aspects of the nature of reality, of the world, and of the human person located in the world. Her characters look at their own fictionality and the fiction-making ability, and introspect over the formation of human identity through many modes of 'fiction' or 'narratives'.

The novel *Loitering With Intent* is described by Fleur as an autobiographical 'account of that small part of my life and all that happened in the middle of the twentieth century, those months of 1949-50' (127). In the narrative her personal reminiscences emerge along with the descriptions of the tension she experienced as a writer. Fleur was a young woman at that time living in London, and she recalls with nostalgia 'what a wonderful thing it was to be a woman and an artist in the twentieth century' (182). Fleur's being an artist in the twentieth century opens up many new areas of self-examination and critical enquiries in the art of writing. While woman-writers had also produced a substantial amount of literary writings – both fiction and non-fiction in the nineteenth century, writing for a woman in mid-twentieth century implied greater freedom – both economic and intellectual. A woman-writer who acquired a name in the literary world came at par with the male writers. She also enjoyed more freedom to express her ideas about issues critical both to men and women in the society. This meant that through the medium of print a woman-writer could convey to readers all over the world her views about serious issues and could expect some effect, even if little, on the society at large.

Fleur Talbot, before the publication of her first novel, works as secretary to Sir Quentin Oliver, who is the founder of the Autobiographical Association. This consists of a group of " 'men and women of great distinction living full, very full lives' " (19) who are writing their memoirs with Sir Quentin's assistance. These confidential memoirs are to be retained by Sir Quentin and are to be published after a period of seventy years. Fleur is employed to type these memoirs, and to edit them wherever necessary.

As Fleur becomes acquainted with Sir Quentin and the members of the Association, she realizes that Sir Quentin is behaving uncannily like Warrender Chase, the protagonist of the novel she is writing. Fleur's Warrender exercises a strong, malign influence on a group of weak-minded people, driving them to madness and suicide by planting in them 'a sense of terrible and unreal guilt' (83). Sir Quentin similarly starts blackmailing the members of his Association by misusing the guilty secrets they have recorded in their memoirs.

Sir Quentin exhibits a strain of authoritarianism in his desire to control the lives of the members. He forces them to fast for self-purification, and also hands out drugs to them, which are appetite-suppressors but which affect the brain adversely: 'he was handing out to all of them, including Dottie, small yellow pills called Dexedrine which he told them would enable them to endure the purifying fasts he inflicted' (117). Like a god manipulating the destinies of his creations, Sir Quentin believes that he has absolute control over the people he has trapped. His dictatorial behaviour brings to the reader's mind the similarity that might exist between him and a fiction-writer. Does the writer control the characters she has constructed through her imagination, or do they become free once a personality has been assigned to them? Are the characters in a work of fiction merely puppets, with the writer pulling their strings, exhibiting his/her innate tendency to control others? Or are they similar to real persons, having a will of their own and shaping their own fates by exercising their choice? Spark explores these issues of the creative process through the character of Sir Quentin Oliver in this novel.

When Fleur is appointed by Sir Quentin as secretary, she is expected to typewrite the memoirs, and also " 'to rectify and lack or lapse in form, syntax, style...' " (23). While memoirs and other autobiographical writing ought to be sincere and written in first hand, the act of editing them transforms their meaning, even if only a single word has been removed or replaced. Fleur is basically an artist, and she finds the memoirs very dull and boring to start with. She feels that 'Typing out and making sense out of these compositions was an agony to my spirit' (31) and decides to enliven them by adding fictional bits to the boring parts. Fleur, through this action turns autobiographers into novelists: 'I had set them on to writing fictions about themselves' (117). This is a significant shift from one mode into another. The shift from merely copying or imitating reality to writing fiction makes all the difference. Spark is concerned with the problematic relationship between fiction and reality as Fleur struggles with the two modes.

Fleur, through the act of rewriting the memoirs becomes a creator of the new texts. She gives a new atmosphere to the scenes presented, and adds incidents, which are more probable than possible, and gives them a humorous turn. Margaret Moan Rowe in the article "Muriel Spark and the Angel of the Body" (1987) comments on Fleur's writing ability as: 'art is the way to power, to control. A control not altogether different from that exercised by Sir Quentin Oliver...' (175). But there is an important difference between Fleur as an artist, and Sir Quentin as one. The changes that Fleur makes in the biographies have an aesthetic purpose while Sir Quentin's desire to control others is a moral sin. Fleur expresses her disapproval of Sir Quentin's interference in the lives of those people when she states, 'I was sure that nothing had happened in their lives and equally sure that Sir Quentin was pumping something artificial into their real lives instead of on paper' (117). Through the character of Sir Quentin, Spark explores the moral issues of power in this novel.

Sir Quentin pushes his followers to the destinies he has planned out for them. He 'insists on complete frankness, forcing them to share their secrets and therefore making them susceptible to blackmail' (98). After having revealed their weaknesses to Sir Quentin, the members of the Association can in no way shake off his dominion over them. Sir Quentin convinces these people that 'there is just one way – *his* way – to interpret their lives and write their autobiographies' (14). Lady Bernice of the Autobiographical Association commits suicide due to the malevolent influence of Sir Quentin. Spark, through the ill effects of Sir Quentin's personality on the other characters, condemns the human tendency to exercise control over others.

The relationship between fiction and reality is further explored when Fleur begins to regard the real-life members of the Association as 'inventions of my own' (36), having revised and rewritten parts of their memoirs while performing her duties as a secretary. Due to Sir Quentin's similarity with her hero Warrender Chase, Fleur feels the same for the former, 'It was almost as if Sir Quentin was unreal and I had merely invented him, Warrender Chase being a man, a real man on whom I had partly based Sir Quentin' (182-83). Through such statements Spark deliberately puts the reader into doubt about the reliability of the mental state of the heroine Fleur. The reader is forced to wonder, who is more real, Sir Quentin or Warrender Chase.

Fleur also has momentary doubts about her own existence, 'For a moment I felt like a gray figment, the "I" of a novel whose physical description the author has decided not to set forth' (95). A person's self includes both her physical self as well as her mental/emotional self. Here Fleur's intellect – her mental self is present in the form of the novel but her physical description, in fact, in Spark's novel, is obtrusively missing. Fleur appears to indicate her awareness of her fictional role of an imaginary narrator in the novel. As if to underline this fact, Wally, a friend of hers once tells her, 'You know, Fleur, sometimes when I'm with you, a very odd thing happens – you're suddenly *not there*. It's creepy' (203). Spark hints that Fleur is essentially an imaginary character, who appears or disappears according to the author's will. Jennifer L. Randisi comments on the satirical elements in *Loitering With Intent*: 'By substituting art for reality and then reminding us that art is a lie, the satirist stands us on a carpet only to pull it out from under us' (142). Spark deliberately confuses the reader about the reality or the unreality of the characters in her novel to belie the expectations of the reader.

Spark in this novel, underlines the fact that language and fiction are human constructs. She questions the mimetic tradition, mainly its tendency to interchange the text for the world. Fleur says of her fictional hero, 'Warrender Chase never existed, he is only some hundreds of words, some punctuation, sentences, paragraphs, marks on the page' (85). At the same time, Fleur reduces the status of the 'real' people, Sir Quentin and his followers to mere words when she says, 'Those people and their Sir Quentin Oliver were sheets of paper on which I could write short stories, poems, anything I cared' (99). Through such statements, Fleur tries to indicate that characters being only a piece of fiction, the moral norms of the human society do not apply on them. Fleur's denial of this fact reveals the tension in her mind about her characters acquiring independent existence, after having been created. Yet words collocate together to build images, which acquire a life of their own, and Fleur cannot negate this fact. Art is a powerful medium, and does influence society, as Fleur discovers in her experiences with the Autobiographical Association, and the writer has to feel a sense of responsibility for her creations. This responsibility is both moral and social, and the writer is expected to represent the society as well as to adhere to its moral principles when producing a literary piece.

In *Loitering With Intent*, Spark plays with the reader's expectations by destroying illusions of verisimilitude after creating them. The writer explores the problematic issue of the human tendency to keep other persons under one's control, and at another ontological plane, the corresponding autonomy of artistic creations. Spark builds up the novel-within-a novel structure and casts doubt upon the reality of existence, fictional and non-fictional alike. By setting up interplay between art and life, Spark explores ethical and moral issues through the artistic problems faced by Fleur. Using a complex story line, Spark seems to conclude in the novel that the desire to control the lives of other individuals is a moral sin.

In the fiction of Muriel Spark, postmodernist tendencies are perceptible in her narrative technique and in her continued inventiveness. In these novels, Spark repeatedly draws attention to the fictionality of fiction through an undercurrent of playfulness, the use of time-shifts and the subversion of conventional expectations. The anti-mimetic mode of narration in her novels foregrounds her search for a narrative style which underlines the complex and fluid nature of reality.

References

Bold, Alan, ed. *Muriel Spark: An Odd Capacity for Vision.* London: Vision; Totowa: Barnes, 1984.

Bradbury, Malcolm. *Possibilities: Essays on the State of the Novel*. London: Oxford UP, 1973.

Cavaliero, Glen. *The Supernatural and English Fiction: From* The Castle of Otranto *to* Hawksmoor. Oxford: Oxford UP, 1995.

Cheyette, Bryan. *Muriel Spark*. Writers and Their Work. Devon: Northcote House, 2000.

Hart, Frances Russel. "Ridiculous Demons." *Muriel Spark: An Odd Capacity for Vision*. Ed. Alan Bold. 23-43.

Kaminsky, Alice R. "On Literary Realism". *The Theory of the Novel: New Essays*. Ed. John Halperin. New York: Oxford UP, 1974.

Kellman, Steven G. *The Self-Begetting Novel*. London: Macmillan, 1980.

Kermode, Frank. "Novel and Narrative." *The Theory of the Novel: New Essays*. Ed. John Halperin. New York: Oxford UP, 1974. 155-74.

Little, Judy. "Muriel Spark's Grammars of Assent." *The British and Irish Novel Since 1960*. Ed. James Acheson. New York: St. Martin's, 1991. 1-16.

Lukács, Georg. *The Meaning of Contemporary Realism*. Trans. John Mander and Necke Mander. London: Merlin, 1963.

McBrien, William. "Muriel Spark: The Novelist as Dandy." *Twentieth Century Women Novelists*. Ed. Thomas F. Staley. London: Macmillan, 1985. 153-78.

McIlvanney, Liam. "The Politics of Narrative in the Post-war Scottish Novel." *On Modern British Fiction*. Ed. Zachany Leader. Oxford: Oxford UP, 2002. 181-208.

Morrison, Jago. *Contemporary Fiction*. London: Routledge, 2003.

Murdoch, Iris. "Against Dryness: A Polemical Sketch." *Encounter* XVI, Jan 1961: 16-20.

Page, Norman. *Muriel Spark*. Macmillan Modern Novelists. London: Macmillan, 1990.

Randisi, Jennifer L. "Muriel Spark and Satire." *Muriel Spark: An Odd Capacity for Vision*. Ed. Alan Bold.132-46.

Rankin, Ian. "Surface and Structure: Reading Muriel Spark's *The Driver's Seat*." *Journal of Narrative Technique* 15.2 (1985): 146-55.

Robbe-Grillet, Alain. "A Future for the Novel." *The Theory of Criticism From Plato to the Present, A Reader*. Ed. Raman Selden. London: Longman, 1988.

Robbe-Grillet, Alain. *For a New Novel: Essays on Fiction*. Trans. Richard Howard. 1963. New York: Freeport, 1970.

Roberts, Andrew Michael, ed. *The Novel: From its Origins to the Present Day*. The Bloomsbury Guides to English Literature. London: Bloomsbury, 1993.

Rowe, Margaret Moan. "Muriel Spark and the Angel of the Body." *Critique* 28 (Spring 1987): 167-76.

Spark, Muriel. *Curriculum Vitae*. London: Constable, 1992.

Spark, Muriel. *The Driver's Seat*. 1970. London: Penguin, 1988.

Spark, Muriel. *Loitering With Intent*. London: The Bodley Head, 1981.

Sukenick, Ronald. "Twelve Digressions toward a Study of Composition." *New Literary History* 6 (1974-75): 429-35.

Weightman, John. "Alain Robbe-Grillet." *The Novelist as Philosopher: Studies in French Fiction, 1935-1960*. Ed. John Cruickshank. London: Oxford UP, 1962.

Whittaker, Ruth. *The Faith and Fiction of Muriel Spark*. London: Macmillan, 1982.

9 Multiculturalism in Margaret Drabble's *The Witch of Exmoor*

Nidhi Singh

Commenting on *The Witch of Exmoor*,[1] Drabble in an interview says 'It was written at the end of Margaret Thatcher's regime... when politics in Britain had become so shabby and despairing that even the people who were in power had lost all faith in themselves... There was a feeling of complete cynicism'.[2] The all pervading cynicism finds expression in this particular novel along with the issue of multiculturalism in Britain. Though narrated in a female voice and in the period when feminism was gaining momentum Margaret Drabble, in her novel, depicts concerns which are more comprehensive and cover wider areas of interest. The role of history, both at social and personal levels has been problematized. Margaret Drabble attempts to depict how history is made and remade through the act of narration. The processes associated with the creation and narration of the fictional worlds can also be observed in the making of the real historical world.

The historical developments in Britain since the Second world war reveal an existence of complex relationship between the decline of Britain as a colonial power and socio-cultural changes. The 1970s, in the history of Britain, are marked by the deterioration of welfare state and the loss of empire. This resulted in Britain being marginalised where world politics as well as economic and military powers were concerned. Though one of the leading industrial nations, Britain's role in globalized world economy and balance of power was very small. Britain also experienced an influx of diverse cultural forms as a result of immigrants from different regions of the defunct Empire. The concepts of 'Britishness' and 'Englishness' were challenged by the resultant multiculturalism. These changes in the post-war and post-imperial period undermined the importance of history of Britain in context of global scenario. Steven Connor holds, 'Britain came progressively to lose its confident belief that it was subject of its own history'[3]. The challenge to the 'Englishness' by the hostile 'other' and multiplication of alternative cultures and ways of self-definition find expression in Margaret Drabble's *The Witch of Exmoor*.

The writer explores the implications of immigration and hybridity leading to multiculturalism in the context of Britain in the latter part of twentieth century. This was the period of unprecedented migration to Britain, and the opportunities for employment, business and education brought about a historic change. Britain became an increasingly complex, multicultural, multi-religious, post-imperial society. This was the direct result of the British Nationality and Status of Aliens Act in the beginning of the century, i.e. in 1914. This act defined British citizens as 'any person born within His Majesty's dominions and allegiances' and confirmed their right of entry into Britain. Due to immigration and hybridity the concept of 'Britishness' as an aspect to be preserved and protected received a set-back. Margaret Drabble, writing in 1990s, is aware of the changing scenario. Drabble in this novel conveys the sense of self and culture not as absolutes but as constructs which are constantly changing. In a country where discrimination is based upon the colour of skin and different speech habits, the act of self-definition and identification becomes problematic even for the second generation settlers. The struggle to relocate themselves is further hindered by the complexity resulting from migrations which involve adjustment with more than one migratory experience and cultural past where character has to come to terms with not only his immediate past but also his racial past. Will Paine, the 'hybrid' character in the novel *The Witch of Exmoor* gives expression to the impossibility of the task:

> He couldn't credit some of the rubbish he heard from Afro-Brits, about African roots. He could just about get his mind as far as Jamaica, and one day he'd go there, one day he'd go and see where he came from, but as for going all the way back again, back through history, back to Africa, and the bush and the jungle – no way (80).

Dislocation, the need for identification, political participation, self-individuation, search for roots are aspects of late twentieth century immigrant and hybrid consciousness which enact the historical dislocation and marginalization experienced by Britain, stripped of its empire and political relevance in the emergent global power equation.

Margaret Drabble combines the nineteenth century realism with post-modernist challenge to it, shattering the balance envisaged between the self and the society. Contrasting strains of cultural, social, political and economic life of Britain are put through the melting pot of Drabble's novel. The complex network of subjects in this novel is reflective of ethnic complexity in multi-cultural British society. A search for origin emerges as a dominant motif in the novel. Displacement and alienation is experienced not only by the outsider, David the Guyanese, Nathan, the Jew, and the hybrid Will, but also by Frieda who tries to come to terms with her past by writing about it. A successful writer of social-history, a failure as an authoress of historical romance, Frieda finds it extremely difficult to write a memoir based on memories which are implicitly unreliable.

The need of going back historically and even geographically for self-individuation finds an echo in the narrative which is self-reflexive and overlaid by the intrusive narrator's voice. The act of narration becomes problematic owing to the writer's profession of limited knowledge and control over the subject. The novel opens with the intrusive narrator, almost in the voice of master of the ceremony declaring, 'Begin on a midsummer evening. Let them have everything that is pleasant' (1), and then goes on to describe a very English meal interspersed with reminders of global influence in the form of bowls and dishes from Spain and Italy, French wine, and apples from New Zealand. The narrative voice however changes its stance while describing the characters. It becomes limited like that of an observer making intelligent guesses: 'Rosemary has style. She could be an actress, or a television presenter, or a journalist' (2). The narrator's voice fluctuates between omniscience and that of an outside observer disrupting and fragmenting, and at the same time, carrying the narrative forward.

Drabble presents the saga of Palmer family. Four generations are linked together by the memories and legacy of Frieda Haxby Palmer, the idiosyncratic writer. Frieda, a successful writer in her 60s, decides to lead a life of a recluse in a gothic 'Victorian castle' at Exmoor, built on the edge of the mountain facing the sea. There is a movement away from the metropolitan centre of London to the province, on the margins. The possibilities as suggested by this conscious choice points at the alternative possibilities existent in the British society.

Frieda's family consists of the lawyer son, Daniel, with a very English lifestyle and his wife. Patsy, their precocious daughter, Emily, and the drug-addict son, Simon; Gogo, the second offspring, is a consultant neurologist married to David, who is a good looking Guyanese, with keen political aspirations. David hopes to represent the ethnic minority in his constituency. Benjamin is their imaginative and sensitive son. Frieda's youngest daughter, Rosemary, marries a Jew, Nathan who is into advertising. Drabble sketches characters who caricature middle-class British attitudes as opposed to the emergent stances exemplified by characters who are second generation immigrants and diaspora. Will Paine, the hybrid character though not belonging to the family, emerges as integral to the novel. All the characters put together reflect the various facets of the multicultural British society. While David, Nathan, Benjamin and Will are outsiders,

Daniel, Patsy, Gogo and Rosemary form the inner circle with middle-class British way of life.

The disappearance of Frieda, the self-proclaimed Witch of Exmoor, brings to surface the submerged rivalries, suspicions and reservations among the rest of the family members. Her children are more concerned about the inheritance than about finding Frieda. The final will makes Benjamin the major beneficiary and endows upon him the title deed of the house at Exmoor. Dissatisfied, Daniel looks for a former will. Much to the consternation of the family, the major part of the fortune is willed to David for establishment of a '... Just Society, to be founded on the principles of social justice' (198) at the Valley of Eagles, David's ancestral land. David and Benjamin inhabit the no-man's-land located between the opposing pulls of two cultures, that of the country of origin and of the country of adoption. Though a migrant faced with geographical and cultural displacement, David has done well in life aided by good-looks, intelligence and a devoted English wife. The intrusive narrator addresses him as 'the New Millennial Black British' (21). He is intelligent enough to be aware of the strengths and weaknesses of his minority ethnic background and so makes the most of it. Commenting on the white scholarship on post-colonial culture, he calls it 'a new kind of colonialism, cultural colonialism' (55). Seminars become an excuse for holiday at exotic locales involving theorizing 'on behalf of the benighted disadvantaged tinted folk who haven't yet learnt that its their duty to reject all representation and represent themselves' (56). The theme of powerlessness and power form the sub-text in the novel in relation to the conflict arising out of a sense of proprietorship of a group representing the British way of life threatened by the other, here comprising of multicultural community. Despite his apparent confidence, even David is keenly aware of his position as a 'parliamentary candidate for a marginal constituency in West Yorkshire' (21), contesting for 'marginal seat'.

When confronted with the clause in the will, David is forced to acknowledge the sense of displacement. 'The D'Anger do not know their ancestral land. Politics drove them out, and now they live in perpetual diaspora' (207). When Frieda's will provides him with an opportunity of reclaiming his lost cultural and ancestral heritage, he wonders 'Does it really exist, out of family mythology' (206). He is not sure of even the existence of the Eagle valley, his ancestral land. The act of looking back over the shoulder at a culture and country of origin, idealizing and theorizing about it contributes tensions to the multicultural aspect of British society, the unwilling recipient of cultural baggage brought along by the immigrants and the diaspora. Faced with the choice between country of origin and the country of adoption, David chooses the reality of experienced life in multicultural Britain over and above the imagined and idealized ancestral one.

The concept of conscious choice is further heightened when merged with the issues of hybridity, immigration, appropriation and the conflicts related to individuation. The game aptly named 'the Veil of Ignorance' (4) as suggested by David, reinforces the concept of free choice. In this game the participants were expected to unimagine everything they and the existent social-set-up stood for, and as if by pushing a button rip the veil of ignorance and wake up in a society based on 'social justice'. Frieda's offspring with 'Nordic' looks and affluent upwardly mobile British middle-class attitude are not ready to risk their comfortable existence for a society where they could end up amongst the very poor who are necessary for the proper functioning of this ideal society.

David finds no takers for his game except his Jewish brother-in-law, Nathan. With a gambler's instinct, a job of marketing executive and his racial background, Nathan is ready to take his chance. When questioned closely about the intricacies of the game, the one time academician David defends himself saying that the game should not be taken literally as it was only 'a philosophical concept. A hypothesis', as was the concept of 'social justice'. Drabble here makes explicit the disjunction that exists between the world of academic and the day-to day world, questioning the credibility of concepts which can have no truck with real life. 'Dreams survive in an academic set up, at conferences and congresses where students and lecturers and professors still discuss the concept of the fair, the just and the good. But they have no connection with the world of ring-roads, and beef burgers, with a world of disease and survival' (47).

Diverse strands converge and the notion of indigenous national identity becomes suspect, as suspect as the personal history Frieda aims to write in her 'memoir'. At one point referring to her ancestry Frieda ruminates about claims made by Gladys, her mother, 'Her forebears had come across the North Sea from somewhere' and later, 'she had claimed for her children a Nordic inheritance which, who knows, may well have been fact, not fiction' (140). Frieda's tentative explorations of her roots is in no way reflected in the confident appropriation of the British way of life by her offspring. Nathan reflects upon it, 'Daniel, Gogo and Rosemary might seem to carry the assumptions of the British middle classes, carried on from generation to generation. But they come from nowhere. They have turned themselves into members of the English middleclass by sleight of hand' (20). Their successful identification and acceptance is in stark contrast to the alienation and rootlessness experienced by Britain born Will Paine with a Jamaican father. He realizes '... no one will give him Wolverhampton or Stoke Newington. They won't give him anything' (80). Helped by money forced upon him by Frieda, Will reaches Jamaica, his fatherland, only to experience a new sense of displacement. He realizes that there he is neither a tourist nor an indigene and wonders, 'Is he a Jamaican, is he a Wolverhampton man, is he a North London man? Is there a place in the world for him?' (183). The intrusive narrator intervenes on his behalf and decides to 'liberate' him since, '... there are many plots that could enmesh and entangle and imprison him... Are there any plots that will let him free? Not in this country, that is clear' (261). The alternative is Australia where he finds refuge and settles down – Australia, a land of opportunities where multiculturalism forms the matrix of the society.

The other 'outsider' who has been portrayed sympathetically is Nathan. He however is not allowed to escape, and mystery surrounds his death which though declared as the result of a heart failure, also points at a possibility of suicide. Nathan as a young man opting for a career in marketing, the high priest of the market-culture in Britain eulogized, 'Shopping was indeed our new religion. Consumer choice, in a post-industrial society, was our area of free will, informed perhaps by grace' (18). The marketing culture, a by-product of global economic mobility was another major force which Britain had to reckon with. It was an aspect which affected all, irrespective of their nationality and colour of the skin. As a competent professional he had successfully marketed 'the myth of the rural England' to affluent English, superimposing the advertising commercial of rural England on the 'palimpsesty of England of Hampshire in 1990s, and that again is superimposed upon the reality of the past, the unknowable reality of History' (18). Like other characters he wonders about his own ancestry which can not be traced and almost envies and disapproves of the complacency of Palmers. The optimism of youth declines into macabre thoughts of death, 'could he market, not life, not health, but death? Could one take up on oneself the challenge of changing the corporate identity of death?' (191). He realizes his insignificance and death is a release for him. In a world dominated by demands of market, human beings play a very insignificant role and are dispensable.

Benjamin, the recipient of Frieda's dubious munificence, is weighed down by the guilt of imagined responsibility for her death by drowning. A sensitive and imaginative adolescent, Benjamin tries to come to terms with the hybrid legacy received from maternal British world and the exotic paternal world. Praying to be spared the agony, 'he promises God, he promises Jesus Christ of the Christians... he will renounce all his kingdom' (208). The Guyanese writer and friend, David Saul Sinnamary feels 'Benjamin D' Anger is suffering from exile ... He needs ancestral images' (213). After a near fatal experience of drowning in the bath tub, Benjamin is able to come to grips with depression. Accompanied by Emily, his cousin, he visits Exmoor. Emily and Benjamin seem to have emerged stronger from the 'test' (179) that Frieda had put the whole family through. Water in the last lines emerges as a challenge to be accepted and overcome. The novel ends with Emily encouraging Benjamin to take on the incoming tide 'Jump for it! cries Emily Palmer, as the tide comes in. And Benjamin D'Anger jumps' (276).

Drabble also explores through the character of Frieda the limitations and possibilities inherent in literary genres like social histories, historical novels, romances and memoirs. Drabble at one point questions the reliability and adequacy of 'memoir', a saga of personal history. Frieda constructs two versions of a single incident where the positions of the tormentor and the tormented are reversed based on the point-of-view from which the incident is narrated. The act of narration becomes suspect. Having nothing but her own memories and 'interpretations' to go by, Frieda decides to 'write a record without records. Her last testament' (75). Personal history emerges as innately unreliable and fragmented. Use of literary form of 'memoir' by Frieda to present the fragmented memory of the personal history as a continuous whole is undermined by her dissatisfaction with and alienation from the world she inhabits. She declares, 'I look to the past because I have no future' (117). The irony lies in the fact that she cannot be too sure about her past too.

Going through the files in Frida's computer, Emily, the granddaughter, locates the memoir. It is marked by her need to come to terms with a past overshadowed by debilitating matriarchy of her mother, Gladys, and destructive sibling rivalry with sister Everhilda. Rooted in matriarchy and sibling rivalry the relation between women characters emerge as destructive of individuality and growth. Mutual suspicions and suppressed envy negate the concept of female bonding pointing at the obsessive rivalry and hatred which outlives even death. This 'Mother' figure has been portrayed in unsympathetic light, as was prevalent in feminist writings of early years of women's movements. It is only after the death of her mother that Frieda feels free.

The Witch of Exmoor is constructed from the points of view of different characters involved in the dialogics of ethnicity. About the memoir Frieda holds 'There were so many versions of story, and all of them were false' (113). The act of writing is fore-grounded. The linear narrative of the novel is disrupted by the intrusive narrator's voice guiding the readers backward and forward in time. The fragmented and disrupted narrative reflects the similar fragmentation in personal as well as historical past of not only immigrant cultures but also in the lives of those who form the core of the British society.

Multiculturalism as it existed in late twentieth century in British society and the related issues of hybridity, diaspora, alienation, cultural appropriation and the act of self-individuation find due and successful expression in *The Witch of Exmoor*. By focusing on the marginalised characters, Drabble brings out the changes taking place within the contemporary British society. David's statement sums up the multicultural dilemma as it existed in Britain:

> It's the new white man's burden. He is not allowed to write or speak *as* a black man, but he's damned if he doesn't recognize their existence and their otherness. Damned if he appropriates, damned if he neglects. It's a fine line. (54).

The *Witch of Exmoor* successfully traverses along the 'fine line' to present a comprehensive view of multicultural Britain.

Notes

1. Drabble, Margaret. *The Witch of Exmoor.* London: Viking, 1996. All subsequent references are from this edition.
2. Interview. Online. Available on Internet at google.com http://www.
3. Connor, Steven. *The English Novel in History.* London and New York: Routledge, 1996.

10 *Nights at the Circus*
Multiple Directions in Narratology

Sudha Shastri

On the very first page of *Nights at the Circus* (henceforth NC), right in the first paragraph, a remarkable feature of the narrative vies for the reader's attention: the heroine Fevvers, who spans in her unique person the label of 'Cockney Venus' on the one hand, and the lineage of Helen of Troy on the other. And this is not just an exaggerated manner of speaking. '- for I never docked via what you might call the *normal channels*, sir, oh, dear me, no; but, just like Helen of Troy, was *hatched*' (NC 7). The wings that she sports on her shoulders, which are described rather painstakingly for us a few pages later, substantiate Fevvers' claim.

NC is no fairy tale, where winged heroines belong quite naturally; the story is rooted clearly in time and place: London (except where the circus is travelling to Petersburg and Siberia), and the turn of the nineteenth (into the twentieth) century. Such a combination invites the reader to locate this story in the genre of magic realism, where a winged woman finds, quite naturally, a job for herself in the circus as a trapeze artiste. Her spectacular story is initially rendered to the reader through Walser, a young reporter who 'filed copy to a New York newspaper for a living' (NC 9).

Walser's professional scepticism of such a marvel as posed by Fevvers (a lady with wings) enables the reader to identify with him, and this is what, paradoxically enough, makes the reader believe Fevvers' (tall) claims. Walser's credentials make it unlikely that he would be bamboozled by a tall tale. One of Walser's initial discoveries is that 'the girl went no further than any other trapeze artiste...he was astonished to discover that it was the *limitations* of her act in themselves that made him briefly contemplate the unimaginable – that is, the absolute suspension of disbelief' (NC 17, emphasis mine). 'He smiled to himself at the paradox: in a secular age, an authentic miracle must purport to be a hoax, in order to gain credit in the world' (NC 17).

Walser's strenuous effort towards realism (which is also the novel's predominant mode of representation) is overturned by NC, which thereafter turns into an enchanting pastiche of various narrative traditions and modes, including magic realism, the tall tale (oral tradition), metafiction, and intertextual allusions.

Fevvers' wings do allow themselves to be interpreted metaphorically. Such an interpretation is made for us at the end of the novel, when Fevvers tells Lizzie, her foster-mother, on the eve of the twentieth century: 'And once the old world has turned on its axle so that the new dawn can dawn, then, ah, then! all the women will have wings, the same as I' (NC 285). However, this metaphorical explanation is not something that one can reconcile with a literal understanding of the role that wings play in NC, the very literal manner in which Fevvers' wings determine her adventures and experiences. This is magic realism at its most sophisticated, where magic finds a place for itself in the ontology of realism, causing disruptions in the process, which, nevertheless, are not large enough to topple the framework of realistic representation.

After negotiating with a human being who sports wings, the next hint of disorientation for the reader comes in the bizarre behaviour of time. Fevvers recounts the story of her life to Walser after her performance, who, scrupulous journalist that he is, takes copious notes down even as he is increasingly tired as the evening wears away into night. By degrees, Fevvers comes to the point when she first flew; at this juncture, 'the wind blew Big Ben, striking midnight, so lost, so lonely a sound it seemed to Walser the clock might be striking in a deserted city and they the only inhabitants left alive' (NC 37). The ambience seems appropriate for just such an incredible stop.

Fevvers continues with her story, while Walser takes notes down mechanically. After some time lapses Lizzie, Fevvers' foster-mother, goes out to fill water for tea, when 'the chimes of Big Ben came drifting towards them once again on the soundless night'. striking twelve, once more. 'For the first time that night, Walser was seriously discomposed' (NC 42). Fevvers does not notice anything irregular; indeed she asks him to check his wrist-watch which, he finds, shows midnight.

This temporal anomaly repeats itself twice. A progressively weary Walser hears the chimes of Big Ben ring midnight, for the third time that evening: 'Big Ben had once again struck midnight' (NC 53). The gilt clock in the room corresponds to the time outside, which only adds to the inexplicable nature of the mystery.

Towards the end of the section, Walser finds that his own watch had stopped at midnight – as if the text has found a need to provide an explanation of the bizarre event. Much later, Fevvers herself confesses that she had played a trick with the gilt clock, but there is no explanation for how Big Ben could have been co-opted by Fevvers in her mischievous meddling with time.

It is left to the narrator to clinch matters by providing a larger, magically pitched explanation once Fevvers has reached the end of her interview with Walser. As morning dawns, Walser has the curious sensation that in the night, for the duration of the tale, the room had, 'in some way, without his knowledge, been plucked out of its everyday, temporal continuum, had been held for a while above the spinning world and was now – dropped back into place' (NC 87).

Magic spares nobody in the world of NC. In Section 3, it is Fevvers' turn to be at the receiving end of the propensity of time to deceive. Stranded in Siberia, the circus has lost Walser for a week, and when they see him next, he has 'gone native' with a vengeance, and is unable to recognise his erstwhile companions. Fevvers is shocked, for she believes that one cannot change so drastically in a week, but Lizzie wonders if it is only a week, considering the length of his beard since they last saw him. Lizzie's audacious explanation is the only one that the reader is vouchsafed: 'Something's going on. Something we *wot not of*, my dear. Remember we have lost our clock; remember father Time has many children and I think it was his bastard offspring inherited this region for...time has passed – or else is passing – marvellous swiftly for these woodland folk' (NC 272).

Brian Finney's essay talks about the deliberate confusion with time that Carter perpetrates, and comments that she 'might well be parodying the most famous instance of a double time scheme in *Othello*, especially as she twice quotes from this play (228, 264)' (Finney 3).

Let me offer one more instance of magic from NC: the magic of the tigers vanishing into the mirrors. The circus troupe is travelling on the Trans-Siberian railway, into the land where all laws of physics are bent to accommodate the freedom of narration, when their train has an accident. At this point Fevvers shares the honours of narrating the tale with the narrator:

> Of my young man, no sign.
>
> Then, amongst the ruins of the 'wagon salon', I beheld a great wonder. For the tigers were all gone into the mirrors. How to describe it. The 'wagon salon' lay on its side, ripped open like the wrappings of a Christmas toy by an impatient child, and, of those lovely creatures, not a trace of blood or sinew, nothing (NC 205).

The very offhand and casual manner in which magic is periodically introduced into the story, as well as the realistic tone in which it is narrated, balance the element of fantasy and infuse that of realism, achieving thereby precisely the defamiliarising aim of magic realism, whose technique consists in perceiving the conventionally fantastic as real, and vice versa.

And finally, the narrator explicitly *mentions* the mode of magic realism in the context of Walser's experiences with the Shaman, thus creating an intersection between magic realism and metafictional self-reflexivity. Commenting on the inability of the Shaman to make a distinction between seeing and believing, the narrator says that 'for all the peoples of this region, there existed no difference between fact and fiction; instead, a sort of magic realism. Strange fate for a journalist, to find himself in a place where no facts, as such, existed! Not that Walser would have known what a journalist was, any more' (NC 260). Magic Realism thus becomes as much a way of life as a mode of representation.

NC frames its spirit of magic realism within the oral tradition as a tall tale, which is Fevvers' mode of recounting to Walser in the first section of the novel. By then, Fevvers' own larger-than-lifelikeness has been so incontrovertibly established that even after the omniscient narrator takes over she retains in her persona this tall-(tell)tale feature.

Traditionally, a tall tale is a narrative that depicts the wild adventures of extravagantly exaggerated folk heroes. The main character of a tall tale is quite Fevvers-like, larger-than-life/super-human, and the tale itself employs exaggeration to good effect. It is an oral form of entertainment, and generally speaking, its audience appreciates the imaginative invention rather than the literal meaning of the tales (a point that Walser takes time to internalise, since this conflicts with his journalist persona) – and this is a significant factor favouring the subversive approach of the genre of the tall tale to the realistic tenor of the novel.

Consider the following two of the several definitions of 'circus' from the Wordnet, Hyper Dictionary: 'a travelling company of acrobats, clowns and trained animals;' and 'a frenetic disorganised (and often comic) disturbance suggestive of a circus or carnival'. By privileging the carnival element of the circus in NC, Carter shows how postmodernist fiction can compensate for the loss of the social context of the real carnival with its liberating influence from monologic (and masculine) authority.

The threads of fantasy, hallucination, and grotesque imagery of the body, are various ways in which the carnival makes its entry into NC. Carter situates the genres of magic realism and the tall tale in the image of the circus, which in turn embodies the spirit of carnival. The circus becomes a fitting trope for the carnival as a socially accommodated domain of fantasy where normal laws and regulations are challenged. Carnival 'denotes any atmosphere of sanctioned indulgence and illusory disorder preceding, surrounding or permeating a holiday or sacred feast... (it) permits the debasement of social institutions and personalities which are normally feared/respected' ("Carnival"). The spirit of carnival was and continues to be one of the most powerful forces of subversion. Carnival suspends normal law and order and inverts them with parody, melodrama, farce and irreverence. 'Representations of circuses, fairs, sideshows, and amusement parks often function as residual indicators of the carnival context in postmodernist fiction' (McHale 174)[1].

As a potent tool for inverting accepted order, it may be argued that the circus signposts the similar power of the novel to challenge the direct, monologic genres like the epic and lyric, as well as canonical conventions of representation like realism, replacing them with a world of parody and laughter.

The name almost unanimously recalled with reference to the carnival element in the genre of the novel is that of Mikhail Bakhtin. In his essay entitled "From The Prehistory of Novelistic Discourse", Bakhtin catalogues various parodic-travestying forms, both oral and written, from the Greek and Roman periods through the Middle Ages, which paved the way for the birth of the novel in the late seventeenth century. The prehistory of novelistic discourse comprises the parodic-travestying forms of the Middle Ages and the ancient world which 'modeled themselves on folk and holiday merrymaking, which throughout the Middle Ages bore the character of carnival' (Bakhtin 153).

This parodic literature, says Bakhtin, took over the function of doubling, in a comic manner, the theme and intent of their serious literary/artistic counterparts. He cites the fourth drama as a case in instance, which followed upon the tragic Greek trilogies and 'developed the same narrative and mythological motifs as had the trilogy that preceded it' (Bakhtin 134). This tradition had a social extension, too. 'We recall the role of medieval clowns...who with the doubling effect of their laughter insured the wholeness of the seriolaughing word'. Moreover, "Echoes of this comic parallelism can still be heard today – for example, in the rather common doubling by a circus clown of the serious and dangerous numbers of a program' (Bakhtin 153).

Thus, Carter's assimilation of the carnival in no uncertain terms presents NC as a watershed or milestone, urging the novel to take a look backwards at its carnivalesque origins, in the spirit of postmodernism. The pre-eminence of the circus in Carter's scheme of things is indicated at the outset, in the title itself. Furthermore, Carter's plans to ensconce the spirit of carnival include bringing in the tradition of the clown within the larger arena of the performing circus. When Walser joins the circus he does so as a clown.

Walser is also a *picaro*. For McHale, 'the typical plot of carnivalised narrative is that of a picaresque adventure-story in which the *picaro* seeks not social and economic advancement, or not only that, but answers to 'ultimate questions' (172). Walser fits this description very well indeed, since his adventure, initiated by his meeting with Fevvers, and involving, among other risks, that of being a human chicken in a performance, takes him over the terrain of the magical, where he tests the limit of human experience after meeting the Shaman in Siberia. In a larger context, by being part of the travelling show moving into Siberian wastelands, he also functions as an agent of disruption, a vehicle "for insinuating the supernatural or paranormal into 'normal' reality" (McHale 174).

In NC, the animals run the circus. Sybil, the pig, makes all the decisions for the manager; the Professor (an ape) is so clever that he sees through the manager's pathetic attempts at cheating him; the tigers simply vanish...in short, this circus expertly fits the definition proffered by the Devil's Dictionary as 'A place where horses, ponies and elephants are permitted to see men, women and children acting the fool' (Hyper Dictionary).

The liberating power of the circus which stretches limits is thus comparable to that of the novel itself, and Carter creates a novel of the circus to produce a carnivalesque world that challenges the staid, the mundane and the expected, through laughter and burlesque. The (literary) world of the novel has an affinity and empathy with the (social) world of carnival, and both perform same functions.

Laughter is one of the most important characteristics that Bakhtin identified in the prehistory of novelistic discourse. The parodic-travestying forms, according to him, constituted 'an extra-generic or inter-generic world' which was

> unified by a common purpose: to provide the corrective of laughter and criticism to all existing straightforward genres, languages, styles, voices; to force men to experience beneath these categories a different and contradictory reality that is otherwise not captured in them. Such laughter paved the way for the impiety of the novelistic form (Bakhtin 139).

It is more than a coincidence, then, that NC closes, literally, with peals of laughter: Fevvers laughs as she recollects that she succeeded in fooling Walser. "Her laughter spilled out of the window and made the tin ornaments on the tree outside the god-hut shake and tinkle" (NC 294) and her infectious laughter reaches out to the baby, the Shaman and even the bear:

> It seemed this laughter of the happy young woman rose up from the wilderness in a spiral and began to twist and shudder across Siberia....The spiralling tornado of Fevvers' laughter began to twist and shudder across the entire globe, as if a spontaneous response to the giant comedy that endlessly unfolded beneath it, until everything that lived and breathed, everywhere, was laughing (NC 295).

Postmodernism has found myriad ways of presenting metafiction; the presence of the carnival (in the form of the circus) goes some way towards enabling novelistic self-awareness. Carnival embodies 'otherness', the otherness of the marginal, and infuses a new 'language' that reveals the presence of more than one voice in the text. In Bakhtin's words, 'Novelistic discourse is always criticising itself' (131); metafiction is the first step towards paving the way for self-consciousness, self-critiquing, and self-criticism.

Bakhtin defines the genre of the novel in contradistinction to other "straightforward" genres like the epic poem, the lyric and the drama: 'All directly descriptive and expressive means at the disposal of these genres, as well as the genres themselves, become upon entering the novel, an object of representation within it' (131-32).

There are significantly pointed ways in which metafiction occupies the space of NC. I will discuss one of them at least in some detail here.

Metafiction's conventional way is to produce recursiveness through Chinese-Box worlds, and then create *trompe-l'oeil* devices such as that of illicit animation. Here, "a nested 'still' representation is transformed before our eyes into an 'animated' sequence with every appearance of belonging to first-order reality" (McHale 117-18). McHale gives examples where dynamic episodes derived illicitly from static representations (like paintings or cards) collapse back into stills.

Carter adapts this device brilliantly in NC: just before the circus leaves for Siberia, Fevvers finds herself accepting an invitation by the Grand Duke to his house for an evening, at the end of which he forces himself on her. Desperate to escape, but finding no means, the narrative opts a way out for her at this critical juncture via illicit animation.

How is this accomplished?

Earlier, Fevvers had noticed among the Grand Duke's collection of curios, an egg containing a model train. It is described as having 'an engine, in black enamel, and one, two, three, four first-class carriages in tortoiseshell and ebony, all coiled round one another like a snake, with, engraved on the side of each in Cyrillic, the legend *The Trans-Siberian Express* (NC 191). Fevvers asks for this toy, but the Grand Duke refuses her, promising in its stead, another egg topped by a swan and containing a cage. (The symbolism of this is quite explicit).

At this point, 'Fevvers did not shrink; but was at once aware of the hideous possibility she might do so. She...contemplated life as a toy' (NC 192). She is of course thinking of the cage, but the narrative has other ideas for her. As the Grand Duke climaxes and loses consciousness for a few seconds, 'Fevvers ran helter-skelter down the platform, opened the door of the first-class compartment and clambered aboard' (NC 192), the compartment being that of the toy train we have just had described for us.

Here, then is a narrative sleight-of-hand that simply takes your breath away. The tone of the narrator wavers not a whit in racing the story along a different mimetic level. Illicit animation is one of the ways in which a text can produce metalepsis, which is an offshoot of imaginative metafictional embedding. Metalepses or strange loops produce a 'disorienting transgression of narrative logic', a 'tangled hierarchy' which occurs 'when what you presume are clean hierarchical levels take you by surprise and fold back in a hierarchy-violating way' (Hofstadter, qtd in McHale 119).

A less dramatic metafictional effect is achieved in the switch in narrative voice in the third section of the novel, which opens with the voice of Fevvers (NC 197) and after some interruptions/interspersed narration by presumably the omniscient narrator (of events that Fevvers is not witness to), reverts to Fevvers' voice in chapter five. In chapter nine, the omniscient narrator displaces Fevvers' voice in a categorical fashion, and from thereon her representation is re-appropriated by the omniscient narrator.

I have tried to show some of the major narratological signposts that NC displays, within (and because of) its postmodern temper. In its admirable coalescing of so many narrative strands and identities, NC achieves the status of what Susan Sontag describes as *Camp*: 'Camp is a vision of the world in terms of style – but a particular kind of style', which 'responds particularly to the markedly attenuated and to the strongly exaggerated' (279). 'It's too much', 'It's too fantastic', 'It's not to be believed' are standard phrases of Camp enthusiasm' (283). Again, "Camp taste is, above all, a mode of enjoyment, of appreciation – not judgement" (291). And, again, 'The hallmark of Camp is the spirit of extravagance. Camp is a woman walking around in a dress made of three million feathers' (283), and I would like to stop at this juncture with the comment that in this respect, NC, in no uncertain terms, 'outcamps' camp.

Note

1. McHale in fact draws a distinction between reduced and displaced forms of carnival, and full-fledged popular carnivals. According to him, 'the point where representations of carnival converge with carnivalised literature's Utopian themes we find the postmodern topos of revolution. This is not political or social revolution, however, so much as it is ludic and sexual revolution, revolution *as* carnival.' (McHale 175).

References

Bakhtin, Mikhail. "From the Prehistory of Novelistic Discourse". *Modern Criticism and Theory*. Ed. David Lodge. London: Longman, 1988. 125-156.

Carter, Angela. *Nights at the Circus*. London: Chatto & Windus, The Hogarth Press, 1984.

McHale, Brian. *Postmodernist Fiction*. London: Routledge, 1987.

Sontag, Susan. "Notes on 'Camp'". *Against Interpretation and Other Essays*. New York: Picador USA, 1966. 274-292.

Online

Finney, Brian. "Tall Tales and Brief Lives: Angela Carter's *Nights at the Circus*". 1998.
<http://www.csulb.edu/~bhfinney/AngelaCarter.html>

8th July 2005 Copyright 1998 Brian Finney

Howard, Donald. C. "Carnival and Pilgrimage"
http://lonestar.texas.net/~mseifert/carnival.html 8th July 2005

"Carnival" http://www.ot.com/skew/eleven/carnival.html 8th July 2005

Hyper Dictionary [The Exploding Dictionary]
http://www.hyperdictionary.com/dictionary? 8th July 2005

11 Challenging the Male Gaze and Motherhood in Doris Lessing's *The Summer Before the Dark* and *The Fifth Child*

Mini Nanda

> Long ago, a young girl lay on her back in a bed with a hand-mirror held close to her face, and she was thinking: That is what he is going to see... (Lessing 155).

In these lines Doris Lessing in the novel *The Summer Before the Dark* (1973), presents an interestingly layered study of the theme of the female body-image and its construction and the dominance of the male gaze. Lessing centres her narration on the power of male gaze; she lays bare the pressures it builds upon the observed and controls on their behaviour.

Rosalind Coward writes in the *Female Desire* (1984) that in society 'looking' plays a crucial role in sexual relations, not because of any natural impulse, but because it happens to be a way in which domination and subordination are expressed. The relations involved in working enmesh with coercive beliefs about appropriate sexual behaviour for men and women. It leads women to a narcissistic preoccupation with self-image, and, as Laura Mulvey suggests, it enables men to cope with the threat which femininity presents. It distances the image of women, fetishizing her and regarding her voyeuristically as a 'spectacle' (1975: 6-18). Women perhaps achieve some narcissistic pleasure, on being the centre of 'the look', but pay a heavy price in terms of their identity (1979: 3-10). Lessing critiques the degree to which a woman's identity and her sense of reality in the society depends on her position as the focus of 'the look'.

Doris Lessing focuses on the myriad images of Kate Brown in *The Summer* and the different identities she dons like different dresses. Kate had, for years, spent a lot of time in front of many different mirrors and had been able to see exactly what 'he' would be seeing, when his face would be above hers. For the whole of her life since she had was sixteen she looked into mirrors to see what other people would judge her by. She had been very fastidious about her appearance, full of exquisite taste appropriate to her position as her husband's wife and the mother of her children. suitably dressed with shoes and stockings, her red hair falling in soft waves over her face, though she would have preferred to walk bare-feet on the lawn, wear something exotic like a mum-mum, or a sari or a sarong and her hair straight on her shoulder.

Kate Brown/Catherine Brown/Mrs. Michael Brown always "sealed" herself down to please her husband and her children, for they disliked her giving rein to her own nature. From her teens in her grandfather's strict household she was 'sheltered and distrusted, she was precious and despised'. At the same time she was aware that she occupied a carefully defined subordinate part in her grandfather's life, as her grandmother and aunts had done. She saw herself as a delicate girl as "fragile as a camellia", with her dead white skin and heavy dark red hair, sitting on a swing chair in the verandah, as one willfully and whimsically play acting, of being an object sexual attractive before all the young men present. She also saw herself as one speaking fluent Portuguese as she was soaked in the 'spirit of the language', as her grandfather had said to her: 'Catherine! The way to learn a language is to breathe it in. Soak it up! live it' (24). She had immersed herself in the language of the home-maker as well for more then two decades, for language had become a patriarchal given to her as well.

That summer there would be a hiatus in the family life, as each member had plans to go off in different directions. Suddenly she feels the "cold wind" blow at her from the future. She picks-up the threads of her expertise in language again – French, Italian and Portuguese. She chooses a suitable dress and makes all the inner adjustments to be away from being Mrs. Michael Brown temporarily. Smoothly she slips into the role of a translator in an international organization as one language would flow into her ears and another from her mouth. Whether at home or outside, she feels like a "migrant" silently observing everything. She feels more comfortable in her small box of a room than she did in her large Victorian house. She now has only a bed, a chair and a mirror, she reinvests herself with a cosmetic make-over, chic hair-style and stylish dresses, while she parries offers from black, brown and olive-skinned men in the conference on Global Food. She basks in the state of eternal youth, as she did not look her forty odd years.

She turned her internal thermostat to 'low' when men gave her 'that skilled, professional inspection, with which we size each other up in such encounters of the sexual and professional mart'. Soon she would rearrange her posture, huddle and sag and let her face droop and the attention would be switched off dramatically. Which in turn would give her a dislocated feeling, as if something had slipped out of alignment.

In her mind's eye, she sees all over the continent, the girls – friendly, perky and attractive, employed in airlines and on various committees, who are intoxicated by their own attractiveness. They would float about like 'weather balloons' as they would walk up and down, up and down, smiling and being admired by men as well as by women. Then Kate concluded in her mind's eye that these girls marry and it would be just like walking off a stage where there were hundred of people applauding into a small dark room. Then the balloon of admiration and adulation would burst. Kate realises that the girls would miss the bright lights, the adults who had admired them would now turn away bored. They seem to have forgotten her, no matter how she would dance, pose and shout, "Look at me! Look at me!" They would turn around and say, 'Be quiet. Run along and play' (56).

There begins the process of individuation for Kate, which runs parallel to the 'simple, epic and direct' dream of the seal. Ralph Beret (1980) perspicaciously points out that Lessing is playing on the word 'seal'. Here it means both the animal and the stamp of authenticity and approval.

The dream begins with the image of a dead slug on top of a mountain, which stands for her past, the dark shadowy past. On closer examination it is not a slug but a sick, wounded and dying seal. As Beret observes, the seal is the dreamer (Kate) herself in the Jungian interpretation of dreams. Both, the seal and Kate are out of their natural habitat, Kate makes both a conscious and subconscious effort to restore it back to its environment.

Lessing confessed in a interview to Jonah Raskin:

> Dreams have always been important to me... the unconscious can be what you make of it, good or bad, helpful or unhelpful. Our culture has made an enemy of the unconscious... other cultures have accepted the unconscious as a helpful force... with a few symbols a dream can define the whole of one's life and warn us of the future too (172).

Kate works out her own liberation from despair in her dream. She begins to feel that the dream will become a path back to herself which when completed will lead her back to her familial and community relationships.

Working on and accepting the unconscious part of herself she holds her marriage up like an object between her finger and her thumb to analyse it. She resolves to 'nourish and to nurture in herself that person which was all warmth and charm' that personality which has nothing to do with her... the individual who sat and watched from behind the warm brown eyes, the cared for skin and the heavy curves of her dark-red hair' (48). In her dream as Kate chews and applies the bitter shrubs to heal the wounds of the seal, she begins the process of healing herself from within.

Lessing ironically compares a woman to a sunflower who turns towards one man, holding in the palm of her hand, something precious and attempting to offer it in vain to her husband and her children, who never notice it or take it (123).

This was the real being in her which had been overwhelmed by the different roles, its aspiration lost in the crowd of the world. She compares her marital status with that of a nun in Spain, The 'bride of Christ', content in her self chosen prison. While the men and women of the world appear 'mad' to her, in their binges of self-indulgence, she saw her husband Michael as one gorging on the various exotic chocolates, tasting one and discarding another.

Her own sexuality appears to her like an organ, lifted out of her body and laid by her side like 'a deformed child without function or purpose' (122). She seems to emerge from a spell of madness and sees that her face has aged, the mirror reflects the face of a 'sick monkey'. There is a spring in her step for she feels her self-definitions would now be straight.

The seal in the dream is restored to its habitat, healed back to its community. Kate finds that the snow had gone from underfoot and she was walking over spring grass. She resolves to walk into her house with her hair undressed, the grey steak widening like a statement of intent. She realises that she had been used just like words, but now she would be understood.

She who had been a scientist's rat, giving a Pavlovian response to the appropriate levers would now be saying no, no and no-'a statement which would be concentrated into hair' (233). The relevance of Lacan is evident here, in the treatment of language. Lacan describes the unconscious as structured like a language, like language its power arises from the sense of openness and play of meaning.

Another paradigm controlling women's lives is that of motherhood. Lessing recognises its political content in the modern society. Adrienne Rich (1980) observes that 'motherhood is not only a core human relationship but a political institution, a keystone to the domination in every sphere of women by men'. The dichotomy of maternal power/female powerlessness is central to the novel. Julia Kristeva makes the succinct observation that 'A mother is a continuous separation, a division of the very flesh', that in the experience of giving birth paradoxically the 'wounds but increase' (The Kristeva Reader 178). There is also the recognition of the unconscious, of the strangeness of the other and the strangeness within.

Lessing focuses and balances on both the vulnerability and the strength of a woman like Harriet who has given birth to a monster in the novel – *The Fifth Child* (1988). Giving birth to four children in six years she was the picture of fulfillment in her large Victorian house, overflowing with relatives and guests each year for Easter. Her fifth child changes it all right from the foetal status, it was a 'wrestler', trying to tear its way out. The expectant mother – Harriet used sedatives to keep the 'enemy' insides her quiet. At other times she would take up frenetic activities to keep her mind off the ordeal. She would run through the streets hour after hour, at other times clean and scrub the house to deny the pain. She is alone in her physical ordeal. 'Her time was endurance, containing pain' (52), felt as if hooves and claws were cutting her insides, she fantasised that she had cut open her own stomach with the kitchen knife to pull out the child.

The monstrous child is called Ben, his abnormality is a given in the novel. Born in the eighth month, he weighed eleven pounds, he did not look like a baby nor did he cry at birth. He had a heavy shouldered hunched look and green-yellow eyes like lumps of soapstone. The child gives everyone the creeps and Harriet, the mother, is made to feel like a criminal:

> I suppose in the old times, in primitive societies, this was how they treated a woman who'd given birth to a freak. As if it was her fault. But we are supposed to be civilised (74).

As Kate Brown cries out in *The Summer* about her own experience of motherhood, she who had given her years to her family was now treated like an old curse and as one who must be put up with. She felt like a wounded bird being pecked to death by the healthy birds or an animal teased by cruel children. Lessing sketches the darker aspect of motherhood and the sad realisation of the 'empty nest syndrome'.

Harriet tells Dr. Gilly the specialist in London. 'It nearly is extraordinary ! No one has ever said to me... "How clever of you to have four marvellous normal clever good-looking children! They are a credit to you. Well done Harriet".... But about Ben – I'm a criminal' (25).

The Fifth Child lends itself to an interesting intertextual contrast and parallel with Mary Shelley's *Frankenstein* (1818). In Mary Shelley the monster is produced by the eponymous scientist who runs away in despair at the horror of his creation. In Lessing the child is critically examined by the mother as a "creature" whom she disliked intensely. But she tries valiantly to be kind to him and to draw him into the circle of the family.

Both the creatures are monstrous agents of devastation for the family, its peace and warmth. Harriet has the uneasy feeling that the house is not the same that there is a wariness in every body. Six months old Ben twists the arm of his elder brother and sprains it. Less than a year old, he quietly walks down the stairs from his room and kills the family dog and then the cat. The other children feel threatened and the mother locks Ben in, 'if he could kill a dog, then why not a child?' (76)

In Mary Shelley the Alps and the Arctic wastes are the landscapes of isolation from society. In Lessing the barred cot, the locked room and, later, the institution where Ben's father David banishes him become spaces of contempt and isolation. With Ben institutionalized, the children bloom again and there is a sense of relief in the family.

But Harriet is stricken with guilt, she assert her maternal concern and retrieves Ben from a virtual hell of an institution, where children are kept drugged in strait-jacket in sub-human conditions. She brings him back home against the wishes of her family and nurses him to some semblance of normalcy. Harriet stays with Ben most of the time for days and night, shielding her other children from him, though her family felt that she has turned her back to them and gone off to an alien country (108). The children avoid home and family and gradually move away.

Unlike the scientist in *Frankenstein* who escapes from the reality of the monster, Harriet's integrity as a mother is remarkable, even though she feels that he has reached the dark edges and would vanish one day. She implores the doctor to pronounce that Ben is a strange and an abnormal creature from another planet, even as she watches the horror in the doctor's stare, horror at the alien outside the human limit, 'horror of Harriet, who had given birth to Ben' (125). In Mary Shelley, the scientist goes to the criminal judge beseeching him to seize and punish the creature. Harriet felt as if the strain of her life had stripped off a layer of her skin (135). For both each day is a living nightmare.

Watching Ben standing at the open window as a child, the mother regrets having come in to prevent his fall, or chasing him across the road she longs for someone to run him over. She realises sadly that by saving Ben from being murdered at the institution, she had destroyed her whole family. Especially the fourth son, Paul who needs psychiatric help and is the worst hit.

In the whole sordid incidence, Harriet is seen by the family as 'Irresponsible Harriet, selfish Harriet, crazy Harriet' (140) and as the destroyer of the family. While she tells her husband, David, that they are being punished for their presumptuousness, for planning, for thinking and believing that they would be having their large bungalow, would have six children at least. She feels her own mother, Dorothy had paid a heavy price by working herself to the bone in their household and David's father James too who had supported them financially for years.

In a strong voice Lessing expresses the unspeakable agony of motherhood, as one who realises the harsh truth about her child. He belongs to that group of the uneducable sediment in school who move from class to the class and play truant from school, to everyone's relief.

Stripped of all maternal concern, she watches dispassionately, as her adolescent son moves progressively away into the circle of gangsters. They stomp in and out of the house, hooked to the tv, watching and cheering gory violence on the screen. Technology had enmeshed them and replaced home, love and care, Harriet is convinced that there will be a link with the growing crime in the neighbourhood and this gang. With years of suffering she has been able to slough off guilt. She knows that she has lost Ben to the world of crime and violence, just as she knows that her other children would never return. Nevertheless she would wait for them.

Ben becomes the symbol of the mechanised technology driven life. Devoid of family bond and full of hatred, irresponsible and unconnected with his mother and the rest of the family, he does not feel the agony which the Frankenstein monster felt that he was born with the monstrous frame, there was no love of a father or a mother for him. He had been denied human intercourse and had no friends, violence becoming his only mode of self-expression. Both live in a sterile world devoid of spirituality and grace.

Both *Frankenstein's* monster and Ben cannot be contained by the text; while one is lost in the icy wilderness, the other disappears into the world. Lessing treats motherhood and male gaze as a challenge to a woman's position. By 1960s Lessing herself had become disillusioned with politics, for her too, like others it was a god that had failed. She confessed that it was madness to believe that Communism could come up with any answers. The point of rest for an artist, she wrote, would be the recognition of the responsible individual making his own public and private judgement before any act of submission (*A Small Personal Voice* 12).

Both Kate Brown and Harriet Lovatt achieve individuation through suffering, they rid themselves of guilt with the unswerving acceptance of failure.

References

Beret, Ralph. "A Jungian Interpretation of the Dream Sequence in Doris Lessing's *The Summer Before the Dark*." *Modern Fiction Studies*. Vol. 26 No. 1, Spring 1980.

Coward, Rosalind. *Female Desire: Women's sexuality Today*. London; Paladin, 1984. *Contemporary British Fiction: Narrative Practice and Feminist Theory*. Ed. Paulina Parmer. New York: Harvester Wheatsheaf, 1989.

Lessing, Doris. *The Fifth Child* (1988) London: Flamingo, 1993.

Lessing, Doris. *The Summer Before the Dark*. (1973) London: Paladin, 1990.

Mulvey, Laura. "Visual Pleasure and Narrative Cinema" *Screen* 16, number 3 (1975): 6-18.

Mulvey, Laura. "Feminism, Film and Avant-garde" *Framework,* No. 10 (1979): 3-10.

Raskin, Jonah. "Doris Lessing at Stony Brook: an interview". *New American Review*, 8 (1979): 172.

Rich, Adrienne. *On Lies, Secrets and Silence: Selected Prose* 1966-1978. Virago 1980: 216.

Shelley, Mary. *Frankenstein* 1818. Ed. Anjana Sharma. New Delhi: OUP 2001.

12 Anita Brookner
A Reluctant Feminist's Fictional World

Bandana Chakrabarty

The charge levelled against Anita Brookner (1928–) that her novels are predictable and that she is recycling the same material does great injustice to an exquisite craftswoman like her.[1] Brookner's editor at Viking, Juliet Annan, says that she is one of the most misunderstood writers of her time. Internationally eminent as an art historian and critic, she became the first woman to hold the position of Slade Professor at Cambridge. It was in her early fifties that she published her first novel *A Start In Life ((1981)* and has produced a novel every year since then – the latest being *Leaving Home (2005)* which is her twenty third novel. The essay proposes to consider some of Brookner's novels and explore the relation of her women protagonists to their essentially male-dominated milieu as well as to investigate the gradual change that is coming over the lives of (her) girls and women.

Many women novelists in the twentieth century have been revalued in recent times. Brookner's narratives are 'women-centred'. A 'woman-centred' novel is one which in some way or other illuminates female attitudes to experiences and throws light on the texture of women's lives. A 'woman centred' novel may or may not be feminist, whereas a feminist novel 'foregrounds consciousness-raising', says Rosalind Coward.. Raising one's consciousness means heightening one's awareness, becoming attuned to the evidence of male domination to which previously one paid little attention or ignored altogether (Einstein 35). According to Brookner, feminists are naive, if not dishonest so long as they refuse to acknowledge the degree to which most women are locked in a competition that she describes as "inborn", a biological given (Haffenden 67).

In defining her opposition to feminist thought Brookner has told John Haffenden in an interview, 'I do not believe in the all-men-are-swine programme' and she has deliberately distanced herself from feminist politics. In her novels, Brookner shows that the 'liberated alternative is seen as producing loneliness, absence of love and family.' She has confessed that she is successful on two counts: as an academic and as a novelist.

Olga Kenyon in *Women Novelists Today: A Survey of English Writing in the 70s and 80s* says that Anita Brookner 'observes the constraints on women, yet cannot reject them as a feminist would, because she feels their continuing hold on the female conscious and unconscious' (1988:164). Brookner possesses 'the ability to represent the social frustrations and intimate thought-processes of gifted undervalued women.' Her protagonists have inherited values of 'seriousness, self-control, rectitude' from the eighteenth and nineteenth century societies but are still part of the twentieth century which no longer values them.

When Brookner surveys women today she finds them all wanting. Her characters are inheritors of the Victorian ideals of dignified behavior. Her concern continues to be with lives of women and their often reluctant preoccupation with their emotional lives. They learn at times that emotional fulfillment is often frustrated by intellectual achievement. Her experiences as an academic have to some extent shaped the subject matter of her fiction. Her first novel *A Start in Life* (1981) opens thus, 'Dr Weiss, at 40, knew that her life had been ruined by literature' (7). The name, Ruth, is suggestive of the biblical Ruth standing 'amid the alien corn.' Since childhood Ruth Weiss has been escaping from life into books. She is a beautiful and intelligent woman'. She remembers her childhood, her friendship and doomed love affairs and finally her marriage to Roddy. During the six months of their marriage, Ruth felt a great sense of security which, as her friend Anthea believed, is what 'every woman needs' (172). Roddy dies as a result of a motor accident and Ruth and her father 'could not believe that such a thing had happened, that they were both once again, survivors' (173). She knows that once again she must make a start in life. She picks up her work on Balzac again and she was able to plan the second volume (174).

Hotel Du Lac, Brookner's fourth novel, made her visible overnight after she won the Booker prize. Edith Hope the heroine is an English woman, approaching middle age, a writer of romance novels who secretly believes in the happy endings they offer. She puts her London friends to shame by transgressing their unwritten sexual codes. When Edith saw her fiancé on the registry steps, 'then she saw in a flash, but for all time, the totality of his mouse-like seemliness' (129). From a marriage of convenience Edith departs to a quiet Swiss hotel in the hope that she would once again become her former respectable self. During her sojourn at the hotel, she writes her experiences into the long letters she writes to her married lover, David Simmonds. This relationship does not provide her with any permanence. At the hotel when Philip Neville, a diabolical man, proposes to her, Edith thinks of accepting him. She writes to David about her views on marrying Philip, 'I shall try to be a good wife to him. One does not receive proposals of marriage every day in this enlightened age' (181). But when she sees Neville come out of Jennifer's bedroom, Edith responds decisively and with a new knowledge of herself, 'And I should lose the only life that I have ever wanted even though it was never mine to call my own' (184). Malathi Rao is of the view that *Hotel Du Lac* offers her heroine 'in place of family and children and home – a flat of her own and a drifting relationship which satisfies the home making instinct of Edith Hope who is content to cook and feed elaborate meals for her itinerant lover.' In the novel Edith leaves England and home for a journey to a foreign hotel but it is also a journey into the perilous areas of the self. The novel concludes as Edith buys a ticket for London. In the early novels, Ruth Weiss in *A Start in Life* (1981) and Edith Hope in *Hotel Du Lac*

(1984) travel abroad, yet they always return to their old worlds whereas in the novels of the 1990s Brookner breaks this pattern of her previous writing.

In *A Closed Eye* (1991) Brookner presents Harriet writing a letter to her dead friend's daughter, Lizzie, inviting her to spend a holiday with her in Switzerland where she decides to stay after the death of her daughter and her husband. Lizzie's arrival at Switzerland changes Harriet's perceptions and gives her the opportunity to find meaning in her life, to mature and survive. Harriet in *A Closed Eye* is imagined as a good daughter and an obedient girl and, later, as a good wife to Freddie Lytton, the rich but much older husband, to whom her parents marry her. Harriet openly questions the value of goodness. She sees a reflection of herself in Charles Dickens' heroine Little Dorrit, 'But Little Dorrit was beginning to horrify her... An impossible woman, she thought, with a slight but definite sorrow. But good as I always wanted to be good' (71). Harriet is conscious that her parents loved and protected her, and, at the same time, also, of their selfishness: by marrying her off to the wrong man. Though she continues to see them and to love them, neither of them can feel comfortable with each other. 'Now we meet on uncertain terms with little enough to say to each other' (137).

In her rather unhappy marriage Harriet recognizes the shortcomings of her marriage as also her own weakness and her need for the protection, stability and affection she gets from her husband. She compares her own husband with her lifelong friend Tessa's husband who is defined as 'the villainous hero of romantic fiction, the cruel lover who breaks heart and thrills women' (42). Harriet's craving, her sexual dreams and her unsatisfied desire become 'a universal metaphor for the suffering and loss associated with women's destiny' (332).

Feminist theory has defined women's literary quest as tending to be circular. Critics like Julia Kristeva see the enriching cyclic perception as the woman writer's way of disrupting patriarchal linearity. Brookner's novels of the 1990s provide an example of the transformation of feminine "vicious cycles" into feminist open structures, from claustrophobic, matrophobic texts to liberatory revisions. Harriet's decision not to return home seems to be an essential step in acquiring self understanding. The feminine cycle of passive repetition is opened up into new vistas of 'wisdom, of personal growth and creativity' (Usandizaga, 331).

An interesting novelty that this novel provides is about female bonding.. Harriet's isolated existence is relieved by the company of her friends, especially Tessa. When Tessa prematurely succumbs to cancer, Harriet states, 'She had felt so close to them, the girls, as Freddie used to call them. They had spent the afternoons together, unwilling to part, in silence, lying back in chairs or on sofas' (120). At the end of the novel female bonding can be observed when Tessa's daughter, Lizzie, helps Harriet bear her loss and desolation with fortitude. Brookner offers her women a new choice, novel with the *A Closed Eye* as she transforms the destiny of Harriet by changing the bleak perspective of loneliness and lovelessness in which Brookner usually left her female protagonists at the end of the stories.

In her twentieth novel *The Bay of Angels* (2001) Brookner continues to explore changes in women's destiny. Zoe Cunningham and her mother are typical Brookner characters – women who hide their empty emotional lives behind a facade of stoic acceptance. Zoe grows up fatherless and Brookner from the very beginning lays down her dictum of life as a fairy tale flawed at its very centre. A white knight who steps into their lives is neither handsome nor young. He is an older Jewish businessman, Simon, who brings transient comfort to their lives.

Marriage brings Zoe's Victorian mother the company of her husband but she remains lonely in this marriage. Brookner voices her views through Zoe that 'marriage does not always cure the curse of loneliness' (91). Simon dies and Zoe's mother becomes incapacitated. They find themselves once again without a knight, leaving behind him much less to live on than anticipated. During the mother's illness both Zoe and her mother are brought together again in an extraordinary bonding of intimacy. But for Zoe, this bonding deconstructs itself into other relationships. In the end, Zoe, Dr Balbi, and his sister stay together, an arrangement that suits all three of them. Fiction, says Brookner, through Zoe, 'should show other possible lives.' Brookner gives us the other possibility – the subversion of marriage and a new definition of a family. Says Malathi Rao, 'With all her modernity Brookner still seems to operate in a deterministic world where the choice of a woman is narrowed down to final acceptance of duty rather than rebellion and anarchy'. For the first time Brookner advocates single life and in the end shows that one can be single and happy.

In the earlier novels her heroines are 'deceived, disappointed, deeply introspective and deprived.... They embark on an endless and cyclical journey, for them there is no promised land' (Hosmer 55). But from the 1990's Brookner's pattern of previous writing undergoes a change. The world of her heroines acquires specific values and lends itself to 'achievement, to improvement and to actual change' (Usandizaga 329). In the novels of the 90s Brookner's narrative strategies too undergoes a change. These novels have tightly woven structures that help focus the writer's purposes and emphasize the protagonist's awakenings to their understanding of identity.

Brookner's heroines seem to be helpless, yet in a subversive way, they control their world and gain a brief authority. She may be termed a 'reluctant feminist' in the sense of a writer who values the creation of art above all other activities and who depicts relations with other women as the wellspring of that endeavour for the woman artist. In her novels Brookner has reiterated that 'If we are women' and writers, 'we' depend upon the examples and imaginations of other female artists to provide us with inspiration and material."

In Margaret Diane-Stetz' opinion, 'If one can define the championing of literature written by and to women, the valuing of aesthetic or emotional bonds between women artists and their female mentors, and the focusing of attention upon the woman writer as a character worthy of occupying the foreground of a novel, as literary acts that promote the general good, then Brookner and her artist-heroines may stand up after all and receive their feminist honours' (111). Brookner continues to explore changes in women's destiny. Her novels offer new insights into the complexities of women's growth and independence. They may not be revolutionary changes but they end on a more positive note.

References

Brookner, Anita. *A Start in Life*. London: Penguin, 1981.

Brookner, Anita. *Hotel du Lac*. London: Jonathan Cape, 1984.

Brookner, Anita. *A Closed Eye*. London: Jonathan Cape, 1991.

Brookner, Anita. *The Bay of Angels*. London: Penguin, 2001.

Coward, Rosalind. "Are Women's Novels Feminist Novels?" in *The New Feminist Criticism*. Ed. Elaine Showalter. New York: Pantheon Books, 1985.

Diane Stetz, Margaret. "Anita Brookner: Woman Writer as Reluctant Feminist." *Writing the Woman Artist: Essays on Poetics, Politics and Portraiture*. Ed. Suzanne Jones. Philadelphia: U of Pennsylvania Press, 1991. 96-113.

Einstein, Hester. *Contemporary Feminist Thought*. London: Unwin Paperbacks, 1984.

Haffenden, John. "Anita Brookner" in *Novelists in Interview*. London: Methuen, 1985.

Hosmer, Robert E. Jr. "Paradigm and Passage: The Fiction of Anita Brookner." *Contemporary British Women Writers: Narrative Strategies*. New York: St Martin's, 1993. 26-55.

Kenyon, Olga. *Women Novelists Today: A Survey of English Writing in the 70s and 80s*. Sussex: The Harvester Press. 1988.

Rao, Malathi. "The Anatomy of Loneliness." *Deccan Herald*. Sunday, May 5, 2002.

Usandizaga, Aranzazu. "The Female *Bildungsroman* at the *Fin de Siecle:* The Utopian Imperative in Anita Brookner's *A Closed Eye* and *Fraud*". *Critique:* Summer 1998, Vol. 39, No. 4.

Waugh, Patricia. *Feminine Fictions: Revisiting the Postmodern*. London and New York: Routledge, 1989.

13 The Stories Ghosts Tell in Muriel Spark's *The Portobello Road and Other Stories*

Urmil Talwar

Do ghost's 'Tell' stories? Yes! My first encounter with Muriel Spark was through the ghost of Needle, the narrator of the story "The Portobello Road". Ghost, the first person narrator, is made to behave like a living person narrating the story. There is nothing eerie or fantastic about the ghost. In this paper I propose to take up the narrative technique in the postmodern fiction that lays emphasis on the 'telling' of the stories.

Critics have paradoxical views regarding Muriel Spark's fiction. Fredrick Karl describes her fiction to be 'light to the point of froth' (280). Frank Kermode feels that through she is 'obsessed with the medium' (425), she is "a difficult and important artist" (426). Bernard Harrison in his essay "Muriel Spark and Jane Austen" compares her fiction to that of Jane Austen's and finds that her 'books are too spun out'. Her fiction seems all surface, and rather dry and sparsely furnished. Her novels seem 'to be profoundly... preoccupied with morality, not to say moral theology. Indeed, these seem to be about nothing else' (225). Another criticism is that inconsequentiality is the prime source of the thinness of her fiction which:

> partly... stems from Miss Spark's authorial tone of voice, which is characteristically cool, level and uninvolved, and occasionally enigmatically flippant (226).

Are these really her weaknesses? In this paper I wish to present the view that these are the tools which she has consciously employed in her fiction to reveal the kind of contemporary reality that she wishes to depict.

This 'coolness' and 'detachment' are the hallmark of her work. Instead of interpreting events and individuals, she stands aside and shows them unadorned. Authorial detachment or objectivity is an attitude taken as submission to chaos and sometimes as the denial of omniscience and the ghost seems an appropriate device to defy the realistic mode.

In the story "The Portobello Road" she describes situations through action and dialogue, with little or no attempt to explain or reveal the internal, psychological motivation of her characters. This makes reading her work a demanding process since the lack of authorial comment is a means of forcing the reader to engage in his or her ethical evaluations. Like Hemingway, she succeeds in making 'parataxis'[1] statements, leaving it to the reader to ascertain the value for oneself. One has to think about the ethical implications of the murder of Needle and of George's behaviour towards Kathleen and Maltida. George marries Kathleen after a marriage with Maltida, a nigger, in Congo whom he leaves after his uncle settles annuity. Nowhere in the story Needle reveals her reaction to her own death, neither does she condemn the behaviour of George who has murdered her nor does she reveal the feelings of her friends on her death. Muriel Spark reports the action in a God like attitude, totally objective, totally impartial. This may privilege more than one 'point of view' from which the story could be told. This kind of narration has been criticized as worthy of journalism and historiography, and, being unfit for fictional story as it is unlikely to engage our interest unless we know whose story it is. Muriel Spark is a skilled narrator and she sustains the interest of the reader. 'The Portobello Road' could be the story of any of the three major characters involved. The ghost of Needle narrates it but it may just as well be the story of Kathleen or George. Similarly, "Bang, Bang You're Dead" could be the story of Sybil or of Desiree who have similar physical features and look alike.

This multiplicity of 'point of view' or 'objectivity' serves a purpose. Devoid of the expression of shock, horror and moralizing that usually attends death in fiction, we as readers have to exercise our own moral intelligence in each case without explicit authorial guidance. The death of Needle is described in the following words:

> He looked as if he would murder me and he did, he stuffed hay into my mouth until it could hold no more,... he made a deep nest for me.... Then George climbed down, took up his bottle of milk and went his way.... Only a lot of excitement and drinks came of those investigations. The Haystack Murder was one of the unsolved crimes that year. (24-5)

Needle does not reveal any emotions. In fact the story is narrated with such detachment as if the incident does not affect her in the least. The ethical implications are to be construed. Similarly, in the story "Bang, Bang, You're Dead", the death of Desiree and David Carter are thus related:

> A deafening crack from the pistol and Desiree crumpled up. A movement by the inner door and David held the gun to his head.... The gun exploded again and David's body dropped sideways. (61)

In the same story Sybil's husband Donald was on a hunting expedition with a few friends, he was mauled by a lioness and died on the long stretcher journey back to the station. His death is described thus: 'it was done in a flash' (38). Earlier Donald had described the shooting at the infidelity of his subordinate's wife, 'The chap came home unexpectedly and found his wife with another man. He shot them both' (39). At both these deaths Muriel Spark does not reveal the reactions of Sybil or Donald or David. Violent deaths occur frequently in her work, but are always described with extreme detachment and there is no emotion accompanying the incident. She defended her position in an address to the American Academy of Arts and Letters in 1971 and condemned, 'the literature of sentiment and emotion because it enables us to substitute feelings for action.' She says, 'I would like to see less emotion and more intelligence in these efforts to impress our hearts and minds' (25). Certainly, less emotion and more intelligence is the formula for her short stories. Whether it is Needle, Sybil, the Seamstress, or the narrator of "The Seraph and the Zambesi", none of these characters are described with emotional intensity nor do these characters reveal their emotions or judgements on the incidents they describe. Sybil constantly thinks of herself as 'mind' and not as 'heart'. And at the end of the story she remarks, 'Am I a woman, she thought calmly, or an intellectual monster?' (63)

The narrators of the stories "The Dragon" and "The Seraph and the Zambesi" are unnamed but these are first person narrations. Still the emotional content is lacking in these stories. 'Emotion' she believes, is a tool of the traditional English novel. And her refusal of it is the refusal to fulfill the readers' expectations. Nevertheless, some critics like Henk Romijn Mejier, Douglas Reed and Michael Ratcliff assume that it is her shyness and she is embarrassed to reveal her feelings.

This criticism too seems to be irrelevant as the author does this quite consciously and her narrator keeps questioning herself as to why she wishes to be friendly with or be married to a 'Mind'. 'Why men do not like women with a mind?' Sybil questions her inability to reveal her anger or sympathy with other characters – the Dobell boys or Desiree, Donald, Berry, Watson, or David Carter. Maybe she wants to deconstruct the myth that men are intellect, reason, logic...and women are emotional.

All fiction (short story or novel) is narrative and narratives whatever be their medium, hold the interest of an audience or reader by raising questions in their minds and then delaying the answer. David Lodge in *The Novelist at The Crossroad* divides narration into two kinds: one related to 'causality' that answers the question – Who dunnit? the other, related to 'temporality' that answers – What will happen next? Such narratives excite the readers' emotions of sympathetic fear and anxiety and hold the readers' attention to the end. But here is an author – Muriel Spark who in the very beginning of her narration gives away the ending with calculated panache, and allows the reader to see the process of selectivity which leads to it.

"The Portobello Road" begins with a past incident and when the narrator takes over after the first scene the reader is informed that "Needle is no more" and the reader at once realizes that George is hallucinating! The narrator explains 'I must explain that I departed this life nearly five years ago' (1). The story is narrated by the ghost of Needle and is about the death of Needle. It covers a span of about ten years. In "Bang, Bang You're Dead", before the second reel begins to unwind Sybil informs that three of them are already dead. "The Dragon" too begins with the narrator's comment that she felt defeated and she was going to stop all this. However, in all these stories the reader's interest and curiosity is aroused and sustained throughout. Muriel Spark's stories do arouse the questions of causality and temporality as one wishes to know why these people – Needle, Desiree, David Carter, Berry Watson died. The author achieves this through a combination of frequent time-shifts with third person narrative. Time-shift is a very common device used in modern fiction. Normally it is naturalized as the operation of memory, either in the representation of characters' interior monologue (stream of consciousness), constantly shifting from one phase of life to another through memoir or it is done reminiscence. It could be fragmentary, discreet memoir in the form of a collage or a flashback technique in cinema where a word or an incident evokes the past memory of a particular incident.

Muriel Spark has made use of all these techniques. She uses the interior monologue in the story "The Dragon". The description in the story constantly shifts from one phase of life to the other. In "Bang, Bang You're Dead" she uses the flashback technique. This in fact is more than just the operation of memory. The protagonist/narrator is "time-tripping" and it is her past that is narrated through her ghost like appearance in the story where the host family is watching the screening of the film of her past life. Muriel Spark frequently combines time-shift with authorial third person narrative. This is a common post-modernist strategy, calling attention to the artificial construction of the text.

Experimenting with narrative technique, Spark's stories are remarkable for their fluid handling of time, ranging back and forward over the given span of action. "The Portobello Road" begins with the scene of an incident in youth, then the time shifts to 'One Saturday in recent years...' (2), then a few days later, to the present, 'I must explain that I departed this life nearly five years ago....' (4). But two paragraphs later she picks up the earlier frame and describes how the four friends departed after the completion of their education. Except Katheleen, three of them – Needle, Skiny and George were in Africa.

Her frequent time-shifts prevent the reader from getting too absorbed in the temporal continuum of the fictional story or the psychological depth of the central character. In all the stories except "The Seraph and the Zambesi" there are frequent and abrupt time-shifts between various episodes. Through time shift, Muriel Spark allows connections of causality and irony between widely separated events. In the story "The Portobello Road" the synchronic[2] structure of the story and the significance of the name Needle is revealed at the end. At the outset the reader is informed that she is named Needle because she found one in the haystack. Ironically, after her death, the evening newspaper reported – "needle" is found: in haystack!

A shift of narrative focus back in time may change our interrelation of something that happened much later in chronology of the story. Except for "The Dragon" the other three stories peter out into scrapes and fragments of action and conversation. At the end of the story one really absorbs the significance of each dialogue and scene and the part each has in the overall design of things. The pleasure of reading her stories lies in the expectedness and yet the justice of these discoveries.

Another technique of predestined narratives[3] is used by Muriel Spark in her novel *Do not Disturb*. In this novel also the end is revealed in the beginning.

> 'Of course he expected his dinner', Lister says. 'But as things turned out he didn't have to eat it. He'll be arriving soon (11).
>
> But what's done is about to be done and the future has come to pass. My memoirs up to the funeral are as a matter of fact more or less complete. At all events, it's out of our hands. I place the events at about 03:00 a.m. So prepare to stay awake. (12)

There are numerous such statements used by the author, as the event will take place at about 3 a.m. The three – Baron, Baroness and Victor – are due to arrive for dinner. The servants have already planned their funeral and how they will receive the journalists and reporters the death of Baron and that they will sell the story for a movie to the highest bidder. The story is narrated by the servants, traditional filmmakers and reporters of crime. The servants are quite innovative and have learnt the manners of their betters – acquiring press agents, aspirations to film-script writing as well as sharing with their author a gift for forward plotting.

Muriel Spark's fiction is end directed. The end is definite and told in the beginning. She is sure where the events will lead to. The beginning, which creates expectations and freedom, and the middle, which sustains and qualifies it, seems to be absent. The meaning in her fiction is gathered on reading back from the end towards the beginning. Not only the novel but the short stories are also end directed. Frank Kermode in his essay writes that endings in fiction and apocalypse in history are analogous and the author is unable to relate this time of a life to the time of the world and therefore so much significance is attached to time and to the ending (1967: 249).

In an interview with Frank Kermode about creative process in *House of Fiction,* Spark says, 'Things just happen, and one records what has happened a few seconds later' (26). She records what has happened leaving God to pass judgement on it. God, like the fiction writer 'knows the beginning and the end, and the struggles of his characters to evade their destinies' (28). Most of her short stories and novels end with death. This is because she inter-relates morality, aesthetics, teleology and the novel form. Indeed, death and ending is the retrospective subject of her fiction – The life of a Christian is a preparation for death and the plot of the story is an extended preparation for its ending.

Apart from this her work seems to convey a paradox. Inspite of humour at the manifest absurdity of human behaviour and events, there is 'a supernatural process going on under the surface and within the substance of all things' (*The Mandelbaum Gate* 199). This belief, she clearly demonstrates, in her first published fiction "The Seraph and the Zambesi" for which she won *The Observer* award. She said, 'I do not know what gave me the idea for the story, but I certainly believe in angels, and I had been up the Zambesi on a boat' (Spark: 1960, 683). Her assurance in acknowledging both – angels and boat trips – as her inspiration is her characteristic. It is the disclosure of a relationship between the profane and the divine. This is the motivation and ultimately the abiding theme of all her works. She persuades us that angels and demons are neither metaphoric nor outdated. In doing this she has not reverted/ subverted to the old forms of fantasy nor succumbed to the current patterns of magic realism. The device of supernatural element is used in her fiction without any explanation and is quite exciting for the reader as well as the characters themselves. In "The Portobello Road" the ghost of Needle is as confounding to Kathleen as it is to the reader because George can see the ghost of Needle and Kathleen cannot. The characters seldom share their creator's awareness of the supernatural as a part of everyday reality. In the story "The Seraph and the Zambesi", Cramer who encounters the Seraph does not speak about him. The natives believe that there was a leopard in the garage and so set it to fire. Only the narrator and Cramer saw the Seraph, and the unnamed narrator describes the Seraph passing through the jungle and riding the Zambesi.

Along with the inclusion of supernatural machinery her characters too have a ghost like appearance in the stories. She portrays very flat characters, *sans* thoughts, *sans* motives, *sans* emotions. She seldom gives us sufficient background of her characters so as identify with them. The four characters in "The Portobello Road" have a ghost like presence. In the second story "Bang, Bang You're Dead" Sybil has a ghost like presence. The eighteen-year-old Kodachrome reel is about dead people. There are few words that tell us of the present time and these words evoke the memory of past incidents that are recorded and narrated by Sybil in third person narration. The characters of the story "The Dragon" do not have a sense of belonging and it is as if, by isolating them, disregarding the distractions of environment, she immediately gets down to the essentials, as if she is only bothered about or has to consider the state of the soul. I feel that her characters and especially her narrators have a ghost like presence in her work.

Notes

1. 'Parataxis' statement is a rhetorical tactic of juxtaposition.
2. For Synchronic and Diachronic structures of a story see Eric S. Rabkin *Spatial Form and Plot.* New York, 1963.
3. 'Predestined narrative' is a narrative in past tense that allows the future to seep, as it were, into the present and the present into the past.

References

Bradbury, Malcolm and David Palmer eds. *The Contemporary English Novel.* London, Arnold Heinemann, 1979.

Bradbury, Malcolm. *Possibilities: Essays on the State of the Novel.* London, Oxford University Press, 1973

Harrison, Bernard. "Muriel Spark and Jane Austen". Gabriel Josipovici. *The Modern English Novel. The Reader, The Writer, and the Work.* Ed. Gabriel Josipovici. 1976, London, Open Books, 1976.

Josipovici, Gabriel. ed. *The Modern English Novel. The Reader, The Writer, and the Work.* 1976. London, Open Books.

Karl, Fredrick R. *A Reader's Guide to the Contemporary English Novel.* 1959, New York, London, 1963.

Kermode, Frank. *The Sense of an Ending: Studies in the Theory of Fiction.* 1967. London, Oxford University Press, 1967

Kermode, Frank. 'Sheerer Spark'. *The Listener.* 24 September 1970.

Lodge, David. *The Novelist at the Crossroad.* New York, Columbia University Press, 1966.

Lodge, David. *The Art of Fiction.* London: Penguin. 1992.

Meijer, Henk Romijn. 'Het Satirische Talent van Muriel Spark'. In *Tirade* VI. 1962. Unpublished translation by Tony de Vletter. Quoted in "Angels Dining at the Ritz: The Faith and Fiction of Muriel Spark".

The Contemporary English Novel. Ed. Malcolm Bradury and David Palmer. London: Arnold Heinemann, 1979.

Rabkin, Eric S. *Spatial Form and Plot.* New York, Hill and Wang, 1963.

Ratcliff, Michael. *The Times.* London, 6 March 1973.

Reed, Douglas, 'Taking Cocktails with Life'. *Books and Bookmen.* August, 1971. 0-14.

Ruth Wittaker. "Angels Dining at the Ritz: The Faith and Fiction of Muriel Spark", Ed. Malcolm Bradbury and David Palmer *The Contemporary English Novel.* London, Arnold Heinemann, 1979.

Spark, Muriel. "How I became a novelist". In John O' London's *Weekly* III, 61, 1 Dec. 1960.

Spark, Muriel. *Not to Disturb.* London, Macmillan, 1971.

Spark, Muriel. *The Mandelbaum Gate.* London, Penguin Books, 1965.

Spark, Muriel. *The Portobello Road and Other Stories.* London, Penguin Books, 1995.

14 The Nowhere People
Paul Scott's *Staying On*

Veena Singh

Independence of the colonies in Asia and Africa impacted the status of the white races both at home and abroad, and the process of Great Britain being reduced to Little England was set in motion. Political power through the intervention of the United States in the Second world war had already changed hands and imperial stature was also on its way out. The liquidation of the empire left an in-between generation on the peripheries. They were the people in the shadow. They were the '... new race of sahibs and memsahibs of international status and connection who had taken the place of Generals and Mrs. Generals...' and, who '... had become for them almost as far down in the social scale as the Eurasians were in the days of the Raj' writes Paul Scott in *Staying On*[1] (*SO* 215). They were a tribe of people no longer at home in their own culture but equally out of place in the countries they had ruled once. In India many of the hill stations, climatically more congenial to them, were dotted by an aging population of the British who chose to stay behind, a generation reluctant to go back, to being on the margins, but, at the same time, unable to foresee the marginalisation which awaited them in an independent India.

This paper proposes to take up for exploration Paul Scott's *Staying on*, which forms an appendage to Scott's well known quartet, the Raj Quartet and is in this form, a contrast to the earlier four novels where the dimensions of dynamics of power are very different. The white races, in a mood of ascendancy, had gone on from one victory to another, both through territorial expansion and through consolidation of power in their own hands. Scott's sympathies were with the underdog. In a large measure his work offers an interesting comparison to the work of other liberal writers who had preceded him. But as he moves to his fifth novel about India, he is able to see the underside of marginalisation. Power in itself has no race or colour, it is not a matter of masculine qualities. It is, instead in a fluid state, and as Foucault has observed, is circulatory (98). *Staying on* offers some remarkable insights into the nature of both freedom and power, concepts which are abstract enough in themselves but are transformed into concrete realities, the moment they are placed within interactive relationships.

The interactive relationship in the quartet is across race, culture and history. Scott's novels trace the history of India over a period of a hundred years, from the Mutiny to the post independence period, but the history which is narrated is not only the victor's history; it is also the loser's. When there is a clear cut division on the basis of race, culture or history then it is possible to talk of resistance literature or of post colonial writing. But in the case of sympathy being extended to the 'other', such an easy classification eludes one. Locating *Staying On* in this in-between state, the present paper seeks to problematise the notion of exile, concept of alienation and the idea of homeland. Simple concepts on the face of it but the moment one delves deeper, they became shifting concepts.

In the pre-independence period, India had its own set of expatriates and exiles, its 'nowhere' men. In fact Kamala Markandaya titled one of her novels *The Nowhere Man*, where Srinivas, the protagonist, had escaped to England to avoid police enquiry against his anti-British activities. But the host country is inhospitable and he is always on the margins. By borrowing half a title from Markandaya, I intend to make the point that affiliation has a connection with power and with the value of the individual.

Edward Said in his Reith Lectures on the Intellectual Exile observed that 'Exile is one of the saddest fates.' This was applicable in full force to the empire-builders, specially when they were engaged in the task of conquest and administrative residence. The loneliness of Flory in *Burmese Days,* or the gradual erosion of Ronnie's humane qualities in *A Passage to India* are examples of this kind. Scott's Quartet gives several examples of this kind.

The Raj Quartet traces the cultural encounter and the power struggles from 1857 onwards till the division of the country. He looks at the race relations very sensitively and brings out the complexity of the social scenario. He reveals how sympathy can cross cultures, for instance, the relationship between Sarah and Kasim in *Jewel in the Crown*. Scott also depicts how education is both an enabling as well as an alienating factor. If, on the one hand, the missionary school teacher Miss Edwina Crane feels 'conscious of a duty to promote the cause of human dignity and happiness' by teaching '....blacks and half-castes, cut off from her own kind' (*JIC* 217), on the other hand, Hari's 'Englishness' alienates him from his own Hindu society. For him England is back 'home' (*JIC* 287-289).

In the Quartet he moves geographically across the country, travels from north India to western India and central India and historical, cultural, geographical, and racial expanses. *Staying On* is not only literally an appendix but also a metaphorical one. The house in which the Smalleys live, known as The Lodge, is an annexe of The Smith Hotel.

The Smalleys are now outside power. Tusker, after an early retirement, has chosen to stay on in India to avoid anonymity in England.[2] The Smalleys have been living in India where they have been part of the ruling class. The colour of their skin, their accent, their life style and clothes, have distanced them from the ordinary people of the country. They have once commanded the people. But now the contract is at an end. One cannot help but go back to Foucault especially when he discusses two major systems of approach to power. The 'Terms of the contract' (Foucault 91) were transgressed, and in this case freedom, that is, the right to govern one's own country, the right to the sovereignty of a nation is a formal delimitation of his power (93). The Smalleys were simply the vehicle of this power. And now as the centre of power has shifted, they are bereft of it.

Tusker and Lucy, minor characters in the Quartet, are the central characters of *Staying On*. This dark comedy takes place exactly a quarter century after Independence. The imperial arrogance has now been replaced with Indian corruption in the form of Mrs. Bhoolabhoy. The center of power has shifted. The British have gone back home. The Indians are their own masters. The Smalleys, unpromising nobodies in the Quartet "stay on", "hang on" in Pankot. They are the last surviving members of the old school of British and as their circumstances decline they themselves gain in human poignancy. The surname Smalley becomes a metaphor for their over all degradation and their diminutive social status in free India.

The Tuskers decide to stay on not for love as their reasons for staying on in India are purely economical, the main being that Tusker (Smalley) had realized that the 'pension would go further in India than in England' (*SO* 231). Even earlier he was a petty official on the margin of power, now they are on another margin. The *nouveau riche* Mrs. Bhoolabhoy, has the power to dislocate them by asking them to vacate the Lodge, withdraw the mali or take back her tools. Their total subordination and marginalization affects their acceptability as well as respectability in the environs which they now inhabit.

In the days of the Raj, personal servants were a status symbol, controlled by the gaze of the ruler but now the Smalleys are being observed and also being depicted through Ibrahim's (the house boy) gaze. The look of surveillance returns as the displacing gaze and 'the observers' have now become the 'observed' (Bhabha 89). There is an absolute reversal of roles. Ibrahim tells Joseph that the Smalleys 'although still pukka they were often very peculiar like most old people' and adds 'its different kind of pagal. English kind' (62). Knowing fully well his own worth and importance in the household and also the Sahib Membsahib's temperament, when Ibrahim is sacked by Lucy, he knows Tuskar would call him back and when Tuskar sacks him he hangs around waiting for Lucy's return.

Though a servant himself, Ibrahim tells Joseph, 'the new mali', to take orders only from him suggesting that Joseph bypass the Membsahib, for the helpless Membsahib would not be able to say or do anything. Furthermore, he not only argues with Tusker but answers him back when he asks him to take the dog out for a walk and get a shaving stick for him (SO 15). Since Ibrahim has no illusion about Tusker's impotent anger the question of being cowed down does not arise. Moreover as Ibrahim is their sole support in case of illness it is he who looks after the Smalleys like a parent taking care of 'demanding and unreasonable children whom it was more sensible to appease than cross' (*SO* 20).

Location is also of great significance in this novel. It is not only that the Smalleys are located in India which is a free country but they are now tenants in an annexe. The very word annexe evokes the colonial past. The walls giving the house a status of a separate compound have been 'knocked down and a path trodden to create an illusion of connection between hotel and annexe', and, 'the old gateway' now a 'side entrance' opens on to a lane (*SO* p5). The Lodge, which had always been 'diminutive' is now over-shadowed and blocked out by the big Shiraz Hotel. The Lodge is surrounded by wilderness as the garden is unkept and unattended, 'The jungle advancing' (*SO* 22) as the mali had been withdrawn by the land lady. The wild garden, symbolic of disorder and lack of control is also akin to being lost in the wilderness.

In the days of the Raj the Smalleys had also lived in the spacious beautiful Rose Cottage, 'a large rectangular structure with cream stucco walls and colonnaded verandahs at front, back and sides' (20). Rose Cottage itself is a metaphor of the ideal British India in the Quartet. The mention of the rose garden in the Cottage being converted into a tennis court reiterates the changed British status and their lost identity in India.

Houses, which one occupies, impact one's psychology, way of thinking and of security. From these standpoints, the dilapidated state of the house sends its own signal. The inside of The Lodge is cramped and needs maintenance as much as the garden does. In fact it is not a proper house. A towel is hung over the shutters to show that bathroom-cum-WC is occupied as there is no proper door in spite of a doorway between the bathroom and the bedroom. Having chosen to live in such a house, the Smalleys, "Sahib and Memsahib", have also chosen to compromise with their sense of privacy and decency. Furthermore, the fact that flush toilets have been fitted in the hotel but not in The Lodge is a comment on their status. The reference to the toilet seats as "Viceregal Thrones" paradies the lost glory; indicating ironically that the Smalleys are regal only in this and here.

Like the private spaces, Paul Scott very brilliantly marks out the shrinking public spaces to reinforce the reversal of power. The Holi party of Colonel Menektaras in which Tusker plays the role of "a gesticulating clown" is one such instance. In trying to adapt to his changed position and situation, and in order to look like and be accepted by Indians, Tusker only ends up looking a fool, which for Lucy is the "final disgrace". In the days of the empire the white man was the role model for the Indians but in independent India with its changed political set up, no longer was the white man's behaviour the role model. The Indians were the role models, for it was the authority of power which had placed the Indian is an assertive role, Mrs. Bhoolabhoy being a minor representation of it. One finds that the whole concept of Bhabha's mimicry is reversed.

The Smalleys in post independent India have neither authority, force and control nor money. Foucault in his "Two Lectures" on Power and Knowledge argues that though very few means would be available 'to conduct a non-economic analysis of power', yet 'Power is not primarily the maintenance and reproduction of economic relations, but above all a relation of force' (89). Thus both money and force constitute power. The Smalleys are not in a position to exercise any authority directly as now neither their racial background nor their economic or political status can be of any help to them. Whatever little power they can exercise has to be through manipulations and through appeal to sympathy. For instance Lucy employs a mali, through Ibrahim, which is kept a secret from Tusker. Also the mock sacking of Ibrahim by Lucy and Tusker, by turns, makes them feel that they can still exercise power. In other words the mechanism of asserting power has changed and what is more important is that this seemingly discharge or assertion of power is only limited to the household and the servants.

In this changed situation where the agencies of power, like church, military, color and race are reversed, the Smalleys' sense of loneliness and alienation deepens. In the hotel in full view of the Indians eating there, the argument between Mrs. Bhoolabhoy and Lucy over the shears ruffles Lucy. The humiliation in public mauls her. At this time no body present there intervenes in her support. This is a reminder to her of "her place" and "an evidence that times for them had changed" for the worse. She retreats to the Lodge mourning the loss of a support system and centrality that was.

Fretting, fuming, drinking, using abusive language for Mrs. Bhoolabhoy, arguments with Lucy and Ibrahim are both articulation of Tusker's unhappiness and deliberate self deception. Lucy on the other hand resists this loneliness, the circumscribing of her life and narrowing of her world by modes which make her move out of the present space on to surer grounds, for instance going to movies, listening to old war time records, dancing with an imaginary partner, looking at the old snaps, and through letters to Sarah she establishes a spatial passage between India and England. The long imaginary trip in which Lucy takes Mr. Turner around the place makes Lucy feel once again that she is in a commanding position. It is through memory that Lucy recollects the past and connects with "Home", things that she had left behind and time that has gone by.

Lucy's experiences for sure have made her realize her social status in the inverted hierarchy but more so when she thinks of Susy William, the Eurasian woman, who continues to search for her identity. Her experiences could have lead to an inner collapse had she not 'had the tendency to imagine, to fantasize, to project' (162). Actually the reality through which she has lived and the one in which she is living make it impossible for her to live totally in the present.

Her imaginary sojourns are only escapes but she longs for 'Home'. It is not strange that she can communicate with Sarah, going into history across geography, but cannot connect with the people around her as the racial hatred still exists and in her the sense of not belonging here in India is very strong. Before coming to India as Tusker's wife, for Lucy India was the land of 'Maharaja.... pearls looped around his neck and the Star of India in his turban' (*SO* 162), India was the 'gorgeous East' (163) but very soon the fascination withered. She realized very soon that there was a hierarchy and that society was stratified. She was treated by some of those 'awful women who had condescended and taken every nasty little advantage of her as a junior wife who was not in a position.' She also realized that Tusker was 'a man without manly ambition'. In fact there is an incompleteness where their personal relationship is concerned. In her own words, 'His silence is his silence and my loquacity is my loquacity.... I can't hear what he is thinking and he does not hear what I am saying'.

In addition to this distancing between husband and wife, Lucy is distanced from the people she is living with – the Indians. The renewal of contact through Sarah's letter brings out in her the sense of alienation and loneliness and the sense of economic insecurity in a 'foreign country' more pointedly. She is greatly disturbed and frightened at the thought that should something happen to Tusker she would find herself 'alone here and weeping amid the alien corn' and that 'there would be no one of her own kind, her own colour, no close friend by whom to be comforted or on whom she could rely for help and guidance'. For her, 'the nice civilised thing in India' is that which has 'British influence'. Men like Nehru are praiseworthy as he 'an old Harrovian, had backed Dickie Mountbatten'. In short she is one of those who believed that the British had 'the whole burden to bear and without whom India would just have fallen apart...' (*SO* 95-105). India had never been a home for her and it could never be one. The idea that they as white were hated and were being avenged for the colonial times is firmly fixed in her mind. After the showdown with Mrs. Bhoolabhoy in the hotel she notices the Indian businessmen and thinks 'as if for further evidence that times for them had changed for the better and that their own old humiliations were being adequately paid for by new' (*SO* 223).

The Smalleys even after having lived in India for several years are still foreigners, not Indians and they are expatriates from their own culture and land. In fact they are expatriates at three levels, culturally, as they still have not got over the feeling of alienation, emotionally, as their support is gone, and politically, as they are not the centre of power.

One finds Paul Scott's approach and attitude towards the Raj very different from his predecessor E.M. Forster. Unlike Forster, Scott looks sympathetically at their agony and analyses power as it has vitiated the relation of the two cultures. By the end of the novel the reader looks at the Smalleys with sympathy as individuals no longer placing them in Imperial history. They are a childless couple, expatriated from their own culture but not at home in the country of their adoption. They are the in-between people reminiscing about the empire, bearing the brunt of the loss of the imperial glory, in a way trapped in their ineffectuality, waiting for the end. This stay in India, almost at the very end of their lives, critiques not only the imperial adventure, its human fallout but also calls for a revision of racial relations, national histories and power structures.

Notes

1. Paul Scott. *Staying on*, (1977), London, Granada Publishing Ltd., p. 215, Henceforth referred to as *SO*.
2. Ashis Gupta, a Canadian of Indian origin, in an interview while discussing the 'outsider' 'insider' situation, very emphatically stated that economic security, position or a family background could make an 'outsider' become an 'insider' in the host country. To support this he quotes the example of Michael Ondaatje, whose brother is one of the richest industrial bankers in Canada, thus Ondaatje was at once an 'insider' in Canada. Further, Gupta states, 'you go to a new society, or a new community you don't have that co-mingling of identity, suddenly

you see that the protective layer is gone.... The profession that you belong to, that becomes a kind of cover and you know, even if no close friends or intimate friends, that there is something'. One is valued and accepted for what one contributes to society (210-211).

3. This choice is governed by the fear of going back to an unfamiliar society. In Osborne's *Look back in Anger* (1956) Alison's father Colonel Redfield, a retired army officer, tells his daughter that he is out of touch with the reality in England. In his own words, he feels he is '...an old plant left over from the Edwardian wilderness. And I can't understand why the sun isn't shining any more.... But it seems very unreal to me out there. The England I remember was the one I left in 1914, and I was happy to go on remembering it that way' (66-68).

References

Bhabha, Homi K. "Of Mimicry and Man: The Ambivalence of Colonial Discourse". *The Location of Culture* (1974) ed. Colin Gordon. London: Routledge, 1977.

Foucault. *Power/Knowledge: Selected Interview and other writing* 1972-1977. London, Harvester Press, 1980.

Markandaya, Kamla. *The Nowhere Man*. New York: John Day, 1972.

Osborne, John. *Look Back in Anger* (1957). London: Faber and Faber, 1968.

Said, Edward. "Intellectual Exile: Expatriates and Marginals (1993)". *The Edward Said Reader*. Ed. Moustafa Bayrumi et al. New York: Vintage Books, 2000. (368-381).

Scott, Paul. *The Jewel in the Crown* (1966) London: Granada Publishing Ltd, 1973.

Scott, Paul. *The Towers of Silence* (1971). London: Granada Publishing, 1973.

Scott, Paul. *Staying On* (1977). London: Granada Publishing Ltd, 1978.

Singh, Veena. 'The Fragile Self-Image of an Immigrant Writer: Interview with Ashis Gupta'. *Writers of the Indian Diaspora*. Ed. Jasbir Jain, Jaipur: Rawat Publications, 1998.

15 Multiple Selves of Kate Brown in Doris Lessing's *The Summer Before the Dark*

Supriya Agarwal

The Summer Before the Dark takes up the narrative of a woman who is at a phase when her children have grown up and now resent being mothered. She is at a midpoint of her life when everyone else has individual plans for the summer while she finds herself at a loose end. For more than twenty years she has given herself up to her marriage, putting aside all her native talents for a career of performing motherly and wifely roles. Kate Brown is on the verge of growing old when she begins her journey of self-discovery, which leads to an acute searching of her lost self and personality. She gradually sheds off some of the masks, disguises, roles, attitudes and customs, which she had adhered to in life, laying bare the crucial issues of feminism. In the character of Kate Brown, the writer has identified femininity with a number of undesirable attributes like passivity, dependence, indecisiveness and a propensity for excessive self-sacrifice, which are viewed as a kind of disorder or mental illness and for which women need treatment. From the very beginning we sense conflict in the protagonist's personality who is torn between the expected role model of a mother and wife and her desire to understand and identify her own individuality.

Doris Lessing consistently refuses to follow a prescribed line or to become a spokesperson for any kind of movement but the swing in her novels emphasize a social and critical evolution. It seems that her principal interest lies not in any specific ideology or empirical truth about any section of society but in the nature of change itself. In an interview published in *A Small Personal Voice* she says, 'what interests me more than anything is how our minds are changing and how our ways of perceiving reality are changing.' Though rejecting the label of a feminist, in her novels she has always been concerned with the condition of women and their search for personal identity. Ruth Whittaker, who has analyzed a few of her novels says, 'she has never been a feminist rather she is a woman novelist whose antennae sensed the crucial issues of feminism and wrote about them long before they were common currency' (9). Contrasting the nineteenth century options for a woman to get married, have children and live happily thereafter, Lessing has looked at woman's personal identity from a changed perspective; questioning the old values of dying for love and romanticism, she has focused on the evolution of consciousness and various psychoanalytical issues.

Published in 1973 *The Summer Before the Dark* belongs to Lessing's middle phase of writing where taking Kate Brown as an example, the phenomenon of housekeeping, aging, of becoming physically unattractive and gaining independence has been taken up, exposing the multiple selves of a woman. Catering to the needs and wishes of her four grown up children varying between the age of twenty three to seventeen, she feels as if 'she were locked in a large box with four exploding egos… that nothing had happened to her for a long time and she could look forward to nothing much but a dwindling away from full household activity into getting old' (9). Unexpectedly an opportunity comes her way and allows her to come out of her confined self. She emerges out of her cocoon and crosses boundaries.

Kate crosses the boundary not only of home, language and sexuality but also becomes conscious of her body and the self. At some point during that week she rushed to buy the dresses that would admit her 'like a passport to this way of life' (29), and thus begins the change and the process of self-realization and exploration. She stands in front of a large mirror to look at herself to affirm that there stood in front of her a pleasant looking fashionable woman on the verge of middle age. The viewing and parading in front of the mirror has been used by Lessing as a device to trace the various stages of psychological development. Many a times it is the hand mirror, she looks in and the middle phase of her journey can very well be called the 'mirror stage' in reference to the Lacanian notion. It is the stage formative of the 'I' as revealed in psychoanalytic experience, leading to the development of the individual. As Lacan says, 'This development is experienced as a temporal dialectic that decisively projects the formation of the individual into history' (4). Doris Lessing has used this image very explicitly as part of the narrative:

> Kate was now grimacing into the handglass, trying on different expressions, like an actress – there were hundreds she had never thought of using! She had been limiting herself to a frightfully small range, most of them, of course, creditable to her and pleasing or non-abrasive to others (156).

A number of narrative strands are interwoven by the author to present the psychoanalytic aspect of Kate's fractured self. To convey the inner workings of the mind there is a serial dream of the protagonist which is very much central to the plot. The dream acts both as a continuous motivating force for the heroine and as a commentary from the unconscious on her behaviour. Kate dreams that she has found a seal lying stranded on dry rocks in a northern landscape. She begins to carry it downhill to get it to water. The seal has been defined variously by critics but even without its symbolic meanings what strikes us is that it is helpless and stranded and Kate's discovery and rescue of the seal parallels her gradual discovery and rescue of her own self, the self lost for the past twenty five years. In her second dream Kate becomes more involved with the seal by trying to cure its wounds with herbs but in the following dream the seal disappears and is replaced by a turtle. The turtle having been irradiated after an atom bomb test, walks away from the sea towards its death in a dry hinterland. Kate searches in anguish for her seal without success. This dream comes at the point in the novel where Kate herself has taken a wrong turning, a bad decision. Instead of pursuing her own quest, however painful, she agrees to go on a holiday with a young American; she then confesses,

> She ought to go straight back to England, ask for a room in a friend's house, or rent a roof for herself and sit quietly and let the cold wind blow as hard as it would...she already knew that Jeffrey Merton when she looked back would seem to her all dryness and repetition (68).

While she is in Spain with Jeffrey, Kate dreams that she is carrying the seal to a house in which she performs motherly and housewifely duties for her family. She makes love with a young man, but refuses to stay with him, telling him that she has to get the seal to the sea. In a later dream Kate and the seal are threatened by wild animals in an amphitheatre and Kate has just sufficient strength to save them both. She begins to realize that her survival is bound up with that of the seal. During her illness, back in England, Kate dreams that her love, a king, has danced with her and then abandoned her for a young girl. She is imprisoned in a pit and criticized by her former lover. This dream seems to symbolize Kate's youthful marriage and her subsequent domestic imprisonment as well as the more subtle incarcerations of aging. The seal, her selfhood, is deserted but it is found again in her next dream, near to death. Kate revives it and continues her journey northwards, towards the sea. After her illness Kate dreams less about the seal but when she is with Maureen in the flat, she tells her the dream, which returns night after night. It is no longer distinct but leaves her with a feeling of difficulty and loneliness. Maureen tells Kate that she must not go back to her family before she has finished dreaming her dream to its conclusion. Once Kate is able to acknowledge the constrictions of love and duty and the 'shoulds' and 'oughts' in her life, the dream becomes clear to her. This time as she carries the seal towards the sea, she sees a pink flowering cherry tree in bloom in the snow and picks a twig. She realizes that the dream is nearing its end. At last Kate dreams that the snow has stopped falling and that the seal is 'full of life and like her of hope' (227). She sees grass growing and spring flowers and looks down onto a sunlit sea;

> Her journey was over. She saw that the sun was in front of her, not behind, not far far behind, under the curve of the earth, which was where it had been for so long. She looked at it, a large, light, brilliant, buoyant, tumultuous sun that seemed to sing (228).

Kate's journey is always northwards with the seal, through snow and ice. And yet paradoxically, when she arrives at her destination, the sea, the snow has melted and the sun is shining. We understand the northward journey to be a metaphor for the pain of self-discovery. The south for her symbolizes warmth and ease and Kate has to turn her back on easy options. The journey is cold and lonely and the metaphor used during the novel for Kate's waking life is that of a 'chill wind' blowing through it. Nevertheless, having persisted in carrying the seal to the sea, Kate discovers the sun, blue sky and warmth. Her persistence is rewarded and her self-knowledge is achieved by a letting go rather than by a process of rational accumulation of knowledge. This brings unexpected light and joy and after this dream Kate is able to return home. Kate who was living in a frozen state of personality is able to find a congenial atmosphere when at peace with herself. When Kate reaches the ocean and sets the seal free, it joins the others in the collective unconscious. Kate then recognizes the possibility of letting go that burden of 'personality' she has carried around and protected for so long. Kate must overcome the obstacles posed by the adversity of nature and the backward pulls of human desires on her perilous journey to return the seal to the ocean. The animal's suffering in its bitterly cold environment away from the sea corresponds with a description of Kate sitting with 'her shoulder hunched: they were set to withstand the sort of cold a living animal must feel if its skin is ripped off...' (50). The general movement within the dream – Kate dragging and carrying the heavy seal in her arms – symbolizes Kate's growing awareness that during the years of being conditioned into her role as lover, wife and mother:

> All that time she had been holding in her hands something else, the something precious, offering it in vain to her husband, to her children, to everyone she knew – but it had never been taken, had not been noticed. But this thing she had offered, without knowing she was doing it, which had been ignored by herself and by everyone else, was what was real in her (126).

The symbolic weight of the seal is meant to suggest more than a metaphor for Kate's self. A characteristic feature of dream logic is, the way images may actually be condensations of clusters of associations. An image could suggest the object it depicts but that same image might also refer to other meanings. A 'seal' is an animal, true enough but the same word denotes a mark or a brand, it can be a sign of individuality or ownership. In this respect, the seal can symbolize what is unique in Kate. Kate's dream sequence has been interpreted variously by critics also. Ruth Whittaker in her essay "Madness, Dreams and Prophecy" considers Kate's dream as 'a counterpoint to the realist action and as a technique to expand her range to include the conscious and the unconscious self' (87). Ralph Berets regards the seal as the symbol of Kate's 'injured self' (124) while Sydney Janet Kaplan has suggested a spiritual evolution in Kate's journey. Istanbul and Spain, the two foreign destinations of Kate's initial wanderings are both centres of ancient Sufi wisdom. Watching a bird fly past her window in Istanbul, Kate feels 'that subtle approaches were being made to her from an unknown world' (53).

Kate's journey with Jeffrey is another effort to project her multiple selves. Though she fails to establish any real connection, the affair indicates a liberating pattern and moral boundaries imposed on women. Lessing has said goodbye to the ideals of romanticism and the idea of dying for love. Kate finds that Jeffrey's illness brings out the maternal more than the sexual self in her. Playing mother to a sick man, not her son, enables Kate to spend sometime with her thoughts. Leaving Jeffrey, Kate comes back to England, to a hotel room in Bloomsbury where she has two insights. She realizes that people are judged by the degree to which they conform to social patterns. She revisits her home and is unrecognized by her best friend. She sees that without the mask of her person she is unrelated to the continuing existence of her former life. She feels freed by the realization that the social patterns can be separated from herself. 'She was relieved that Mary did not know her. More: she was elated, as if she had been set free of something' (144). Kate's second insight occurs when she attends a play, where she wants to see people dressed up in personalities not their own. At a Turgenev play, Kate free of the restraints of being Mrs. Brown openly applauds or derides the actors. Kate has a vision of the players as mere voices of outworn ideas and of the audience as a group of animals programmed to respond to these well worn attitudes. Kate discovers that the note she has been playing and the mask she had worn had received social approval.

Portraying multiple selves of Kate Brown, Lessing has taken up the question of woman's sexuality very realistically, through the medium of the three women-Mary Finchley, Kate herself and Maureen. It is ironic that the aspect by which women is most defined by the male hegemony – her sexuality, is also the aspect by which she is most alienated. Though, appearing sexy is a prescribed part of the curriculum, women have been prohibited from enjoying sex. Denying the whole idea of romanticism, Mary when attracted by a man, does not restrain herself from having sex and is gradually accepted as she is by her children and husband. Kate, on the other hand, has passively accepted her husband's affairs, tending the image of marriage, serving as a good wife and mother for more than twenty years; then there is Maureen, an extraordinary charming young woman whose freedom encourages Kate to find her own liberation. Lessing's analysis of Maureen's particular stage of development includes a prediction that Maureen will marry to satisfy her biological needs. Kate understands this when she imagines Maureen and William 'in their large house in Wiltshire or somewhere, deep in plentiful horses, children and dogs, everything according to the pattern, including their humorous comments on it' (236). Maureen's youth and money, her relatively uncompleted self offer her choices among so many things; she has many hours, days and years ahead but Kate's vision is narrowed. It is her summer before the dark and her need is to complete one dream.

Commenting upon the contemporary literary scene Foucault in his work *History of Sexuality* says, 'Never did sexuality enjoy a more immediately natural understanding and never did it know a greater felicity of expression' (77). The novel also talks in detail about unconditional acceptance of our body. Kate discovers her own body and learns to love and honour it in its different shapes and sizes. Fat, thin, soft, smooth, puckered, our bodies are our own. By nourishing our body we care for and love our self on the most basic level. A lot of stress is given to Kate growing thin, her hair changing colour, her dress getting loose and to her recognition by other people. Kate becomes oppressively conscious of the power which 'the gaze' wields in dictating and controlling not only her appearance but also her identity and sense of self-worth. Paulina Palmer has analyzed "Femininity and its Construction", as she calls it, by pointing out the strategies of symbolic narrative used by the author as a means of illustration in feminist theory. By means of frequent changes of dress, make up and hair-style, Kate remodels herself into a series of contrasting images of woman – sexy and glamorous, or drab and down-at-heel. She studies the way men respond to these various images and is appalled to discover the power the gaze possesses to confirm or erase her identity.

Towards the end of the novel Kate deliberately re-enacts the sexual scenario with workmen on a building site. She walks in front of them wearing her jacket and is not noticed. Then she removes her jacket, revealing her fitted dress and ties her hair back with a scarf. She walks past seductively, this time to a chorus of wolf whistles and invitations. She again puts on her jacket and again walks back unnoticed. She becomes very angry with the realization that all her life has been a performance to gratify other people 'this is what you have been doing for years and years and years' (210). With this in mind, Mary Finchley's warmhearted amorality becomes not only tolerable but the only sensible way of living. Reviewing her own life Kate says:

> There are times, you know, when there's a sort of switch in the way I look at things – everything, my whole life since I was a girl, and I seem to myself like a raving lunatic. Love and duty and being in love and not being in love, and loving and behaving well and you should and you shouldn't and you ought and oughtn't. It's a disease. Well, sometimes I think that's all it is (218).

In the final section of the novel we are given glimpses of Kate's basic self, of her new relationship to the world and of the nature of her new perspective on life. Kate begins to assert a sense of self in her relationship with Maureen and we perceive that Kate's interaction with Maureen has more reality than her lifelong friendship with Mary Finchley. Kate sees Maureen as someone who is more free than she is, at that stage of life. Also she feels assaulted by 'the marvellous assurance of the girl's youth. Of her courage in doing what she felt like doing. Yes, that was it, that was what she, Kate, had lost' (163). Kate suppresses herself for convention's sake, Maureen rejects all convention. The relationship with Maureen has about the same function as the trip with Jeffrey as both provide important opportunities for Kate to develop.

The fatalistic end and the title seem to suggest that for most women there is no escape from the prison constructed for them by society and their own sexual vulnerability. But the collapse of present system is very predominant and Lessing's concern seems to be the evolution of consciousness from the multiple selves of a woman. The end of Kate's journey is a return back to her home, her husband and her family but it is not a return to her old depersonalized self, Kate returns on a higher plane of understanding and experience. There are hints given by the writer that Kate has changed. She resolves not to dye her hair any more. It is a significant symbolic action, which informs us that Kate has reached the end of functioning at the level of conditioned responses to the world. Having restored her scarred and wounded self, she can begin anew anywhere she chooses, even in her old environment.

References

Berets, Ralph: "A Jungian Interpretation of the Dream Sequence in Doris Lessing's *The Summer Before the Dark", Modern Fiction Studies*, 1988.

Kaplan, Sydney Janet: "Passionate Portrayal of Things to come: Doris Lessing's recent fiction" *Twentieth Century Women Novelists* Ed. Thomas F. Staley. London: Macmillan 1982.

Lacan, Jacques. *Ecrits: A Selection*. Translated by Allan Sheridan. London: Tavistock Publication, 1977.

Lessing Doris: *The Summer Before the Dark* (1973). Great Britain Flemingo: 1995.

Palmer, Paulina: *Contemporary Women's Fiction: Narrative Practice and Feminist Theory*. London: Harvester Wheatsheaf, 1989.

Whittaker, Ruth: *Macmillan Modern Novelists: Doris Lessing*. London: Macmillan, 1988.

"A Small Personal Voice". *New American Review*, 8, New York, New American Library, 1970: 61-76.

16 The House and the Church in Michèle Roberts' *Daughters of the House*

Krishna Sharma

Michèle Roberts' novel *Daughters of the House* (1995) locates the formation of female identity in the frameworks of religion and gender. The young female protagonists travel through hybrid spaces of nationality and narrate the conflicts they go through growing up in a world ravaged by the second world war.

This paper will explore the writer's constitution of the female subject, located at the intersection of sex and religion, represented with the backdrop of the House and the Church: how far are these women able to 'step forward into the darkness'? (172) how far is Michèle Roberts able to make hybridity the source of the creative energy and what degree of success does she achieve in re-forming and re-shaping the image of female subjectivity? The shaping of this paper is dictated by the impact of the Church (religion) and its doctrines (particularly Catholic) on the feminine identity, requires the questioning of the facts and the views held by religion. In the text to be analyzed the author's manner of contending with the complex and contradictory socio-cultural, religious imperative, which underline the gender construction, will be examined.

The delineation of native/alien historical and cultured instances deftly woven into the fabric of the novel make it a hybrid narrative. The writer herself half-English and half-French, born to a Catholic mother and a Protestant father in 1949, lives in London, England, and Mayenne, France, with the artist, Jim Latter.

The narrative spans the past and the present in a complex, yet rhythmic manner like a pendulum. *Daughters of the House* (short listed for the 1992 Booker prize and winner of the prestigious W. H. Smith Literature Award) is a hybrid narrative of two women: Therese and Leonie. The main plot is their recounting of an episode in their childhood, framed at the beginning – now the girls having become adult women, twenty years later. In between there are secrets and lies, friends and enemies. There is paganism and religious mysticism, love and hate. There is the maturing of the young girls, physically alongside the frailties of their elders. There is a red vision of the Virgin Mary (seen by Leonie) and a blue vision (seen by Therese). The novel seems to run up and down, around and through the events it describes interweaving in its fabric the very different voices and stories of the two sisters/daughters. The form of the novel is full of shapes, which seem to play games and tricks with the reader. The text is resonant with sounds, words, food and scents of French provincial life sprinkled as a contrast to English life.

Thus hybridity is one of the poignant themes of the novel as Kumkum Sangari points out, 'The hybrid writer is open to two worlds and is constructed within the national and international, political and cultural system of colonialism and neo-colonialism. To be hybrid is to understand and question as well as to represent the pressures of such historical placement' (114). Hybridity need not be an east/west binary, 'it should incorporate the complex cultural intersections of regional, linguistic, caste, class and gender affiliations' (144), asserts Krishna Sarbadhikari.

As the title indicates, the novel is about the 'daughters of the house'. It opens with a description of the old Normandy House, in which Therese and Leonie, French and English cousins of the same age, grow up after the war. Intrigued by parents' and servants', guilty silences and the broken shrine (with dead bodies of Jews and English men in it), which they find in the woods, the girls weave their own elaborate fantasies. Leonie and Therese are given different versions and stories by their neighbours, servants and villagers about the shrine, the cellar, the Germans, the Jews and the war. The daughters imagine, dream and build up their own visions and wrap their lives with them.

The novel comprises of fifty chapters out of which the first eight chapters and the last five chapters describe the adult sisters, while the thirty seven chapters in-between are a vivid delineation of the daughters' childhood in flashback. These parts, if one may call them, are marked by the icon of the house. The chapters are very short with different headings for each. Interestingly all the headings are related to the house or household items such as Dress, Kitchen, Bathroom, Decoration, Drawing Room, Cellar, and bedroom etc. Some of the headings are 'The Wall', 'The Writing Table', 'The Bed', 'The Holdall', 'The Carpets', 'The Statue', 'The Altar', 'The Sack', 'The Cake Tin', 'The Blue Skirt', 'The Dust', 'The Cigarettes', 'The Words' etc. The cover of the novel also shows the house in the backdrop with the sisters (almost identical) standing close, hand in hand, laughing. The foreground of the cover page is occupied by a saintly figure, with a yellow star between her and the sisters.

The opening lines of the novel are very suggestive: 'It was a changeable house, sometimes it felt safe as a church, and sometimes is shivered then cracked apart... The house was strict. The rules indicated the forbidden places. Chief of these was the bedroom at the back on the first floor, at the top of the kitchen stairs' (1).

The house is invested with the power to influence the lives of its inhabitants, so that it becomes itself a character rather than a setting. Roberts invests a special symbolic meaning in the house. The house both limits and protects women, who can transform 'the wall' in to 'a world'. 'The Normandy House' evokes the novels like *Mansfield Park*, *Wuthering Heights* which demonstrate how women turn a restrictive building into a potent social, moral and even emotional image.

In this house one of the daughters, Leonie, married to Baptiste, is longingly waiting for her sister Therese, like a lover. 'Her mind bristled with knives... Its tip vanishing into Therese's soft flesh' (3). Therese is returning after spending twenty years in the Convent. Leonie fears that Therese, after the long absence, during which she could pretend she (Therese) was dead' (24), would claim the house as hers. To the question 'why you have come back?' (21) shot by Leonie, Therese ambiguously replies 'Oh I don't know exactly, something unfinished here. Something to do with what happened here during the war' (22). She wanted to know about the reopening and desecrating of graves; about lawyers coming down from Paris and journalists poking around, about all the scandals coming out and everybody's secrets being dug up in ghoulish manner. She wanted Leonie to help her remember the past.

In this flashback we see Leonie, a child, coming with her mother, Madeline, to France to visit Antoinette, Louis and their daughter Therese in the Normandy House. Towards the end of the novel, Leonie is the owner of the house living there with Baptiste and her daughters.

Therese, inspired by Saint Theresa of Avila, the Spanish mystic writer (Saint Terese of the child Jesus, The Little Flower) as Michèle Roberts states in the Author's note, belies the vulnerability she shows as an adult through the narrated accounts of her as a child. There is something spiteful about her teenage behaviour and something smug about the way she relates her Visions of the Virgin Mary. Leonie's more negative adult behavior, on the other hand, is gradually understood to be due to her difficult position next to the apparently saintly Therese as a young girl. Intrigued by the parents' and servants' guilty silences and the broken shrine, the young girls weave their own fantastic imagination and eventually uncover a family secret, which is to haunt their past, present and future.

The symmetry of the two girls growing up together has become warped with time. It is as if the two strands have got entangled in to a tight knot where one strand cannot be distinguished from the other. The reader cannot help but wonder whether there is an autobiographical element within the novel, a self questioning of two different dimensions to one character.

Michèle Roberts could be labeled a 'feminist' writer. As such terms are immediately defining and therefore, rather limiting it is interesting to take into consideration Roberts' own hope that in future there will be 'male writers and, female writers, rather than as at present, female writers and writers.' Much of Roberts work deals with the issue of female sexuality and religion.

Roberts skillfully expresses the feelings and experiences of the child Therese, who was fostered by Rose. Therese knew Rose's smell, her milk and sweat, her brown skin. She knew the shape of her hips, from riding on them (32). Rose was a world that curved above her when she took her first tottering steps. Her first word was 'Rose' not her 'mamman' Antoinette.

The pleasures of adolescent age and their awakening to bodies has been delineated through the dichotomy of religion and sex. When, as children, the sisters played games, Therese always played the role model of the chaste, the pious, the holy. In the game called Carmelites (which Therese called: All for love), Therese played the role of Carmelites – the hermit; while Leonie played Charlottes – the wicked women who tempt hermits. In the other game Martyrs, Therese is the martyr, the Christian and Leonie is the Lion, who tortures holy Christian. Leonie punishes, drags, tortures the Christian Therese by stretching her 'on the rack until her bones cracked, tore off her breasts with red hot pincers, then flagged her with twigs' (64) the point was that the Christian had got to die without any fuss. At last they were exhausted and rolled in dust 'then side by side they lay still.. They were sweaty and hot. They let the warm air roll over them like water. For a long time they did not speak. Their fingers slid inside each others' clothes, over each others' skin, stroking, testing. Then further into little purses that must never be talked about, that they weren't supposed to know they had.' (65) They shut their eyes, breathless. Therese called it dying. But Leonie thought: 'how could it be called dying, more intensively more living like' (65).

Similarly, the reaction of the girls at their menstruation periods is deftly described by showing Leonie rubbing Therese's stomach up and down as if 'her hand had a mouth and could talk' (80), and Therese bringing up her fingers from under the sheets staring at the bright red fingers said: 'It must be what they told us about. That thing women get. When you cannot go swimming' (80). In an interview with Linda Richards, Robert states, 'I try and get into the skin of the person or the place or the food and really convey the sensual reality of it' (5).

It is interesting to observe that sensual/sexual scenes have been juxtaposed with visions of Virgin Mary or on the premises of holy shrines/chapels. One does not stop from thinking that both the sisters want to attract attention and are jealous of each other. One takes recourse to seeing holy visions and the other indulges in sexual pleasures. Whereas Therese steals Leonie's Vision of Holy Mother in red, Leonie steals Baptiste, who, she thinks, is attracted towards the voluptuous Therese. Thus on the Harvest Féte when Therese falls into a trance after seeing the vision near the Shrine in the woods, the crowd is attracted towards her, then in the middle of a 'Gloria' she stretched her hands, bowed and knew exactly what to do. She began the hymns 'Salva Regina' and 'Mater misericordia'. But soon the tune changed half way through and the people clasped their hands and arms and began dancing. The dance culminated in sexual physical orgies later, when the children and some others left. Leonie, partly to attract attention and partly jealous of Therese, goes to woods with Baptiste and enjoys the forbidden pleasure of the body as she had enjoyed reading forbidden books from the library. Therese condemns this act, 'the thing is Leonie, its rather vulgar, isn't it? There's our Lady appeared to us and you let your self be pawed by some boy from the farm' (109).

When reviewers discuss Michèle Roberts' works, the adjectives they use tend to run to words like 'sensuous' and 'voluptuous'. 'It's a compliment" Roberts says, "I want to put the body always into language....'.

The dichotomy is again reinforced when Leonie learns about the secret of her birth from Therese, who tells her that they are not cousins, but sisters-twins. Both do not want each other for sisters. Therese claims to know the secret through the letters of Antoinette and Doshitte, which were sent back to her from the convent after their death, as memorial. Therese had burned those letters after reading. Leonie feels it was all Therese fault; first she stole her vision, now she wants to steal her mother (Madeline) and her identity. So, deeply hurt and full of anger, she goes out for a walk near the chapel/shrine in the woods and laying down curls her head on the her arms on the pews of carpet. Baptiste arrives there and she confides her secret words to him. Baptiste doesn't believe it and retorts that 'it was just another of Therese's made up stories like seeing the Virgin Mary' (151). He does not believe Leonie to be 'half-German, half French' (152), (because Antoinette was allegedly said to have been raped by the German soldiers during the war in the cellar of the house.). Eventually, Leonie rips off her Englishness and becomes totally French. She steals the affection of Baptiste for herself and seduces him and feels owned by Baptiste. Thus becoming one with Baptiste she becomes aware of being purified by her relationship with him by taking and giving body. She waited 'for the priest and the Bishop and Therese to come running, to come upon this sinful worship on the ground' (153).

The developing sensuality of both the girls is interwoven with highly mystical visions, not dissimilar to some of the famous mystic women writers, such as saint Theresa, Margery of Kempe, Julian of Norwich. Roberts seem to be implying that the physical awakening of the girls is the experience which eventually leads them to enjoy higher transcendental experiences. The finding of the hidden shoe and stone statue of the Saint in a heap of sand in the cellar expresses a raw dichotomy of sensuality and religion and hints at a perverted sexual relationship culminating into rape by the Germans soldiers. The subtle but powerful delineation of sand falling through a metaphorical time glass as years go by, cannot hide the past (2.2).

Michèle Roberts very skillfully presents the social frustrations and intimate thought processes of undervalued women. She understand the suffering of women (like Antoinette, Rose, Madeline and others) morally alone, unnamed and unknown. She visualizes the individual woman as a representative of universal women on a larger scale. Roberts displays what might be termed 'feminine' sensibility in the subtle descriptions of the appearances, textures, gestures, social and religious nuances. She links the character and background, representing the restrictive effects of environment on the female psyche. There seem to be only female voices in the texture of the novel and it is also the voice of the 'self – the Author? She is making the 'marginal' the 'central'.

bell hooks views the decentering of the self as offering opportunities for 'new and varied forms of bonding' among people, for artistic and intellectual engagement with popular culture, and for creating transformative subjectivities that express and exhibit the 'multiple aspects' of identity; the different location from where we see and think...Through such embodiment, the elements of identity developed 'at the margins' are brought to the 'centre'. Only then can hegemony of existing culture of subjectivity be challenged.

There are no male voices in the text. The male characters referred to are just hinted at. Infact, it is the men who have been 'marginalized' in the novel. Louis, Antoinette's husband, and Theresa's father, 'was only the son of poor neighbor who managed the farm for the three girls (Antoinette, Madeline and the eldest Marie-Josephine, later named Soeur Doshittee, as a nun).' By marrying Antoinette 'He'd done very well for himself, marrying in' (28).

Maurice, Madeline's English husband, Leonie's father, died in the war. He is just casually referred to as a soldier – dead.

Baptiste, who later married Leonie, is again no match to the girl in any way. He also is the son of Rose – a neighbour who came to help in the house, whom Leonie marries simply to possess him fearing Therese might take him away.

The other men like Bishop, or the priest too have no powerful voice. Interestingly, like the two sisters, their two mothers have no brothers and neither does Leonie have sons. She has only daughters.

The space given to the women is comparatively much larger than that accorded to the men in the novel. It is the sisters who display their anger and jealousy against each other for occupying the 'centre' the attention, and the space, leaving the 'other' at the 'margin'. When Therese returns as an adult from the convent, she observes then she had not observed the size of the house she left twenty years ago, 'her child's eye had not been overwhelmed by these chilly mausoleums Antoinette called sitting rooms, had created the spaces she needed', (121). Leonie, she ponders, 'could choose to sit in any one of the these 'salons', small, medium, big or in the conservatory. More rooms upstairs, on two floors. How dared she have so much choice, so much freedom of movement?' (12). On the contrary, Therese remembered the bare cell of the convent, where she walked up-down dully between two brick walls. In this house you could stride. She had practiced detachment for twenty years and had failed as soon as she entered the house. She calls it 'My house. All of it' (13), correcting herself.

On the other hand, Leonie keeps counting the items in the house, and the house as hers. 'They were hers. As the house was... she would not share them with Therese, she had cared for the house, spent money on it....' (13). Roberts deftly brings out the possessiveness of each sister who considers the house and the items of the house as her own.

Michèle Roberts has been regarded as 'hotly controversial'. Much of her work, as stated earlier, deals with female sexuality and religion. As a young girl Roberts wanted to be a nun, the Catholic Church had a deep influence upon her work but there was also something against which she reacted powerfully. In an interview she considers her work being reviewed as 'sensuous' and 'voluptuous' to be a compliment. She says

> 'I was brought up in a tradition of reading and thinking at university that, in a sense, left the body out. It was all about

> your mind. That good writing didn't have a 'self' in it, didn't have an ego in it. I had so much to unlearn when I became a writer ! And because I'd been a Catholic and the body is very scorned in Catholicism – particularly the female body – I wanted to rescue the body, cherish it, love it and touch it and smell it and make it into language. Make language actually a body, as it is to be human (Her Story, 5).[1]

These feelings can also be witnessed in the text too. When Therese returns from the convent enroute the village, she observes the church, and the cemetery beyond it, where her parents were buried. She wants to visit the church and the cemetery, but decides to visit it the next morning (incidentally the day of Harvest Festival Mass) to check the evidence about the news of graves being 'newly opened and desecrated, swastikas in red daubed on the tomb' (7) with her own eyes.

The church sometimes becomes mysterious, foreboding and dark; while sometimes it is open, peaceful, flooded with light and fire. Sometimes it holds the darkness as a curved shell holds water. When Therese is asked to attend the church by the village priest, as a punishment for making up the story of the Vision of Virgin Mary, the church, the sermons of the priest and Therese's reaction to it are discussed in detail. The theme of the sermon was reverence and obedience, 'Waywardness of certain elements of the youth in the Parish....' 'Adolescent frailty and need of guidance' 'Saint Paul and Saint Augustine on women' (115). Therese sweated with shame she forced herself not to open her mouth so that 'torrents of lava could not tumble out to force fire down his throat, torch his tongue' ...(115). She was red and dangerous. She wanted to damage the priestly flesh, 'But suddenly she felt God was with her. White peace descended upon her. She could not hear the priest. She saw God. She fainted' (115).

Again, when she visits the church the next morning, after her arrival from the convent, it was decked ready for the Harvest festival Mass. She found the Church small and light, 'Airy cream coloured stripped... gone was the old smell of damp stone and incense and decay. The Church smelled of bees wax and grass and flowers' (165).

As the early light of the day strengthened inside the Church. Therese saw 'the statue of our lady of Belmont-la-Fontaine. Therese's statue. Our Therese's lady' (164), ready to be taken out for procession. Roberts seems to understand the psychological condition of Therese, who had been brought up by Rose despite her mother living. Therese had lost her mother during the war when thirteen, whom she wanted to see, to possess; that's why perhaps she created the vision of Virgin Mary. She had found herself another mother 'Perfect... a holy doll who never felt angry or sexy and never went away'. 'It couldn't console her any more for Antoinette's loss. What she needed now was a funeral, a fire' (166). Therese lit the flames into the heap of harvest offerings. Then, after all those, years, she saw the red and golden lady for the first time leaping towards her, Therese ran, cried 'Mamaan' and flung herself at the church door (166).

Leonie, on the other hand, who was afraid of the word, the buried past for twenty to thirty years, is seen boldly going and opening the door of the forbidden room. 'She twisted the handle of the door opened it, paused and went in. She felt that Therese along with Jewish family, and Maurice was waiting for her on the other side of the door. The voices came from somewhere just ahead, the shadowy bit she couldn't see. She stepped forward into the darkness to find words' (172).

These last lines of the novel may suggest Michèle Roberts' hopes of the realization of the female voice as the voice of religion, Church, without any discrimination of male and female and the voices of the house – which will be open and frank for all. Roberts affirms that all these voices/words/language will finally be made real and concrete by the sensuality and earthiness of words/ Language (1 of 2). Thus towards the end of the novel it is the women who open the closed door just as the woman writer gives word to their experiences, to those voices. Roberts who does not want to be treated as only writing about women, however, has written about their experiences sensitively.

Notes

1. She states "The way women were treated in the religion I grew up in, which was Catholicism, made me a write because women were seen as a source of evil in the world, the source of sin. We led man astray, we had to be forgiven for being women before we even began to try and be good, we had to get over having the bodies we had. This really pushed me to wanting to write as a way of opposing what was very constricting and actually painful in my life."

References

Roberts, Michèle. *Daughters of the House.* London: Virago, 1995.

Roberts, Michèle. "Her Story/B.B.C. World Service. Internet 9 March 2002. Available http.//www.bbc.co.uk/world service art/features /women writers/roberts me.htm/.

Sangari, Kumkum. "The Politics of the Possible". *The Post-Colonial Studies Reader.* Ed. Bill Ashcroft, Gareth Griffiths and Helen Tiffin. London: Routledge, 1995.

Sarbadhikari, Krishna, "Mapping the Future: Indian Women Writing, Female Subjectivity." *Articulating Gender: An Anthology.* Presented to Prof. Shirin Kudchedkar. Ed. Anjali Bhelande, Mala Pandurang. Delhi: Pencraft International, 200.

Singh, Sushila. "Multiplying Identities: Theorizing Difference." *Feminism: Theory, Criticism, Analyses.* Delhi: Pencraft International, 1997.

17 Growing Up in Wilderness
African Stories of Doris Lessing

Madhuri Chatterjee

Doris Lessing spent her childhood and the first twenty five years of her life in Southern Rhodesia (now Zimbabwe) and her background there has been a powerful influence on her fiction. She was born to British parents, Alfred Taylor and Maud Me Veigh in 1919. Her father after the first World War injuries had migrated to Africa after purchasing three thousand acres of land to do farming. Her parents and her isolated and lonely childhood influenced not only the themes in her fiction but also shaped her as a fiction writer.

Doris Lessing, whose position as one of the major women writers of the twentieth century is now assured, stands quite apart from the feminine tradition of sensibility. Her fiction is tough, rational, concerned with social roles, collective action and conscience, and she is unconcerned with the niceties of style and subtlety of feeling for its own sake. The prevalence of colonialism in Africa is important to her, moulding her outlook towards people. African identity is seen as the product of Europe's gaze. For Lessing, there are two Africa – the continent which always belongs to the Africans, and the label or veneer which the white colonial has imposed upon it. The notion of Africa also emerges as the homeland of dispersed population in search of solidarity and to the construing of black identity as creolized and dislocated. The term "Black" at times deployed as a multi-accented signifier of oppression and resistance has energized a discursive stance. As Benita Parry puts it "Negritude is not a recovery of pre-existent state, but textually invented history, an identity affected through figurative operations and a topological construction of blackness as a sign of the colonized condition and its refusal" (45). Such multivalence prompts both closure and fixity, making it available to other modes of oppression.

In Doris Lessing's writing there is a detachment and marginality as she belongs to neither of these two worlds. There is no significant connection between the white and the black worlds because of the restraints on a socially formed and positioned author, and the "objective narration" of African culture is related to the writer's refusal to violate its rhythms, meanings and mysteries. It seems that the composite image of Doris Lessing is very different from the self image which she presents in her autobiographical novels, even though the facts themselves often concur. The composite portrait has its own reality. The experience of the white Rhodesian who came to settle in a culture foreign to his British tradition, raised and educated his family in the wilderness, created a productive agriculture for this land and then saw the British motherland turn against her own progeny in the political economic feud over Rhodesian racial policy. Lessing herself became a prohibited immigrant to Rhodesia after 1956. Thus, there is a strong dichotomy and ambiguity in her African short stories and in her non-fictional world. The different voices are not all written as "heard" by their white "interlocutors" and the multiple differences are also not erased by a generic otherness. As Lessing writes in *Going Home* 'Africa belongs to the Africans, the sooner they take it back the better. But a country also belongs to those who feel at home in it' (16). Being a colonial means essentially that one is living in a strange land and this applies even when the family has lived for generations in a foreign country. The 'home' is thus alien and growing up here means deep cultural difference of being one and yet an outsider in the country they have adopted. In order to maintain their separateness and their identity the whites generally carried their own cultural distinctiveness imposing it where it could be imposed and distancing themselves where it could not be.

The source of all her "African" stories is found in her own experiences as a girl in southern Rhodesia. Somewhat solitary and in a manner tending towards what would in such a society be regarded as "tomboyish", she grew up bound by her father's farm and her mother's house. The recurring feature in Lessing's fiction dealing with this period in her life is that of a young girl hovering between these two self-contained but related worlds. In the story "The Flavours of Exile", the English family shares the language of nostalgia and despite rich and luxuriant vegetables, always longs for their inheritance of Brussels sprouts, cherries, English gooseberries while the children enjoy the 'inheritance of veld and sun' (50). The story subtly captures the pangs of love and desire in the heart of the adolescent narrator towards William Mc Gregor, the neighbor's son. These youngsters do not have the option of braking out of the social and educational 'traps' set for them, they can only religiously build their adolescent dreams. The golden pomegranate in the narrator's courtyard epitomizes her love and infatuation for William which ripens and grows and suddenly her whole life becomes concentrated in ripening of that single fruit. But when the boy Mc-Gregor visits the family, he casually snaps the fruit with a stick and shatters here illusion 'it was bad, after all the ants had got it. It should have been picked before' (56). This brings her to a new realization and awakening. She accepts the verdict and her position as an outsider in his life. Adolescence can be assessed in terms of the unique orientation to the natural and interpersonal world it represents. The encounter between the self and the world is the first essential crisis and encounter with experience and outside world, which gives the person knowledge, recognition, also shock and conformity.

Another story, "Traitors", captures the excitement of growing childhood years, where the children discover the Thompson's house in the wilderness. The story rightly captures the beauty of the bush, the growing up fears, the excitement, the guilt and their innocence.

> We were stopped again where the ground dropped suddenly to the vlei, a twenty foot shelf flattened grass where the cattle, went to water, sitting we lifted out dress and coasted down hill on the slippery swathes, landing down with torn knickers and scratched knees in a donga of red dust, scattered with dried con parts and bits of glistening quartz. The guinea fowls stood in the file and watched us, their heads lifted with apprehension (84).

Doris Lessing captures the beauty of her house, a thatch of wild grasses, the uneven walls, the leaking roof in *Going Home,* even after it was overrun with ant heaps and mingled into the bush, it was home in Lessing's imagination. The Lessings lived in real poverty in a pole and dagga (mud) house. She described this house in her book *Going Home* as 'like a living thing responsive to every mood of the weather and during the time I was growing up it had already begun to sink back into the forms of the bush. I remember it as a rather old, shaggy animal standing still among the trees lifting its head out over the vleis and valleys to the mountains' (41). The primitive nature of the house, the talk of the adults, the sense of space and isolation all these were potent factors in Lessing's growing up years.

The stories also capture the colonial society. In the story 'The Black Madonna', Lessing is 'full of bile' for the white society in Rhodesia as she 'knew and hated' it (*African Stories*). The story constructs a two fold process of displacement and ends with an ironic twist whereby the native refuses to yield to the white colonizer's demand for supremacy. Michelle, the artist, paints a black peasant Madonna in Zambezi which is a tough, sun burnt, virile, positive country contemptuous of subtleties and sensibility Zambezi, as is to put it mildly, 'unsympathetic to those ideas so long taken for granted in other parts of the world, to do with liberty, fraternity and the rest' (93). The 'culture loving ladies' of the society only offer sentimentality and gushing patronage to the artist, their notion of culture and art extending to little superficial knowledge. The black country is in fact a occupied German village and when it is shelled the church, the hospital building and everything collapses but the picture is saved by Michelle for the captain. The author, like Sartre, applauds the act whereby the oppressor seizes a word hurled as an insult and turns it into means of vindication [See Notes]. The captain's realization is the story's conclusion as in saving the picture , he shields and protects the captain's world represented by Nadya and his black child. Doris Lessing grew up to be a writer in such a society and had to find a way of dealing with these polarities. By 1930s and 1940s, the maintenance of the white superiority was becoming increasingly difficult to justify in economic and political terms. Poor whites and educated blacks muddled the simplicity of earlier categorization and redefined the composition of the 'proletariat'.

The strength of Lessing's fiction comes from her comprehension both of the prevailing myths and of the forces, which challenged them. She explores many of the cultural myths in the white dominated society of Rhodesia in her short stories. 'Pig' is another story, which explores the sexual dichotomy in a straight, broad, direct and much less beguiling manner. It begins with a generalized description in which a character is etched against a landscape:

> 'The farmer paid his laborers on a Saturday evening when the sun set down. from the kitchen door, where the lantern hung... bars of yellow light lay down the steps, across the path and lit up the trees and faces under them the dark' (79).

Dialogue is introduced when the mutual distrust between the employer and employee has been carefully delineated and then the story bifurcates. The farmer, wanting to put a stop to the thefts of his mealicobs, refers to culprits as pigs knowing well that pigs are his own farm hands. Jonas, the gunman is assigned the job to shoot the pigs as they destroy acres of cultivation. Instead, he tracks down and discovers in person the black young man who visits his wife, also a black woman, at night and had been 'thieving his wife'. 'A pig' said Jonas aloud to the listening moon, as he kicked the side gently with his foot 'nothing but a pig'. He wanted to hear how it would sound when he said it again, telling how he had shot blind into the grunting invisible herd (81). The story concerns itself with the male exercise of power and its frustration. With indirectness and irony, the author through the structure of the story provides implicit moral comment on the relationship of a man with another man. It is not an idealized monolithic, homogenized Africa which valorizes indigenous culture; the plot and characterization are sufficiently powerful to convey the message. Each story is a process of growing up, of explaining the conflict between white sensibility and African culture. The fact that each displacement and alienation of the characters ends with forced compromise creates an awareness of the impossibility of setting in this African ethos.

A child's perception about the surrounding is another closer device used by the author in the story "This was the old chief's country" providing her with an openness and honesty to explore the land and the circumstances. The child's life clearly mirrors the ambiguities of rejection and affirmation, revolt and conformity, hope and disenchantment observed in the culture at large. The story "This was the old chief's country" has a fourteen year old narrator who, despite her African nurturing, feels greater proximity with the English tradition and landscape. The oak and the ash trees are more close to her than the African bush and shrubs. She befriends an old tribal chief in the bush and her attitude towards the natives changes. 'It seemed it was only necessary to let free that respect that I felt when I was talking with old chief Mshlanga to let both black and white people meet gently with tolerance for each others differences, it seemed quite easy" (*Collected African Stories*, 17). The chief's son works as a cook at her farmland and she undertakes a journey to his house through this unfamiliar bush, experiencing new terror. The formal welcome by the chief further leaves her non-plussed. She returns feeling excluded 'there was now a queer hostility in the landscape, a cold sullen indomitability that walked with me, as strong as a wall, as intangible as smoke, it seemed to say to me; you walk here as destroyer' (22). This belief is further emphasized when her father usurps the goats of the natives who have his crops. The loss is a big one for the chief, especially when they face a dry season ahead. As an indirect result of this alteration the villagers are moved from their kraal to a distance reserve emphasing the white/colonial take over of the black native land. The girl's final realization is that no easy apologies will make her any less a usurper; neither will Africa or bush ever belong to her. Her confrontation with the old man of grace, dignity and reserve provide a moving contrast to values of her mother and her father. It also initiates a revaluation of the white ethics and confounds the sexual polarities inherent in it: 'I had learnt that if one calls a country to heel like a dog, neither one can dismiss the past with a smile in an easy gush of feeling saying I could not help it. I am also a victim' (24).

The next story perhaps captures part of their boyhood years-Doris and brother Harry Taylor spent most of their time hunting in the bush searching for duck, wild pig, antelope, guinea pig or whatever around. Her autobiographical essay "Myself as a sportsman" also reflects her childhood skills. The story "A Sunrise on the Veld" peeps into the psyche of a fifteen year old boy who starts on his morning expedition, feeling strong and invincible, 'There is nothing I can't become, nothing I can't do, there is no country in the world I cannot make part of myself if I choose' (28). He is appalled to discover a dying buck, eaten by a swarm of ants, a part of the 'vast, unalterable cruel veld'. The buck had fallen a prey to ants as native hunters had broken his leg. The story ends with the boy's moral realization of his action who himself had often shot animals, without bothering for the consequences. The author in one shift explains the impersonal forces of the veld shifting from the boy's feeling of triumph to impersonal stoicism to his own role and place in this suffering.

Doris Lessing works on her colonial experience in these African stories. She speaks of her own life, her own early perception of the prevailing racist values. She also portrays the class bound life of English settlers and her 'colonial bile' becomes more bitter when directed towards metropolitan culture. Some of the stories are also a reaction to Gambeson's insensitivity. She also tries to retrieve the value and dignity of a past insulted by European representation. Her integrated self is in vital interaction with an authentic culture community. She looks beyond the English myths of white superiority and the black and white detachment. She comprehends her work as a quest into the hidden places of the unconscious. Her total work fits into the quest pattern and the mythical cycle described by Northrop Frye. Lessing's central character are poised upon a dialectic of openness and cynicism, between 'the integrity of the innocent world and the assault of experience" (*Frye* 87). They pass through two phases in their quest-an early initiation into adulthood and later a renewal of energy before some cosmic disorder in which society breaks up into small units or individuals. Gradually Lessing graws out of this wilderness and moves on beyond this continent to gather in more experiences and knowledge both thematically and technically.

Note

1. Sartre's essay *The Black Orpheus* which Fanon designates as a "date in the intellectualization of the experience of being black''.

References

Benita Parry. Post *Colonial Studies; A Materialist Critique.* Landon: Routledge, 2004.

Doris Lessing. "*The Sun Between Their Feet*". Collected African Stories. Vol. II, Flamingo, Harper Collins, 1953.

Doris Lessing. "*This was the old chief's country" Collected African Stories.* Vol., I, 1973.

Doris Lessing. *African Stories.* 1964. New York; Popular Library, 1965.

Doris Lessing. *Going Home*. New York: Panther, 1968.

Franz Fanon. *Black Skin, White Masks,* London: Lunto Press, 1986.

Northrop Frye. *The Anatomy of Criticism*. Princeton: Princeton University Press, 1957.

18 Shadows of 'Bloody Past and Uneasy Present'

Space in Paul Scott's *The Jewel in the Crown*

Ila Rathor

In rewriting the history of the Raj, Paul Scott was faced with a gigantic task. He chose to look into the volatile ruler-ruled relationship by analyzing the last decade of the colonial rule in India. To read the colonial discourse in all its complexities he had to recreate the two centuries of subjugation and retaliation. Scott uses symbolic characters, situations and places that encapsulate this love-hate union. A major part of Scott's *The Jewel in the Crown*[1] deals with the violence of the Quit India Movement, India's last major confrontation with the British, the rape of Daphne Manners by a gang of Indians, its repercussions and the ruler-ruled situation in the consequent confrontation between Hari Kumar, Daphne's Indian lover and the British police officer Ronald Merrick. In an attempt to depict the dilemmas of the British-Indian discourse these events are revised and examined, by Scott, thereby presenting a string of superbly crafted portraits.

Dealing with the last phase of the British in India the novel presents an India at the peak of the freedom struggle. The ruled were no longer ready for anything short of complete independence and the ruler was not ready to hand over the power, they simply could not afford to lose their superior imperial status. The political situation was made more complex by the social and economical connotations. Moreover, the ruler-ruled psyche in the colonial world on the eve of independence invited an open confrontation between the two. Gandhi had shown the way and men and women were all set to follow. But even the non-violent preaching of the Mahatma could not stop the confrontation from taking a violent turn. Scott is able to read this delicate political situation. The rape of an English woman at the hands of the Indians gives Scott an opportunity to analyse the situation and to study various types of characters and the ramifications of their lives. As a result of the vicious rape of Daphne Manners, her Indian lover Hari Kumar is wrongly accused and cruelly interrogated by the policeman Ronald Merrick. This provides the novel with a realistic central metaphor for British India.

In Scott's novel events and characters operate within an ambience that is strictly anti-imperial and anti-ruling class (Royle 6). He realizes that in reality the colonial discourse of power and fear was very much different from the sepia-tinted images conjured up by the Raj nostalgia. The image presented a completely different past preceding the present reality. So much so that the conventional image of the Raj,

> the great Delhi Darbar with squadrons of exotically uniformed cavalrymen surrounding the King Emperor's pachydermal procession might be one, the District officer sitting in the shade of a Banyan tree dispensing wisdom and justice might be another image. These images summon up a way of life that seems so recent is yet far removed from the everyday experience of life towards the end of the 20th century. (Royle 7)

Paul Scott's *The Jewel in the Crown* is 'the story of a rape, of the events that led up to it and followed it and of the place in which it happened' (9). He focuses on 'the action, the people and the place'. The place in which the entire action takes place is of great importance and affords immense symbolic significance. Swinden feels that in most of Scott's previous novels

> the relationships between people were mirrored in relationships between the places in which they met. In *The Chinese Love Pavilion* the position of the oriental pavilion (facing the merchant's house, with the garden of madness stretching between) provided an exotic milieu for the narrative and symbolized much of the passionate activity that was enacted inside it. The same was true of the cage, the island and the encircling estate at Jundapur, with its legend of Krishna's encounter with the prince and the princess that appeared in some of the central scenes of *The Birds of Paradise* (77).

In *The Jewel in the Crown*, to present his central metaphor of rape, which enables him to read the ruler-ruled situation, Paul Scott creates space which is as much symbolic of the colonial tensions as the action that takes place there. Like the people and the events, the different marked places – the MacGregor House, the Bibighar Gardens, the Club, the Sanctuary, the *Maidan* – epitomise the Raj in *The Jewel in the Crown*. Instead of presenting a realistic and accurate historical document Scott's purpose is to convey meaning. Though the places and people are located far from reality in a fictional colonial world they reverberate with echoes of past historical events.

Representing India of the Raj, like E.M. Forster's Chandrapore in *The Passage to India*, Scott's Mayapore is marked by various places reflecting the racial tensions, prejudices and the segregated social structure. The exclusivity of the *Maidan* and the Club, the invisible wall between the wrong and the right side of the river, the unbridgeable distance between the Civil Lines with its Yellow Dragon Chinese Restaurant, the Eros Cinema and the Mission Church; and the native town side with its Tirupati Temple, narrow dirty streets, old alleyway and crumbling houses of the Chillianwallah bazaar – each one of them plays a definite role in giving a complete picture of the colonial power nexus. Chillianwallah bazaar – the very name echoes the sound of Jallianwallah Bagh, the site of the bloody ruthless killing of the hundreds of innocent Indians at the orders of General Dyer who came to represent one of the harshest faces of the British rule in India, and the tragedy as one of the most heinous crimes committed by the Empire. Through apt words, description and symbols Scott is able to delineate the white and the black spaces. We have the native town with its

> narrow dirty streets, its disgusting poverty, its raucous dissonant music, its verminous dogs, its starving, mutilated beggars, its fat white sacred Brahmini bulls and its ragged population of men and women who looked so resentful in comparison with the servants and other officiating natives of the cantonment (19).

Even nature seems to be less benevolent towards the unfortunate natives:

> On this side of the river the sun seemed to strike more fiercely and indiscriminately as though the smells of poverty and dirt would be wasted in shade. Colour was robbed of the advantage of its singularity, its surprise.... Even the scarlet flower in a women's braided hair, lacking its temperate complementary green, was scorched to an insipid brown (149).

In between the Civil Lines and the Chillianwallah stands the sanctuary, a place for the dead, run by Sister Ludmila. In the strife-ridden world of colonialism she takes care of the dead and the dying. The Raj of death, sickness, and madness needs someone like her to provide 'a clean bed, a hand to hold, a word through layers of unconsciousness to reach and warm the cold diminishing centre of the departing soul' (161). In his presentation of a mini India Scott seems to have felt a need to have such a place because, 'India is a place where men died, still die, in the open for want of succour, for want of shelter, for want of respect for the dignity of death' (160). The Raj has robbed it of its life. It is ironical that this place of the dead is the only place where Daphne and Hari Kumar could meet. An uninhibited meeting of a native and a British is impossible among living human beings. Life is overshadowed by the presence of the Raj. And even the Sanctuary does not remain completely outside its clutches. The Hari Kumar-Ronald Merrick affair has its beginning there.

Scott has created the Bibighar Gardens to serve as the stage for the violent rape that reflects the relationship of fear and power. Here again like Forster's Marabar Caves, the Bibighar Gardens lie at the thematic centre of the novel and seem to engender the entire violence that overtakes the country in the last days of the Raj. Scott's creation of the Bibighar epitomizes the two centuries of colonial tensions in a single point of time in a single space, so much 'so that at once past, present and future are contained in your cupped palm' and one gets the feeling as if 'time were telescoped and space dovetailed' (157).

The two major events reflecting the violence, the fear, the distrust and the attempts at subversion were the Indian 'Mutiny' of 1857 and the Amritsar riots of 1919 that led to the Jallianwallah Bagh Massacre. The two assaults on the English women, Edwina Crane and Daphne Manners, in *The Jewel in the Crown* are clear reminders of these two points in the Indo-British colonial encounter. The very name Bibighar is enough to evoke the horrors of the Cawnpore Massacre of 1857 when a large number of English women and children were hacked to death and thrown into a well. Later it also served as the locale for British vengeance that followed. Therefore the very name draws painful responses from the readers besides underlining the cause for fear among the British and the smouldering desire for revenge in the Indian heart. And as Manohar Malgonkar's protagonist remarks in *The Devil's Wind,* 'Bibighar: it means "love nest", and yet what terrible thoughts it evokes! In common with names like Waterloo, or Panipet, or Balaclava, it has its inherent violence, a power to shock. *Its ruins will ever serve as whetstones to sharpen racial hatred*' (72). Scott has resurrected the ruins of this memorial of the Mutiny horrors in his attempt to find the symbols for the complex colonial relationship between the two races. As Gomathi Narayanan states, 'Fit for the juxtaposition of love and rape in the *Quartet* by its name and associations, the ruined Bibighar gardens is also a statement of the foredoomed relations between Britain and India' (21).

Scott completes his picture of the forced imperial rule by creating the MacGregor House and establishing a definite link between the two. 'MacGregor and Bibighar are the place of the white and the place of the black' (178). So much is contained in them that between the two the entire plot is revealed and enacted. MacGregor is the house of Lady Chatterjee, the widow of Sir Nello Chatterjee, who is quite westernized and has an air of authority and power. Her amiable relations with the English are borne out by the fact that Daphne Manners, the niece of Sir Henry Manners, former Governor of the province, is staying with her as her guest. The Bibighar Gardens and the MacGregor House are not just bitter reminders of the horrors of 1857 and 1942, but also reflect the colonial relationship, the love-hate connection between the two races. History recounts that the ruin of one led to the building of the other right from the time when the king built the MacGregor House for his beloved singer only to be destroyed by his son who built Bibighar just a mile away, for his courtesans. Later a Scotsman, Macgregor, burnt down Bibighar and rebuilt the decayed house of the singer. The myth regarding the burning of the Bibighar also has its black and white version. The white community saw the cause of the burning down of the House as an abomination. But the black version had an entirely different story to tell, which rings truer, that he turned it into a ruin because he fell in love with an Indian girl whom he lost to a boy of her own race. Thus these monuments of love reflect the racial tensions. In MacGregor's occupation of the singer's house, his murder in the 1857 Mutiny and the haunting ghost of his wife Janet, the tale of India's annexation, exploitation and sense of fear among the English is retold. A need is felt to warn the white-skinned and for loyalties to be clearly marked.

Once again the Indians rise against the Whites and, Bibighar and MacGregor House get connected, a connection that can only lead to disaster. Daphne Manners is ruined in crossing from one to another in utter darkness. Covering the dark mile was attempting the impossible as, 'no bridge was ever thrown across it and stood'. She had the courage of falling in love with an Indian, Hari Kumar, in such turbulent times, 'to enter the flood and let yourself be taken with it' (178). Their meeting at the Bibighar Gardens and subsequent love making on August 9, 1942, the day Congress passed the Quit India resolution, ends in Daphne's brutal rape by a group of Indians.

At the end of the novel when the narrator leaves India, 'The Bibighar Gardens are dark (now, as then) – but from the MacGregor House there is the burst of light' (574). The darkness now does not seem to be the darkness of evil, of violence, of oppression, as it was then, but a darkness of the place which has been abandoned. The past is long since gone, shrouded in the cover of mystery and obscurity. The MacGregor House, the place of the white, bore the brunt of native fury in 1857 and 1942. It is haunted by the ghost of Janet, who 'comes dressed in the fashion of the times and stands on the verandah' (87), and Sister Ludmila feels that her ghost might be trying 'to warn people with white skins that the MacGregor House is not a good place for them to be' (177). Daphne Manners' continuous presence is also felt in occasional sounds other than those made by Lili Chatterjee and Parvati, the daughter of Daphne Manners and Hari Kumar. Both Janet and Daphne suffered assaults during the two violent points of time in the history of the Raj and their ghosts haunting the house seem to be warning the rulers. Representing India, the house is now free from the British occupation in the post Raj period, and is occupied by Parvati, the legacy of the Raj. The MacGregor House is free from the darkness of the colonial situation. It no longer broods over the past. Lady Chatterjee is seen, 'as the repository of a tradition established for the sake of the future rather than of the past' (575).

Paul Scott has used spaces symbolically in *The Jewel in the Crown* to serve the purpose of going beyond mere historical facts, political issues, and to present, through this fictional world, the colonial ethos with its racial tensions, colour prejudice and social segregation, as he weaves his tale of power and fear.

Note

1. Paul Scott's *The Jewel in the Crown* is the first book of *The Raj Quartet*, the other three being *The Day of the Scorpion* (1968), *The Towers of Silence* (1971), and *The Division of Spoils* (1975).

References

Malgonkar, Manohar. *The Devil's Wind*. New York: Viking, 1972.

Narayanan, Gomathi. *The Sahibs and the Natives*. Delhi: Chanakya Publications, 1986.

Royle, Trevor. *The Last Days of the Raj*. London: Michael Joseph, 1989.

Scott, Paul. *The Jewel in the Crown*. (1966) London: Pan books,

Swinden, Patrick. *Images of India*. New York: St. Martin's Press, 1980.

19 The Aesthetics of Nostalgia in the Films of Merchant-Ivory

Vijaya Singh

Logically, one might ask, why a paper on films and that too on the films of Merchant-Ivory should be included in a collection of essays on contemporary British fiction? Let me clarify in the beginning itself that in the first place this paper is not about all the films of Merchant Ivory – and there are quite a few – the scope of this paper just cannot argue the case of all the films that the celebrated duo have made. This paper is limited to including only those films of Merchant-Ivory which relate to the famous British author E.M. Forster-but then again Forster can hardly be called contemporary. Now for the point as to why this paper should at all find a place in an anthology on contemporary British fiction. My defense is that the films based on Forster produced in Britain in the later part of twentieth century are a critique of Forster and provide an occasion to look afresh at his novels and to review his position as an English novelist. What is more, the films themselves articulate the concerns and anxieties of the 1990's viewer.

Forster is a writer whose fiction is deeply engaged in a dialogue with modernity and brings to surface issues and problems that the modern world still finds itself grappling with. Also the issues that these films raise are at the heart of contemporary debates about the past, identity, gender, sexuality and the ways in which the past comes to haunt the present. In that sense the films based on his novels have a legitimate claim for a place in an anthology on contemporary British fiction.

Having said this I would now like to clarify the terms of this paper. This paper is about the uses of nostalgia and heritage in the films of Merchant-Ivory. I propose to show how these films knowingly or unknowingly mobilize the issues of the relation of nostalgia/heritage to present times; the cultural function of heritage; the past; national identity; film form; the ways in which cinema structures its meaning; the issue of adaptation i.e. what the filmmaker retains from the text and the kind of uses he subjects this to in the formation of what may be termed as aesthetics of nostalgia.

Nostalgia is commonly described as a wistful or sentimental yearning for return to some past period or irrecoverable condition. Similarly, heritage too is defined as something transmitted or acquired from a predecessor. Both nostalgia and heritage are together rooted in the past. The past at the same time is deeply imbricated in the present. There can be no present without the past. Past is everywhere. As David Loventhal in his book *The Past is a Foreign Country,* says, 'All around us lie features which, like ourselves and our thoughts, have more or less recognizable antecedents. Relics, histories, memories suffuse human experience. Each particular trace in the past ultimately perishes, but collectively they are immortal. Whether it is celebrated or rejected attended to or ignored, the past is omnipresent' (xv).

However, it is the distinction of the twentieth century that it has turned the past into a commodity. Heritage has become an industry and every year countries round the globe earn revenues in millions of dollars in the name of heritage and nostalgia. The heritage films of the 1980s in Britain have come to be regarded as a part of the heritage industry of Britain. In fact, in the 1980s a collection of screen fictions were collectively designated, 'heritage films,' these films and television serials included, *Chariots of Fire (1981), Gandhi* (1982), *Brideshead Revisited (1982), Heat and Dust (1982), Jewel in the crown (1984), Another Country (1984), A Passage to*

India (1984), The Far Pavilions (1984), Hope and Glory (1987), Dance with a Stranger (1985), A Room with a View (1986), Maurice (1987), Where Angels Fear to tread (1991), Howards End (1992), The Remains of the Day (1993) and many others. For the purpose of this paper however I will deal with only *A Room with a View, Maurice and Howards End.*

The 1980s represent a very interesting period in Britain's cultural history. This is the period of Margaret Thatcher's premiership. Her style of functioning came to be known as 'Thatcherism', which loosely defined meant, 'the ideological doctrines of the new Right' (Hill 4), a call to social neo-conservatism, an obsession with heritage, national identity and past glory. This in turn gave rise to what came to be known as the heritage industry and heritage culture. The term "Heritage Industry" came to represent an 'important economic activity', (Hill 73) wherein the country's history, its past, its empire its artifacts, buildings, museums were being marketed for tourism and nationalist purposes. A central feature of this 'impulse was the adaptation of heritage properties, whether novels and plays or buildings and values' (Higson 16).

In fact, the industry, Hill says, performed a number of cultural functions as well (74). Cinema in this period became an important heritage enterprise and articulated the concerns and interests of this culture. Hill makes an important point in this regard when he says that the 'meanings spoken by films during this period connected to the broader patterns of social and cultural life' (xi).

Many critics argue that heritage films constitute a genre and are therefore not only inscribed in history but share common thematic patterns and stylistic concerns. Susan Hayward describes the term *genre* in *Key Concepts in Cinema Studies* as a 'tripartite process of production, marketing (including distribution and exhibition) and consumption' (160). Genre, the book goes on to say 'refer to others of their own type and so are both inter-referential and intertextual' (160). Heritage films therefore may be described as a genre, which concerns itself with the representations of and from the past.

Andrew Higson in his essay, "The Heritage Film and British Cinema" in *Dissolving Views: Key Writings on British Cinema,* describes the following characteristics of heritage films:

1. Middle class quality product between art-house and mainstream.
2. Low budget, independent production.
3. Emphasis on authorship, craft and artistic value.
4. Specialized distribution.
5. Known target audience.
6. Adaptations of highly prestigious and canonic literary and theatrical property.
7. Artful and spectacular projection of an elite, conservative vision of the national past.
8. Melodrama of everyday bourgeois life in period setting.
9. Nostalgia.
10. Literary heritage property are however only a small sample of the property on display in such films, which include in general:
    (i) Large and small country houses, select landscapes, interior designs and furnishings, costumes and the social type we expect to inhabit these various heritage attractions, to display them in all their supposes authenticity.
    (ii) Acting: Repertory company of key players who draw on the English theatrical tradition.
11. The narrative pace is slow and episodic.
12. Emphasis on characterization, setting, atmosphere and milieu.
13. Camerawork is fluid, artful and pictorialist.
14. Editing is low and undramatic.
15. Use of long takes and deep focus, and long and medium shots rather than close-ups (233-234).

Heritage films of the 1980s due to their nostalgia for the past, appropriation of culturally prestigious literary texts, museum aesthetics, 'artful and spectacularly projection of an elite, conservative vision of the national past' came to be widely regarded as a part of the heritage industry and culture at large. These films however were divided into two categories, those that dealt with the empire and the ones, which were melodramas of everyday bourgeois life in a period setting. This paper is concerned with the second category, specifically the three films based on Forster's novels: *A Room with a View, Maurice* and *Howards End.*

These three films are a representative case for all the issues listed above. All these films are steeped in heritage property display. To begin with all the three films put a great deal of stress on authentic period settings, interiors and costumes. For example in *A Room with a View* the house of the Honeychurches is showcased as a beautiful Edwardian house replete with antique furniture, oil paintings, crockery, beautiful tennis courts, well mowed lawns and a battery of servants. This is in sharp contrast to the novel where the house of the Honeychurches is something of an architectural anomaly and causes Mr. Beebe the clergyman to laugh every time he catches sight of house. As Forster says '... the house was so commonplace, not to say impertinent. The late Honwychurch had affected the cube because it gave him the most accommodation for his money, and the only addition made by his widow had been a small turret, shaped like a rhinoceros's horn...Windy Corner seemed as inevitable as the ugliness of nature's own creation' (*ARWV 202-203*).

Similarly, in *Maurice,* too the country house of Clive is showcased lovingly in all its minute details. Ivory himself admits that he used Wilbury Park 'one of the most beautiful Palladian houses in England' (Long 151) as Clive's estate and changed the name of the estate from Penge in the novel to Pendersleigh. The opulence of Pendersleigh in the film erases the novel's stark observation regarding the growing sense of impoverishment the upper middle-classes were beginning to feel in the early part of the twentieth century. The film ahistoricizes the economic concerns of the Edwardian period. In the novel Forster is at great pains to convey this sense of gradual collapse. In *Maurice* the protagonist makes a note of the fact that the gate posts were 'crooked, trees stifling, and indoors some bright wedding presents showed as patches on threadbare garment. Miss Woods had brought no money to Penge. She was accomplished and delightful, but she belonged to the same class as the Durhams, and every year England grew less inclined to pay her highly'(*Maurice* 166-167). Similarly in Ivory's *Howards End* too a great premium is placed on the various houses showcased throughout the duration of the film. The houses in the film function as markers of wealth and opulence. All the three houses in the novel, Wickham Place, Howards End, and Oniton Place represent three different qualities so that Wickham Place stands for intellectual and emotional bonding, Howards End serves as the spiritual center of the novel, Oniton Place represents the material, emotionally vacuous house which functions as a property bought and sold at the whim of its owners but never lived in. The film erases all these distinctions and presents them as heritage props of a bygone era.

Similarly, the motorcar and the other means of transport like the horse-carriages, the railways and bicycles become objects of longing and desire in the films. Indeed for Forster the motorcar was a symbol of a 'civilization in a hurry' and was in fact, an example of the disrupting influence of modernity on the English society. The initial phase of modernity which is such a problematic site in the novel becomes for the film an instance to recreate the charms of vintage cars, exclusive costumes, the rich life style of the upper classes, the unpolluted environment, the lush meadows etc. In fact, the onset of modernity itself becomes for the film an occasion for nostalgia.

Visually, all the three films place a great deal of stress on creating a sepia toned look of the film stock so as to situate the film in the past. The various houses in the film are invested with a fading golden light, the mise-en-scenes often resemble Victorian paintings in their composition and in the use of rich colors like rusts, browns, yellows, reds and greens in the background. The Edwardian age is presented as a period of golden autumns, endless afternoons, and unchanging era of comfortable certainties, economic abundance, unhurried desire – a long country house weekend.

The filming style of the films as pointed by Andrew Higson is limited to the use of long and medium shots so as to capture the background details, which in this case would mean the décor of the house. Editing too in these films is slow, episodic and undramatic. The target audience of these films is largely in North America and England. In his delightful essay, "Anglophilmia: Why does America watch Merchant Ivory Movies" Martin A. Hipsky is of the view that these films serve as a 'cultural capital' for their audience. The many references that are central to the film 'constitute a veritable survey course in the art of high culture allusion'. *A Room With A View* alone features references to Dante, Giotto, Michelangelo, RW Emerson, Beethoven, Greek myths, Goethe and Byron' (103). That is to say, that the act of viewing these films results in 'reaffirming one's accumulation of this type of cultural capital' (Hipsky 103). I feel however, that though Hipsky's argument is valid these films participate in what Higson calls the 'democratization of the community of the nation as imagined by cinema…the voyeuristic gaze of one class looking at another' (Higson 17), which means that these films make use of heritage in more ways than one. On the one hand undoubtedly these films serve as cultural capital but on the other hand by recreating the period details of a bygone era they seek to engage even those audience who may not have this cultural capital by providing them a nostalgic trip to a lost world. Because these films are a part of the heritage culture of Britain in general the films ironically allow people from other sections of the society to take a peephole view of the 'Edwardian theme park.'

Forster's novels are deeply concerned with ways in which homosexual elements are forced to be 'submerged into a sub-text within a society dominated by homophobic discourses' (Nelson 311). His *Maurice* is the only novel, which deals overtly with the theme of homosexual love but was published posthumously. Forster in his own lifetime could not risk publishing it. The novel offers a positive vision of homosexual love and contests the dominant discourses in school, university, medicine and church regarding male homosexuality. The novel is also exemplary in the agency it imparts to its protagonist for self-determination and a happy ending. For Ivory however, *Maurice* offered a chance to make a film, which is related to the problem of coming to terms with one's sexuality as he tells Long in *The Films of Merchant Ivory*.

In *A Room with a View* and *Howards End* Forster is concerned with giving voice to a nascent feminism and privileging the feminine perspective over the male one. But the films subdue these themes so that Lucy's quest for selfhood in *A Room with a View* is reduced to making a choice between her two suitors, George and Cecil. Similarly in *Howards End* too Forster privileges the feminine perspective as a necessary step to dismantling male hierarchy but the film turns the novel into a story about property rights and inheritance. The filmmakers by these acts of selective reading retain what they consider will allow them to sell the film thus undermining the more subversive aspects of the novels.

This brings me to the last point of my paper, the issue of national identity in these films. Englishness in these films is presented as the dramatic dissolution of the aristocratic way of life and the loss of its leisure and opulence. This actually creates a very reductive sense of national identity. There is no engagement with the issue that the opulence, which the upper class flaunts, was the result of colonization and a rigid class structure.

To sum up, these films through the use of nostalgia, heritage props, cinematic devices, adaptation of literary texts, create an aesthetics which embody a state of what Jean Baudrillard and Umberto Eco have called 'hyper reality' (as quoted in Boniface and Fowler 7). They present 'an experience of extra authenticity that is better than reality...a souped-up fantastic experience' (Boniface and Fowler 6). To that extent these films represent the postmodernist quest for the authentic, the real in terms of sets, mis-en-scene and costumes.

Films and Works Cited

A Room with a View. Dir. James Ivory. Perf. Helena Bonham Carter, Julian Sands, Simon Callow, Denholm Elliot, Maggie Smith, Judi Dench, Rosemary Leach, Rupert Graves, Daniel Day Lewis, H.B. Carter, Patric Godfrey. National Film Finance Corporation, Curzon Film Distributors and Film Four International, 1986.

Boniface, Priscilla and Peter J. Fowler. *Heritage and Tourism in 'the global village.'* London: Routledge, 1993.

Craig, Cairns. "Rooms without a View." *Sight and Sound.* 1.2 (1991): 10-14.

Forster, E.M. *A Room with a View.* 1908 New York; Vintage International. 1989.

Forster, E.M. *Howards End.* 1910 ed. London; Penguin Books Ltd. 1970.

Forster, E.M. *Maurice.* 1971 ed. New York: Norton and Company Inc. 1993.

Hayward, Susan. *Key Concepts in Cinema Studies.* London: Routledge, 1996.

Higson, Andrew, ed. *Dissolving Views: Key Writings on British Cinema.* London: Cassell, 1996.

Hill, John. *British Cinema in the 1980s.* New York: Oxford UP, 1999.

Hipsky, Martin A. "Anglophil(m)ia: Why Does America Watch Merchant Ivory Movies?" *Journal of Popular Film and Television.* 22.3(1994): 98-107.

Howards End. Dir. James Ivory. Perf. Anthony Hopkins, Emma Thompson, Helena Bonham Carter, Venessa Redgrave, Samuel West, James Wilby, Nicola Duffet. Sony Pictures Classics, 1992.

Long, Robert Emmet. *The Films of Merchant Ivory.* 1991 Cambridge UP Japan: Harry N. Abrams Inc. Pub, 1997.

Loventhal, David. *The Past is a Foreign Country.* London: Cambridge UP, 1985.

Maurice. Dir. James Ivory. Perf. James Wilby, Hugh Grant, Rupert Graves, Denholm Eliot, Simon Callow, Billie Whitelaw, Barry Forster, October Films, 1987.

Nelson, Scott R. "Narrative Inversion: The Textual Construction of Homosexuality in E.M. Forster's Novels." *Style.* 26.2 (1992): 310-326.

20 Fantasy and the Harry Potter Novels

Joya Chakravarty

Welcome to the world of fantasy as popularised by J.K. Rowling. The Harry Potter series have met with resounding success and Rowling has earned name, fame and money. Children all over the world are going crazy about procuring and reading these fantasy books. Adults enjoy reading these stories too. But what is meant by the term 'fantasy'? According to the Collins English Dictionary (1995) the word "fantasy" means 'imagination unrestricted by reality, a creation of the imagination especially a weird or bizarre one, a series of pleasing mental images, usually serving to fulfil a need not gratified in reality, a highly elaborate imaginative design or creation, an illusion, hallucination, or phantom' (559). The word 'fantasy' originates from a Greek word 'Phantazein'. If we keep these definitions in mind then one would say that the term 'fantasy' can be applied to myths, legends, folk and fairy tales, allegories, fables, science fiction and horror stories. This term, therefore, has a broad-encompassing range. Rosemary Jackson in her book *Fantasy: The Literature of Subversion* (1981) defines fantasy both in literature and out of it as:

> an enormous and seductive subject. Its association with imagination and with desire has made it an area difficult to articulate or define and indeed the 'value' of fantasy has

> seemed to reside in precisely this resistance to definition, in its 'free-floating' and escapist qualities. Literary fantasies have appeared to be 'free' from many of the conventions and restraints of more realistic texts: they have refused to observe unities of time, space and character doing away with chronology . . . and with rigid distinctions between animate and inanimate objects, self and other, life & death . . .(1)

It is, therefore, difficult to 'theorize' about fantasy as it resists narrow categorization and definition.

A fantasy can to a certain extent be placed within a social context. People might argue that it is difficult to do so, but no fantasy can be understood in isolation. The same applies to the Harry Potter series. There is a sense of continuity and credibility in all the novels namely *Harry Potter and The Philosopher's Stone* (1997)[1], *Harry Potter and The Chamber of Secrets* (1998), *Harry Potter and The Prisoner of Azkaban* (1999), *Harry Potter and the Goblet of Fire* (2000), *Harry Potter and the Order of Phoenix* (2003), *Harry Potter and The Half Blood Prince* (2005). The omniscient author tells us the story of an orphan Harry who has been brought up by Mr & Mrs Dursleys, his aunt and uncle. The cruel and shabby treatment meted out to him by his relatives including his cousin Dudley makes him feel neglected and rejected. The child here reminds us of Charlotte Brontë's character, Jane Eyre, and the Dickensian characters, David and Pip. Harry Potter, the child, becomes an Everyman type of figure.

For ten years Harry has had a miserable life. He cannot remember his parents and he is forbidden to ask questions about them and, for that matter, about anything at all. Readers are able to identify with Harry Potter because of the element of ordinariness that is there in his portrayal. He is a small and skinny boy wearing hand-me-down bedraggled clothes, 'Harry had a thin face, knobby knees, black hair and bright-green eyes. He wore round glasses held together with a lot of Sellotape because of all the times Dudley had punched him on the nose' (PS 20) . Harry had a scar on his forehead and this was the only thing he liked about his appearance.

He had asked his aunt about the scar and she had replied ' "In the car crash when your parents died . . . And don't ask questions". DON'T ASK QUESTIONS – that was the first rule for a quiet life with the Dursleys' (PS 20). Harry had never seen any photographs of his parents. He had often hoped and dreamed that some unknown relative would come and take him away from the Dursleys. But it had never happened till now.

In the novel it is stated that Harry felt at times

> people in the street seemed to know him. Very strange strangers they were, too. A tiny man in a violet top hat had bowed to him once while out shopping with Aunt Petunia and Dudley . . . A wild-looking old woman dressed all in green had waved merrily at him once on a bus. A bold man in a very long purple coat had actually shaken his hand in the street . . . The weirdest thing about all these people was the way they seemed to vanish the second Harry tried to get a closer look. At school, Harry had no one, everybody knew that Dudley's gang hated that odd Harry Potter in his baggy old clothes and broken glasses and nobody liked to disagree with Dudley's gang (PS 27).

The main idea of these novels is contained in the theme of disaster arising from man's over-reaching himself and misusing his powers. In these novels Lord Voldemort (he who must not be named) loses his power when he tries to misuse magic. Since Lord Voldemort was proud and over-ambitious, he met with disaster. In these novels Rowling shows that the laws of witchcraft and wizardry are to be followed strictly. Underage wizards and witches are not allowed to do magic outside the school. The Ministry of Magic watches over the activities of one and all. Anyone who disobeys or violates the norms ends up in the Azkaban fortress which is guarded by the Dementors who 'suck the happiness out of a place . . . most of the prisoners go mad in there (PA 140). The Dementors' kiss sucks out the life of a person and destroys him utterly. At the start of his third year at Hogwarts School Harry and his friends Ron and Hermione learn that a prisoner by the name of

Sirius Black has escaped from Azkaban. Hogwarts is a likely place that Sirius may visit. Hence Dementers are stationed at every entrance to the ground. The headmaster Prof. Dumbledore tells the students that these guards are not fooled by tricks, disguises or invisibility cloaks.

These novels are written in a racy style and keep the readers spellbound. With the Dursleys' Harry had felt neglected and rejected. But at Hogwarts Harry is able to make friends and they help him. These novels reflect the world we live in. As one reads the novels one realizes that at Hogwarts school also there is peer-group rivalry, peer pressure, sibling jealousy, nepotism and favoritism. Harry, Ron and Hermione are great friends and belong to the Gryffindor Team. They dislike Draco, Crabbe and Goyle who are members of the Slytherin team. Every now and then Draco boasts of his father's influence at the Ministry of Magic. Harry and his friends have to really tax their brains in order to get the better of Draco and his goons.

Fantasy violates what is generally accepted to be possible and probable and therefore upsets rules and conventions that are taken to be the norm. Jackson says that fantasy is the descendant

> of a traditional literary genre: the menippea. Menippean Satire was present in ancient Christian and Byzantine literature, in medieval literature, Renaissance, and Reformation writings . . . It was a genre which broke the demands of historical realism or probability. The menippea moved easily in space between this world, an underworld and an upper world. It conflated past, present and future and allowed dialogues with the dead. States of hallucination, dream, insanity, eccentric behaviour and speech, personal transformation, extraordinary situations were the norm (14).

In the novels Rowling manages to create an anachronistic world. It is a world peopled with wizards and witches. Shorn of the protective umbrella of his parents, Harry Potter learns at a young age that if he wants to survive then he must evolve his own survival strategies. He is, as has been said earlier, miserable with the

Dursleys. But with Hagrid's arrival, at the stroke of midnight on Harry's eleventh birthday a ray of light begins to shine in Potter's life in the novel *Harry Potter and the Philosopher's Stone*. Harry is happy with the books and clothes he buys with Hagrid. Harry looks forward to joining his new school on the 1st of September. On the train and on his arrival at the school Harry discovers that the other students and teachers are aware of his background. But this does not disturb Harry.

The western world has made tremendous technological advancements and this has affected human life. Information Technology has changed mind-sets, opened visions of a world of free communication and interaction and a never before opportunity to seek and obtain information and visuals on virtually anything under the sun. A global netizen is emerging who must transcend the limits of geographical boundaries to fit into this world of computers. Interpersonal relationships are undergoing cataclysmic changes with net chatting and cyber affairs looming large on personal lives and fast diminishing the thin line between reality and illusion. In such a world Rowling's stories also weave together unlikely special effects in ordinary children's lives. The reader gets deeply engrossed in Rowling's works. In fairy tales, romances, and folk tales the stories generally began with the traditional formulaic device 'Once upon a time' . . . and had a formulaic ending that they 'lived happily ever after', somehow down the line we seem to have lost touch with these types of stories. Rowling's fantastic novels give the feeling that all is not lost. Our faith in the basic goodness of human nature gets re-affirmed even though these are imaginative pieces. The activities of Potter and his friends may appear impossible but never-the-less we begin to believe in them. Potter's world may not be established, may not ever exist, but this make-believe world provides us pleasure and delight. When we begin to analyze these novels we realize that it is an inversion of the world we inhabit. We wish to get rid of this world, and only the fantastic mode can transport us to another world, a world that we crave for.

As stated earlier, technology has entered into and affected our lifestyles. People are becoming increasingly self-centered and this is affecting home fronts. Children of working parents are very often lonely as their parents cannot devote a great deal of attention to them. Through the Harry Potter tales and especially through the character of Potter, Rowling is trying to reach out to the lonely child. Lonely children are a widespread social phenomenon today. In *The Philosopher's Stone,* Harry keeps receiving a number of letters prior to his eleventh birthday. The letters come whizzing down the chimney, they are found in the letter box, or they are placed with the eggs in the basket that the milk man hands over to Mrs. Dursley. These letters make us realize that Harry is not alone and friendless. There is someone who is watching and taking care of him.

Once Harry Potter gets to know the Weasleys, he begins to enjoy their company. The Weasleys practically adopt Harry and shower him with love, warmth and comfort. Harry and his school friends, Ron and Hermione, have a series of adventures, some daring, some hilarious. The Weasley twins Fred and George give Harry the Marauder's Map. This enables people to see and understand the activities that are going on at the Hogwart's school. In the second book *Harry Potter and the Chamber of Secrets* the Whomping Willow thrashes and bashes up anyone who comes near it. Wearing the invisibility cloak (which belonged to Harry's father) Potter is able to move around, watch other people's activities and have plenty of fun even though some of the adventures are quite risky. But it is significant to note that Harry never puts the lives of his friends in jeopardy (CS 197-209). He makes every effort to see that Ron and Harmione do not get into trouble. The distinction between the real and the unnatural is a recurring feature in these novels. Initially Harry finds it difficult to maintain a balance, but later on he begins to understand the world of the Muggles and the magical world.

Readers may hesitate to accept the events stated, but they cannot escape the feeling of reality that permeates the novels. As one reads the novels one begins to think of these character as living persons – their world appears to be familiar and one can identify with some of these people. Therefore it is difficult to dismiss these tales as altogether childish.

In these stories time and again Rowling has made use of mirrors, glasses, magical eye etc. These devices enable a person to see only that which he strongly wishes to see. Jackson says,

> The topography of the modern fantastic suggests a preoccupation with problems of vision and visibility, for it structures around spectral imagery: it is remarkable how many fantasies introduce mirrors, glasses, reflections, portraits, eyes – which see myopically or distortedly, or out of focus to effect a transformation of the familiar into the unfamiliar (43).

In *Harry Potter and the Philosopher's Stone*, especially the chapter titled 'The Mirror of Erised', Harry sees that which he most desires, he sees his parents waving at him. The mirror projects what lies latent in his mind, in the unconscious realm.

Rosemary Jackson comments 'In a culture which equated the "real" with the "visible" and gives the eye dominance over other sense organs, the unreal is that which is invisible' (p.45). Visual displays leave a greater impact on our mind. Thus knowledge, comprehension and reason dawn on us in a complete sense when we employ the audio-visual technique.

These fantastic texts follow magic realism in presenting time and space. In the third book *Harry Potter and the Prisoner of Azkaban* chronology is exploded. Dumbledore tells Potter and Hermione that they need more time to rescue Sirius Black. Hermione has a time-turner, which can turn back the hours once again so that jobs, which had been left out, can be completed. It is with the help of this time turner that Hermione and Potter manage to rescue buck beak (the hippogriff) and Sirius. Sirius rides buck beak and flies out of Hogwarts. Time turners are very much a part of fantastic literature and Rowling uses this effectively in the book *Harry Potter and the Prisoner of Azkaban*. Fantastic literature revolves around this problem of making visible what cannot be seen and articulating what cannot be heard. That which cannot be seen, heard and discussed remains a dark and unknown area.

Rowling's books belong to the tradition of fables, allegories etc. In these books good triumphs over evil – truth alone triumphs. In the fourth book, *Harry Potter and the Goblet of Fire* Lord Voldemort returns. But Harry manages to get the better of him and returns to Hogwarts with Cedric's body. In this book *Harry Potter and the Goblet of Fire* emphasis has been laid on qualities like determination and moral fibre. Earlier, Potter has displayed his moral strength during the second task assigned to him at the Triwizard tournament. He displays it once again when he returns with the body of Cedric.

Prof. Dumldedore's concluding speech in *Harry Potter and the Goblet of Fire* is very significant. Talking about the return of the evil genius Lord Voldemort Dumbledore says:

> in the light of Lord Voldemort's return, we are only as strong as we are united, as weak as we are divided. Lord Voldemort's gift for spreading discord and enmity is very great. We can fight it only by showing an equally strong bond of friendship and trust.

He says further that differences of habit and language are nothing at all if our aims are identical and our hearts are open, and that while faced with dark and difficult times 'they must remember Cedric', they must 'Remember, if the time should come when you have to make a choice between what is right and what is easy,' they must 'remember what happened to a boy who was good, and kind and brave, because he strayed across the path of Lord Voldemort. Remember Cedric Diggory' (GF, 627-28).

The fear expressed here is familiar as terrorism has spread its tentacles everywhere in the modern world and badly shaken mankind's need and sense of security. Since terrorism is the most hotly debated issue of the hour, the presence of violence and terrorism has now also permeated children's literature. This violence is visible in the Rowling's fifth book *Harry Potter and the Order of Phoenix* and the sixth book *Harry Potter and the Half Blood*

Prince. In these books Rowling shows the modern assumption that one must make oneself heard by fair or foul means. Manufacturing weapons of mass destruction and using them on hapless innocents is one such means of making oneself heard. In the fifth book *Harry Potter and the Order of the Phoenix* the Sorting Hat sings a new song wherein the Hat laments about the discord that has crept amongst the four houses – Gryffinder, Slytherin, Hufflepuff and Ravenclaw. The Hat goes on to warn the staff and students of Hogwarts by saying:

> 'For our Hogwarts is in danger
> from external, deadly foes
> And we must unite inside her
> Or we'll crumble from within
> I have told you, I have
> warned you . . .' (OP, 186-87)

The students have a new Defence Against Dark Arts teacher by the name of Dolores Umbridge. She makes it clear to the students that '. . . progress for progress's sake must be discouraged' . . . (OP, 192-93). Thus Umbridge who represents the Ministry of Magic would see to it that the ministry has a tight control over the Hogwarts School. As the school term progress, Dolores Umbridge assumes and acquires a lot of power. She is very partial towards Draco Malfoy and his friends. Harry as usual gets into a lot of trouble with her and he is warned by Ron, Hermione and Prof. McGonagall to be careful of Umbridge. Finally, Harry and his friends form a group called Dumbledore's army; Dumbledore has no idea about the existence of this army. Members of Dumbledore's army and supporters of Umbridge are extremely hostile to one another. Rowling has very effectively incorporated the culture of surveillance and group formation that characterize contemporary life. In these novels Harry very often uses the invisibility cloak and Marauder's map to find out what Draco Malfoy is up to so that he (Harry) can be careful.

Umbridge's nepotism and her hostile behaviour leads to a show down between the Minister of Magic Cornelius Fudge and

Dumbledore. With the help of Fawkes, Dumbledore escapes from Hogwarts. Tired of Umbridge's high handedness, the Weasley twins Fred and George fly out of Hogwarts on their broomsticks. As the novel comes to a close, Harry is once again a witness to Voldemort's evil desires until Dumbledore drives out the evil wizard from the Ministry of Magic. In the process Harry's godfather Sirius Black dies to save Harry (OP).

In the sixth book, *Harry Potter and the Half Blood Prince,* Rowling once again upholds moral norms. The Potter novels are written with great imagination. While soothing readers' nerves, these novels help people deal with disaster. In these novels Potter explores the other world, a world that one does not know fully. 'Potterfication', if one is allowed to coin this word, would explain the change in behaviour of readers who stay awake the whole night and stand in queues to procure a copy of the book. After 9/11 there has been a change in readers' attitudes and approaches. The ever-growing menace of terrorism has made the world a complex place to live in. Under such circumstances it is almost impossible to grasp reality.

In the book *Harry Potter and the Half Blood Prince* terror is felt right from the beginning and the reader cannot escape from it. Rowling is an eminently efficient wordsmith and a skilful writer. Rowling pushes the reader's boundaries of imagination further than they were ever pushed. Potter's magic world is sans impossibilities. Draco Malfoy's mother, Narcissa, and aunt, Bellatrix Lestrange, extract a promise from Snape to help Draco in times of need. Thus Snape makes the Unbreakable Vow.

Dumbledore trusts Snape much to Potter's dismay. Dumbledore believes in the essential goodness of human beings. It is this belief of his which is responsible for his being killed by Snape. The book is seeped in terror and violence. In order to achieve specific short term goals, like-minded individuals commit acts of violence by a conscious decision. The violence depicted in the book Harry Potter and the Half *Blood Prince* and also in the fifth book *Harry Potter and the Order of Phoenix* links man's behaviour to that of the behaviour of brutes. That is why violence is so distasteful to the human mind. A person who is violent often feels exhilarated. Thus we have terrorist organisations which take pleasure and pride in accepting responsibility for their violent acts. Rowling tells us that Lord Voldemort feels very happy when he has planned something evil. This is noticed in all the Harry Potter novels. These novels are never dull and routine. The experience of each of the characters erases the notion that life is dull and boring.

It is significant to note that in the sixth book *Harry Potter and the Half Blood Prince* Dumbledore goes at great length to explain to Harry the meaning of the term Horcruxes. The Headmaster also tells Harry that Voldemort must have torn his soul into six parts and

> 'The seventh part of his soul, however maimed, resides inside his regenerated body. That was the part of him that lived a spectral existence for so many years during his exile; without that, he has no self at all. That seventh piece of soul will be the last that anybody wishing to kill Voldemort must attack – the piece that lives in his body' (HBP, 470).

The Horcruxe theory reminds the reader of the transmigration of soul. Dumbledore also feels that since Voldemort is Parselmouth, the sixth part of his soul may be residing in Nagini the snake. Dumbledore tells Harry that despite Harry's knowledge about Voldemort's plans and ambitious, Harry has never shown the slightest desire to become one of Voldemort's followers. Since Harry's mother loved Harry, and died, protecting him, and since Harry has the ability to love, it is this love which acts as a protective sheath round Harry and protects him from powers like Voldemort. Voldemort has never understood the incomparable power of a soul that is untarnished and whole. The Good Lord shall protect the weak and meek and their innocence shall shame and bring ruin on the evil forces.

Talking about Lord Voldemort Dumbledore tells Harry 'Don't you see? Voldemort himself created his worst enemy, just as tyrants every where do! Have you any idea how much tyrants fear the people they oppress?' The answer he gives to this question it that 'All of them realise that, one day, amongst their many victims there is sure to be one who rises against them and strikes back! Voldemort is no different! Always he was on the lookout for the one who would challenge him. He heard the prophecy and he leapt into action, with the result that he not only handpicked the man most likely to finish him, he handed him uniquely deadly weapons!' (HBP 477)

Unlike the tyrant Harry is protected from the evil genius by his ability to love, and his innate goodness.

In the sixth book, *Harry Potter and the Half Blood Prince* memory moves backward and forward and enables Harry to see for himself the memories of Voldemort, Dumbledore, Snape and Slughorn. These memories arouse hope and curiosity in Potter's mind. He begins to understand things in a better perspective. Rowling mixes fantasy and realism and the tapestry that she unfolds reveals fantasy being treated in a matter of fact manner and reality being inverted. Ordinary events like young Tom Riddle's (Voldemort's name) visit to the cave (where he went on a picnic with other orphans) acquires moral and imaginative density when Harry and Dumbledore go there to find the Horcruxes (HBP). The boat, the water, the island, the dead bodies, the chill and terror that grips Harry, go to show that Rowling has produced a tale where fantasy is reality. When Dumbledore and Harry return to Hogwarts they encounter Death Eaters who have been let into Hogwarts by Draco. The Death Eaters belong to Voldemort's group: they are evil and vicious.

Just as Jesus Christ was betrayed by Judas Iscariot and just as Julius Caesar was stabbed by Brutus, similarly Prof. Dumbledore is betrayed by Snape who kills him. Harry had all along disliked and hated Snape and he had voiced his suspicions to his friends and Dumbledore. But Dumbledore did not pay heed to Harry's fears and finally Dumbledore pays with his life (HBP). The novel ends with the hope that Harry would be able to find out the other Horcruxes. Harry hopes that he would be able to wipe out Voldemort, Snape and his evil supporters.

Harry must fight his dreadful enemies. Harry's Muggle world is undercut by the intrusion of inexplicable events. It does not matter if readers have to travel inside a world of magic realism in order to understand the evils of terrorism. Rowling's writings subvert realistic expectations. What appears normal and what one sees as 'normal' are frequently challenged by fantasy where everything is clearly labelled good or evil unlike the real world. The monolithic moral element found in the Potter novels is reiterated time and again. Love, goodness of heart, truth and the courage to hold one's head high are the qualities which will enable Harry to overcome his foes. Harry has now no protective umbrella over his head and as a loner he must evolve survival strategies. Of course his friends Ron and Hermione offer to accompany him as he goes out to hunt down Voldemort. Rowling's novels make us believe in fantasies.

Notes

1. The following abbreviations of J.K. Rowling's books dealing with Harry Potter's adventures have been used in this article:

Harry Potter and the Philosopher's Stone	PS
Harry Potter and the Chamber of Secrets	CS
Harry Potter and the Prisoner of Azkaban	PA
Harry Potter and the Goblet of Fire	GF
Harry Potter and the Orders of Phoenix	OP
Harry Potter and the Half Blood Prince	HBP

Reference

Collins English Dictionary, f.p. 1979 Fifth Reprint, 1995.

Jackson, Rosemary, *Fantasy: The Literature of Subversion*. London: Methuen, 1981.

Rowling, J.K. *Harry Potter and the Philosopher's Stone*. London: Bloomsbury, 1997.

Rowling, J.K. *Harry Potter and the Chamber of Secrets.* London: Bloomsbury, 1998.

Rowling, J.K. *Harry Potter and the Prisoner of Azkaban.* London: Bloomsbury, 1999.

Rowling, J.K. *Harry Potter and the Goblet of Fire.* London: Bloomsbury, 2000.

Rowling, J.K. *Harry Potter and the Orders of Phoenix.* London: Bloomsbury, 2003.

Rowling, J.K. *Harry Potter and the Half Blood Prince.* London: Bloomsbury, 2005.

See Simonsen, Clifford E. and Jeremy R. Spindlove's book titled *Terrorism Today The Past, The Players, The Future,* New Jersey: Prentice Hall, 2000. This book focuses on the evolution of terrorism.

21 "The Cages People Live In"
The Short Stories of Doris Lessing

Manveen Brar

Doris Lessing in an essay "The Small Personal Voice" (1974) writes:

> Post-war literature reveals a confusion of standards and the uncertainty of values; it portrays the individual either as an isolated monad unable to relate to others or as a social being who lacks uniqueness. Both portrayals capitulate to the problems facing the writer, who should try to balance human beings' irreducible individuality against their unavoidably social nature. The point of rest should be the writer's recognition of man, the responsible individual, voluntarily submitting his will to the collective, but never finally; and insisting on making his own personal and private judgements before every act of submission (12).

The careful phrasing of this statement hints at the conflict between artistic freedom and political duty but Lessing never espoused Socialist realism influenced by Marxism. Lorna Sage in *Doris Lessing* (1983) observes that her faith in realism implied not just a belief in 'a tradition and a cluster of stylistic strategies inherited from the nineteenth century but a set of values, an ideology that conceived it as a radical and in some sort revolutionary, literary mode' (45).

The lasting legacy of Doris Lessing's political commitment to Marxism is her dialectical method of working. 'Instead of trying to find meaning in her raw material as it is, she places it in negotiation with its antithesis; the resulting creative clash results in a new synthesis' as Ruth Whittaker notes in *Doris Lessing* (1988). In her short stories apartheid, ideologically opposed by Lessing, is shown in all its tragic potential. Domesticity and motherhood are countered and challenged in stories like "To Room Nineteen" raising questions about the role of women. In *The Golden Notebook* (1962) instead of ordering her material realistically Doris Lessing writes so that realistic conventions are interrogated by a fragmentation of structure and technique in the work.

Doris Lessing's first fictional portrayal of the contemporary British milieu took the form of short stories. An attempt to portray contemporary Britain panoramically, as Anne Wulf in Lessing's monumental *The Golden Notebook* (1962) says: 'the way Tolstoy did it for Russia, Stendhal for France, mutates into an account of social and individual breakdown' (11). In most of the short stories there is a sense of everything 'cracking up' and the stories describe the various manifestations of this implosion: the alienation of people from themselves and from one another; an all pervasive sense of anomie; the ineffectuality of the individual in the face of world scale problems such as poverty, exploitation, famine and war, the atomization of social life, gender conflict, class struggle and personal psychosis. The characters function as microcosms of society and their internal conflicts are homologous to the world they live in.

In more than ten collections of short stories published so far, Lessing's powerful artistry deepens the short story form, giving it unexpected emotional force. Lessing's earlier short stories are all set either in Africa or England. In the African stories Lessing describes the conflict between a white sensibility and the African culture; the European and African experiences of exile and alienation are sensitively explored. In the British stories there is a variety of backgrounds and moods, but certain themes suggest themselves again and again: the bedrock realities of marriage, the dilemmas of the individual in a fluid society, the fate of women. These stories demonstrate Lessing's narrative prowess at its finest.

The focal point of nearly all the British stories authored by Lessing is a modern Britisher. These protagonists are steeped in the British society and culture, and are thus, in radically different circumstances from their solitary African counterparts in the African stories by the same author, but they share with them the fight against existential, if not demographic, isolation.

The structure of the stories is dialectical: each protagonist comes into conflict with a given collective force, and wrests from the ensuing battle her or his identity and self-definition. The collective forces involved generally fall into the broad categories of patriarchy, role stereotypes, politics, history and social ills. The present paper will examine the dialectical relationship of the individual and the collective in the short stories of Doris Lessing. The stories that illustrate these categories of collective forces which will be analysed here in detail are "Each Other", "Mrs. Fortescue", "One off the Short List", "To Room Nineteen" and "An Old Woman and Her Cat".[1]

Through her concentration on the crucial individual, Lessing abides by the traditions of the short-story genre. The individual appears not as an isolated entity, but rather stands silhouetted against a larger collective backdrop. Through this double focus on the human consciousness and the forces that govern it, Lessing broadens and enriches the genre in a remarkable way.

A good half of the British stories have the impact of patriarchy on sexuality as a central motif. Examination of their own sexual roles is the single avenue traveled most frequently by characters in these stories in their search for self. The relationships shown here range from the commonplace to the bizarre and taboo, sexual encounters can express anything from neurotic spite to supreme bliss.

"Each Other" is a poignant story of a brother and his newly married sister who have an incestuous relationship. During their early morning clandestine meetings, they play a ritualistic game with the ebb and flow of sexual climax. For Fred and Freda 'normal' sexual mores are inverted. Their bastion of incestuous ecstasy is the only pure good in a threatening world. Freda's marriage was intended to lend a cover of respectability, but instead, it cheapens and taints their intimacy. They are on the 'edge of disaster' (AMATW192). Both little more than adolescents, he threatened by unemployment and she by a distrustful husband, they close in with each other in a relationship which makes them feel secure. A near metaphysical sexual communion appears here as the only refuge from 'hostile social reality'.

The forces of threatening social conventions are always in the background in the form of Fred's girl friend Alice and Freda's husband. The four characters are entangled in proscribed and prohibited relations-their agony is genuine, but they do not know how they can disengage themselves. Lessing portrays the situation with a detached irony. Repeated references to Fred's girlfriend and Freda's husband succeed in bringing into foreground the socially prohibited relationship of incest. But it is difficult to say whether Lessing feels sympathy for the incestuous relationship or considers them to be weaklings.

In "Mrs Fortescue" sexuality is exposed as a weapon used to denigrate females, Lessing frequently adopts a male viewpoint to demonstrate this mechanism. This technique is convincing as in general the male and female viewpoints are represented with equal insight and sympathy. "Mrs. Fortescue" describes an adolescent boy who suddenly realizes that the grandmotherly tenant of the apartment overhead, whom he has known all his life, is in fact an aging prostitute. He gradually works himself up into an anguished fever of repulsion and desire, until one evening he enters Mrs. Fortescue's flat and rapes her (with her, more or less, indifferent sanction).

The sexual assault is followed by a verbal one: 'Filthy old whore, disgusting thats what you are, disgusting' (TSONM 81). Fred's own sexual initiation is obviously a development of his irrational revenge on Mrs. Fortescue for being an 'old tart' and leaves him with a sense of triumphant superiority over women in general. More important than the story's exceptionally convincing portrayal of the adolescent's sexual ambivalence is the fact that Fred appears not as an exploiting brute, but as a victim of his own misunderstood drives and in a broader sense, of a sexually repressive society which asserts itself by making a stereotypical gendered masculine response of using superior physical strength.

The theme of sexuality as a statement of male domination is developed most incisively in "One Off The Short List". Lessing has described this as one of her favorite stories in a recent interview with Lisa Apignanesi in *Bookforum* (2002). Graham Spence, a middle aged, might-have-been writer distinguished only by mediocrity, compensates in the Freudian sense for his dashed ambitions by systematically compiling a list of women he considers worthy of his seduction. He then savors the brief illusion of conquest, which dulls the taste of his general impotence. Lessing's penetration of the Don Juan complex is superb. Spence, a failure and flunky in all respects, adopts the socially sanctioned defense mechanism of seeing himself in the role of a victor when playing the ladies man.

He is thus a living illustration of Simone de Beauvoir's observation in *The Second Sex* (1988) that even the puniest male becomes a 'demi god' in his own eyes when he compares himself to a female. His illusion is shattered however, by his encounter with Barbara Coles, her refusal to be flattered by her inclusion in Spence's 'list' only aggravates his determination to ravish her. She puts him in the position of 'raping a woman, who was making it elaborately clear that he bored her,' (TRN 234) but instead of relenting, he grows even more hostile. He feels 'dislike,' 'anger', 'annoyance', 'jealousy' and finally 'hatred'. The latter word is used no less than nine times during the seduction scene.

Spence's self-respect rests exclusively on the fact of his maleness, which enables him to 'have women'. Spence is the type of man who refuses to treat a woman as a respectable equal, or superior in intelligence and competence. He experiences a feeling of hostility whenever he comes across a successful woman believing she has usurped the position of the all powerful Male. Like all male chauvinists, he thinks that once he has used his physical power over a woman, he has somehow conquered her. Lessing has cynically presented such a character.

Sex for him is an antagonistic function of a crippled ego. Barbara Coles, on the other hand, personifies the total separation of sexuality from intelligent and coherent thought processes. She cannot be reached 'much less conquered' by the pest who refuses to leave her apartment despite her repeated requests for him to do so.

Barbara Coles is a remarkable female character whom Lessing etches carefully and she epitomizes Lessing's ideal woman – a woman who enjoys her work and lives her life independent of male control. She may have affairs, or relationships with men, as is indicated by Spence quite early in the story but they do not exercise control over her life. Coles is a woman Lessing admires for she does not become a victim of emotional links with a man, nor is she intimidated in the least by men like Spence. She leads a well-regulated life as Spence comments: 'there was about her an assurance, a carelessness, that he recognized as the signature of success' (TRN 213) and she is liked and well-respected in her profession.

Despite his entirely obsequious, manipulative, exploitative behavior, Spence is also a victim of a competitive and sexist society, whose 'losers' take refuge in sexual games, which only further degrade them. The story turns over the stone of machismo to reveal a writhing worm of a man, who has no other place to hide.

"To Room Nineteen" is one of Lessing's most moving and multidimensional texts. It depicts the network of roles and social obligations governing male female relationships which is an ever present motif in the British stories and provides the starting point of "To Room Nineteen". It is a study of a dry, controlled middle class marriage 'grounded in intelligence'. This is clear from the opening sentence of the story: 'This is a story, I suppose, about a failure in intelligence: the Rawlingses' marriage was grounded in intelligence' (TRN 352).

The story traces the fate of a woman, Susan Rawlings, and her husband who does everything intelligently from her well-matched and timely marriage, to the widely spaced children, to the sensibly mortgaged house in the suburbs. As required by the patriarchal rules by which she abides, Susan gives up her own apartment to marry, and then her profession, to raise her children. Yet, after attaining all those goals which society says lead to self-fulfillment Susan Rawlings experiences a growing sense of alienation and depression: 'why did Susan feel (though luckily not for longer than a few seconds at a time) as if life had become a desert, and that nothing mattered, and that her children were not her own' (TRN357).

After years of domesticity, of according first priority to her family, Susan has precious little self confidence left, the husband begins to find 'pleasure' in younger females, Susan's sexual interest wanes, she tries to rationalize this situation: 'There was no need to use the dramatic words, unfaithful, forgive, and the rest: intelligence forbade them. Intelligence barred, too, quarrelling, sulking, anger, silences of withdrawal, accusations and tears. Above all, intelligence forbids tears' (TRN358). She experiences a feeling of emptiness and inertia as there is no intellectual element or creative outlet for her energy. Like most other conventional middle-class housewives, neatly dressed, living in a comfortable house in a posh suburb, Susan turns to the conventional activities like stitching and cooking to keep herself busy but they offer no respite from the growing sense of inner emptiness. Lessing analyses the typical female experience, of a woman who is lonely. When the children grow up and move away from the mother, 'the empty nest syndrome' hits her and she realises her existential loneliness.

The feeling of claustrophobia, of being tied to the house assails her at all times: 'she did not like being in the garden at all, because of the closeness there of the enemy – irritation, restlessness, emptiness, whatever it was, which keeping her hands occupied made less dangerous for some reason' (TRN360), there is a great deal of resentment against the husband Mathew who continues to works in the city and is a devoted husband and father. She wants to escape, to be free of what she terms a 'voluntary bondage'.

In her mid forties Susan stands at the centre of a complicated configuration of household and parental duties, community ties, possessions and social engagements. The paradoxical result of her endeavours is a well oiled machine in which Susan's presence is altogether superfluous, 'all this depended on her, and yet she could not understand why, or even what it was that she contributed to it' (TRN 370). As she oversees life being lived by others, she is increasingly aware that she has no life of her own.

Susan's own identity, which has been obliterated by the demands of her husband and children, seems impossible to recover. She does try to assert herself, rents a room in a hotel where she can be by herself. This provides temporary respite: After these days of solitude, it was both easy to play her part as mother and wife, and difficult-because it so easy: she felt an impostor. She felt as if her shell moved here, with her family, answering to Mummy, Mother, Susan, Mrs Rawlings' (TRN377).

Susan gradually becomes disjuncted from the well-oiled machinery of the household. The urge to be free – to be herself obsesses her at all times. She realizes that she is sinking into madness: Instead of the soft dark that had been the room's air, were now waiting for her the demons that made her dash blindly about, muttering words of hate; she was impelling herself from point to point like a moth dashing itself against a window pane, sliding to the bottom, fluttering off on broken wings, then crashing into the invisible barrier again' (TRN380) how she finds it difficult to escape madness – and ultimately chooses to die.

She withdraws from her family completely, becomes depressive, alienated and finally begins to lose her mental balance. She has hallucinations that the house is haunted by devils and embarks on a search for total solitude, which she is determined to preserve despite her husband's efforts to track her down. The bourgeois suburban paradise-in which her husband has a mistress, the house a maid, and the children a competent au pair girl, she finally withdraws from the world, turns on the gas in her rented hotel room nineteen: She was quite content lying there, listening to the faint soft hiss of the gas that poured into the room, into her lungs, into her brain, as she drifted off into the dark river' (TRNP386). These are the concluding lines of the story.

Susan Rawling's paradoxical fate-she is ruined by the very achievement of her goals is more than a 'failure of intelligence'. It is symptomatic of a great paradox, that it is irreparably wrong to do everything 'right' by society's standards. Susan's mistake was to sacrifice her selfhood to the bourgeois status quo, symbolized by a house, which was not a refuge but a cage. The story clearly implies that without the colossal middle class apparatus to tie her down, and without a patriarchal system which requires that she cheerfully welcome her bondage, her personality would never have eroded to the point of breakdown and suicide.

"To Room Nineteen" examines the condition of the 'well adjusted' socially successful individual *'in extremis'*. Her comfortable niche is a cell padded by role expectations, possessions, marital games and mortgage payments: all of which finally becomes her nemesis. In "To Room Nineteen" the deadening effects of conformity are presented with sufficient voltage to force the reader's gaze beyond the protagonist herself, and onto an oppressive society, which, given the right circumstances easily manages to push essentially sane people over the edge.

In Lessing's later novel *The Summer Before the Dark* (1973) Kate Brown a conventional middle-class housewife, neatly dressed, living in a pleasant London suburb closely resembles Susan Rawlings and like her appears to have nothing in the world to worry about. It is interesting to note that throughout the novel her decorous attitudes are juxtaposed with these of her neighbour, Mary Finchley. Mary has no sartorial or sexual inhibitions and she represents an alternative way of living, instinctual and unrepressed. Married, with three children, she sleeps with whoever she fancies and feels no guilt of shame. Mary enacts the suppressed aspects of Kate's personality and is regarded by her with incomprehension and envy. Kate realizes that Mary is significant to her.

In contrast to her neighbour's freedom and spontaneity, Kate's life seems a network of restricting responsibilities and prohibitions: Looking back over nearly a quarter of a century, she saw that that had been the characteristic of her life, passivity, adaptability to others' (*The Summer Before the Dark* 21) Kate takes up a temporary job as a translator during the summer which through a series of events leads to the rediscovery of her individuality, her own identity which has been obliterated by the demands of her husband and children is painfully reachieved, and *The Summer Before the Dark* is a chronicle of rediscovery and resolution of the issues which in Lessing's earlier story "To Room Nineteen" lead to Susan Rawling's suicide. Susan Rawlings and Kate Brown are in somewhat similar situations but react differently. The greater collective machinery crushes Susan, who commits suicide whereas Kate Brown values her instincts as an individual and survives.

"An Old Woman and Her Cat" presents social criticism applicable to industrialization as a mechanizing force. This story represents the important social group – the old people, who find themselves marginalized and quietly made insignificant to the rest of the society. The old woman in this story, Hetty, finds herself living with a cat, trying to share food collected by the cat.

Hetty is dependent for housing on the regulations of the housing council, and the reader witnesses her descent from a respectable single family dwelling to tenement accommodation for the elderly. She is faced finally with the prospect of being sent to a rest home where: 'The old were treated like naughty and dim witted children until they had the good fortune to die' (TSONM 106), a place from which, adding insult to injury, her feline companion Tibbs would be banned so she chooses to disappear among the homeless on London's streets.

She hides in a condemned house and peers down from a second floor cranny as the frozen corpses of transients like herself are removed each morning by men who, while the: real citizens are asleep....make the rounds of all the empty rotting houses, they know about, to collect the dead, and to warn the living that they ought not to be there at all, inviting them to one of the official homes or lodgings for the homeless' (TSONM 113).

Hetty lives for a time upon the pigeons brought in by Tibbs the cat and eventually dies of cold and malnutrition. And Tibbs' fate applies in the greater sense to all of society's poor and aged misfits: though he: wished to be liked by the human race, he was really too old and smelly and battered to find a new friend'. He is rounded up with the other strays and 'put to sleep' (TSONM 113).

"An Old woman and Her Cat" is a glimpse at a whole social framework, not an appeal for a single reform such as more low cost housing. The story told with empathy, but without sentimentality illustrates how society's anonymous members can slip down into the regions which are 'no longer decent.'

In this respect, the story is typical of all the British stories of Lessing. Their goal is illustration rather than agitation. The individuals profiled here wander through the labyrinthine corridors of stereotypes, history and politics, but most of them do not propound revolution or drastic change of any kind.

These stories propagate the idea that the individual must be seen as both the product and the determiner of intricate networks of personal and extra-personal factors. They also depict that human beings are trapped, boxed and filed inside immutable collective boundaries. Lessing's singular examination of this network gives us not only characters whose habits, loves, failures and successes are eminently readable, but also, the understanding that one's unique and incredible experience is what everyone shares.

Lessing says that individuals must awake from their daily drowse in front of the TV set, question the authority of the group mind and ultimately find the courage to swim against the collective stream because 'the need to break out of our ordinary possibilities-the cage we live in, that is made up of our habits, upbringing, circumstances, and which shows itself to be so small and tight and tyrannical, when we do try to break out, this need may well be the deepest one we humans have' in her Afterword to *The Making of the Representative for Planet* 8 (1982).

Note

1. The short stories discussed in this paper are from Lessing's three short story collections *A Man and Two Women* (1963), *The Story of a Non Marrying Man and Other Stories* (1972) and *To Room Nineteen: Collected stories* (1978).Page references from these volumes will be referred to in abbreviated mention as (AMATW), (TSONM) and (TRN).

Works Cited

Apignanaesi, Lisa. *Bookforum*.net/spring2002 http://wwwbookforum.com/archive/spr_02/interview_lessing.htm.

Beauvoir, Simone de. *The Second Sex*. Translated and Edited H.M. Parshlay. London: Pan, 1988.

Knapp, Mona. *Doris Lessing*. New York: Frederick Ungar Publishing, 1984.

Lessing, Doris. *A Man and Two Women*. New York: Panther, 1963.

Lessing, Doris. *The Summer Before The Dark*. New York: Panther, 1973.

Lessing, Doris. *Afterword to The Making of the Representative for Planet 8 (1982).*

Lessing, Doris. *To Room Nineteen: Collected Stories*. Vol. 1, London: Jonathan Cape, 1978.

Lessing, Doris. *The Story of a Non Marrying Man and Other Stories*. London: Jonathan Cape; New York: Knopf, 1972.

Lessing, Doris. "The Small Personal Voice". *A Small Personal Voice: Essays, Reviews, Interviews*. Ed. Paul Schleuter. New York: Knopf, 1974.

Sage, Lorna. *Doris Lessing*. London: Methuen, 1983.

Whittaker, Ruth. *Doris Lessing*. London: Macmillan, 1988.

22 The Role of Epiphany in the Novels of Angus Wilson

Aruna Pandey

After World War II experimental writers such as James Joyce and Virginia Woolf were pushed into the background and there was a renewed emphasis on the social and moral content of fiction. Writers made an attempt to rediscover the achievements of Trollope, Dickens, Dostoevsky and Thackeray. Britain was definitely undergoing a revolution of manners and mores. Alongwith writers like C.P. Snow who were concerned with Britain's traditional heritage, there emerged Angus Wilson's fiction. Unified Europe, a reality today and a possible nightmare of yesteryears was visualized by Wilson in his novel, *Old Men at the Zoo* (1961).[1] Multiculturalism, its dangers and complications were probingly explored in *As If By Magic.* Foreign violence had been and always would be there, as explored in *The Middle Age of Mrs Eliot.* Wilson's fictional world is one where everything has its place yet the eternal question of man's happiness and integrity lies at the bottom of everything however uncontrollable and overpowering other things may seem to be. Wilson's literary career began as a successful short story writer but the eight novels that he wrote in succession have earned him the position of a major British post-war novelist. He was awarded a Knighthood in 1980. Wilson's fiction originates from a deeper, personal need to seek a synthesis that would explain the disturbing, incessant flux of human experience.

In the many interviews of Angus Wilson we find the writer repeatedly stressing the social role of man although he quickly adds that it is essential to strike a balance between public and private concerns for a happy and meaningful life. In *The Wild Garden* (1963) he expresses this view thus:

> ...the cocktail parties, Christmas dinners and social functions still represent the hell of the human failure to communicate (a sort of blasphemy against life, mocking a communion feat); ...the solitary walks and the meaningless reveries represent the opposed hell of the maze of self-pity and neurosis (*WG* 33).

Wilson's fictional characters belong mostly to the middle class and upper-middle class of Britain of the 50's and 60's. The writer depicts their lives as a series of social get-togethers and parties where human interaction is a juxtaposition of meaningless gestures and postures. The lives of Bernard Sands and Gerald Middleton, the two protagonists of Wilson's first two novels, are shown to be rooted in evasion.

Wilson's protagonists are people who are well past their prime – in fact, they are in what could be said to be their last phase of life where a life of action has been taken up by a life of contemplation. They are sensitive liberals who are scared of treading upon other people's lives. Lionel Trilling in his book, *The Liberal Imagination* (1953) underlines the tendency of the liberal humanist to simplify life a little bit too much. The implication is that the humanist, in his eagerness to embrace the world as it is, is wary of critical analysis. Trilling points out that the very basis of the humanistic creed is the acceptance of variety and possibility, which requires an awareness of the complexity and difficulty in the human situation. The liberals are in the habit of taking themselves to task for every action they perform but the final insights are arrived at only at a stage where it is too late in terms of time as life has already taken its toll, or so it seems. This inner restlessness is born of the realization of the inadequacy of human endeavour to set everything right. It is at this late stage that their own wrongs confront them and become the starting point for an inward journey towards self-knowledge. Many hidden facets of their personalities unravel themselves in the process. The present paper explores this process of unraveling and identifies the new awareness in terms of sudden manifestations, "epiphany" of acute understanding that the protagonists experience.

Epiphany is a Christian feast intended to celebrate the 'shining forth' or revelation of God to humankind in human form, in the person of Jesus. The observance had its origins in the eastern Christian churches, and included the birth of Jesus; the visit of the three Magi (Caspar, Melchior and Balthasar) who arrived in Bethlehem; and all of Jesus' childhood events, up to his baptism. However, James Joyce used the word "epiphany" in a different context. In James Joyce's *Stephen Hero,* an epiphany meant 'a sudden spiritual manifestation, whether in the vulgarity of speech or of gesture or in a memorable phase of the mind itself.' James Joyce believed that it was for the man of letters to record these epiphanies with extreme care because they were 'the most delicate and evanescent of moments'.

The interesting manner in which Angus Wilson depicts the inner tangle and the untangling of epiphany illustrates the writer's keen understanding of man in the social as well as private sphere. The novels constantly move towards the final goal where self-realisation is attained through almost epiphanic perception. This epiphanic moment may be an instant point of time and sometimes a long-drawn climaxing experience with the final confirmation being shown in the protagonist's reversal of decision. These two epiphanic modes may be illustrated through the figures of Bernard Sands and Gerald Middleton.

The opening pages of *Hemlock and After* (1956) introduce the protagonist Bernard Sands as an established liberal humanist who has just received a letter from the Government assuring him of financial aid for his scheme of Vardon Hall. Vardon Hall is meant to be a Utopian retreat for upcoming writers and artists. Bernard

Sands is easily recognized as the "prophet" of the chapter entitled "The Prophet and the Locals". However, for a Grand Old Man of Letters of sixty to whom everything has become "plain sailing", Bernard is wary of the dangers of being over-satisfied and

'...he instantly reminded himself of the histrionic dangers – the knickerbockered, bearded, self-satisfied, quizzing air – of the position he had won in English life' (*HA* 9).

Nonetheless, one finds that such awareness does not prevent him from acquiring a more deep-rooted kind of smugness:

'It was, nevertheless, very gratifying to an anarchic humanist to have the State eating out of his hand, even when the fodder was taken with such primness' (*HA* 11).

So, the reader is quick to see that whereas Bernard resembles a modern-day Socrates in his contempt for misdirected power of authority, he is in fact, in love with his own power over others. Moreover, his habit of self-reprimand does not really puncture his self-assurance and if 'on occasion he mistrusted his own powers, it was not a mistrust that he intended others to share' (*HA* 9).

On the other hand Bernard's private life is empty and miserable. Public elation is followed by despair when Bernard confronts his wife, Ella, who has been suffering from neurotic isolation for years. The 'hatred' that Bernard feels for his wife is coupled with guilt making him all the more anxious. His private grief is further intensified with his new awareness of the existent evil. Wilson felt that apart from a few novelists like Samuel Richardson, Emily Brontë, Joseph Conrad, and E. M. Forster English novelists had not taken up the issues of the "transcendent values" of good and evil.[2]

As Bernard and Ella drive up to their son's home in the country, Bernard catches sight of the 'elephantine figure' of Vera Curry, a cheap and wicked woman (Gardener calls her an 'ectoplasmic' embodiment of evil), who caters to the regressive sexual perversities of the residents of Vardon village. The comprehension of 'genuine' evil and its guises make Bernard re-scrutinise his own motives. Bernard has been suffering from a rare kind of vanity by creating a God-like self-image. James, Bernard's son, is repulsed by his father's position as a liberal humanist, his claims of universal understanding and Dostoyevskeyan emotional "brotherhood," for he feels that, basically, he had nothing but 'utter contempt for nine-tenths of humanity; as for the other tenth he probably hated their guts for not being susceptible to his patronage' (*HA* 21). However, a contrastive view is presented by Isobel Sands, Bernard's sister, who feels that her brother would rise even from his death-bed if there was an injustice to attack. These contrastive views however, cannot quite explain the failure that the protagonist confronts. It is not actually contempt for humanity that Bernard has but a very subtle kind of evasion from the complexities of life. He has chosen to 'travel light' through life like his brother-in-law, Bill Pendlebury.

At first Bernard diagnoses his inner restlessness as a sign of 'literary pregnancy', heralding the conception of a new novel, but he realizes, sometime later, that it has more to do his ever-increasing recognition of the nature of his existence and the deceptiveness of a neatly ordered life that he has built around himself to evade the frightening chaos of the human predicament. Paradoxically, Bernard's evasion stands at one extreme of his basically intelligent understanding of the liberal humanist's tendency to sacrifice his self-interest.

The crystallization of Bernard's intensely-felt perceptions and growing self-awareness takes place as would seem in one epiphanic moment under the ugly neon lights of Leicester Square. It is when Bernard is awaiting the arrival of one of his male friends, Terence Lambert, that he witnesses the arrest of another homosexual by a lurking plain-clothes policeman. For a split second Bernard experiences a certain thrill which he recognizes as the 'hunter's thrill' at the sight of the terrified young man who has been arrested. The revelation comes as a rude shock to him and sends him reeling under the self-knowledge. His past evasions and mistakes suddenly confront him bringing to light the limitations of his path of action so far: 'Truly, he thought, he was not at one with those who exercised proper authority. A humanist, it would seem, was more at home with the wielders of the knout and the rubber truncheon' (*HA* 153).

Indeed, no public shame could be worse than the self-knowledge that has dawned on Bernard Sands. The weight of the burden is physically manifested in a heart attack and develops new insights into the nature of human motives, 'Motives were so difficult, so double; so much hypocrisy might spring from guilt, so much benevolence from fear to use power, so much kindness overlay cruelty, so much that was done didn't matter' (*HA* 153).

Wilson's second novel – *Anglo Saxon Attitudes* (1956), depicts the life of Gerald Middleton who is an academic and whose life is also rooted in evasion. The Melpham Burial is an academic fraud that is carried out by the protagonist with one or two other people in order to create fame and uproar in academic circles. Gerald's personal life is also one of self-deception and fraud. He is evasive of his innermost feelings and has rejected a genuine association with his one-time girl-friend, Dollie Stokesay. The evasiveness of his personal self is akin to the evasiveness of his professional self: in fact, the falsity of the Eorpwald Discovery becomes an objective correlative for Gerald's personal hypocrisies. The fundamental difference between Bernard Sands and Gerald Middleton is that the latter's approach to life is devoid of the refined (but misleading) naggings of the Calvinist conscience that the former suffers from.

The nature of Gerald Middleton's self-realisation, although different from Bernard Sands' could be described as a more 'expanded epiphany' where the protagonist undergoes a series of mental re-livings of major and minor dishonesties. Lounging in an armchair after the Christmas lunch, Gerald is self-induced into a hypnotic state where flashes of the past pass by his mind's eye. The important thing to notice is that Gerald 'sees' the past, catching hold of every detail without any emotionally charged fiction or the need to resist any undesirable detail. With Gerald it is a less troubled self-knowledge – he escapes the entire chunk of what Bernard went through with a shattering of self-image because of his non-commitment to the liberal's way of life. Gerald has led an ordinary life with ordinary aspirations and has nurtured no false notions about himself.

To return to Gerald's mental flashbacks, one finds him deeply in honest dialogue with both his personal life and private professional sphere. In the process Gerald identifies his mistake of having been evasive in almost all matters of his personal life and of having allowed his wife to have her way. When Gerald finds himself finally out of the trance of a reverie, the truth dawns on him like an honest beam of light. He realizes now that his life has been enveloped in 'suspicions engendered by the words of a hysterical woman' (*ASA* 184). A sense of great release follows and he now feels that he is in a position to 'walk or run if he chose' (*ASA* 184). The long-drawn epiphanic experience has given him the courage to "run". The self-knowledge does not shatter him as it shattered Bernard Sands but lends him the wisdom to look ahead.

Meg Eliot of *The Middle Age of Mrs Eliot* and Sylvia Calvert of *Late Call* (1964) are two female protagonists who suffer from the hiatus between childhood and adulthood in slightly different ways. In Meg's case it is the 'preserved innocence' of childhood that delimits adulthood whereas in the case of Sylvia Calvert it is a suppressed childhood that blocks adult self-realisation. Various critics have pointed out the close affinity between Meg Eliot and Sylvia Calvert although the differences in their personalities are as important as their similarities. Again, the epiphanic experiences that are a part of their later lives are qualitatively different too. Meg's could be compared to Gerald Middleton's whose phase was long-drawn and Sylvia's to Bernard Sands' that seemed to take place in an instant.

Meg Eliot is forty three, smart and sophisticated and belongs to the rich and fashionable set. She is associated with a charitable organization called "Aid to the Elderly." Outwardly Meg seems to be a fairly independent woman of the world but the reader is quick to realize that she has been nurturing a kind of 'preserved innocence' in her emotional overdependence on her husband, Bill. Her consciously guarded amnesia of the 'Genteel Penury' of her past is not so much a sin as is her extended infantile existence when she should have been a responsible self-dependent adult. Excessive self-indulgence seems to be Meg's sin. The precariousness of Meg's position is indicated by the image given to her by her friends – she has a house, servants, a flourishing barrister for a husband; in fact, she belongs to the group of the fashionable and lively rich and not to the 'stolid rich'. However, she has private misgivings and some premonitions of a deep-seated threat to her self-esteem are illustrated in the instance when, walking against the 'ghastly yellow buildings of London she feels like an exotic crane in flight' (*ME* 22). Reflexive self-irony instantly overtakes her and she pictures herself almost simultaneously more like some 'greedy, pecking stork.' She resembles Bernard Sands in her 'constant hardworking eagerness to fill life with use and pleasure,' confirming to the belief that 'to let life bore you' is the 'cardinal sin' (*HA* 56).

In the novel the active-passive dilemma, what Bergonzi explains as 'the familiar Wilcox-Schlegel opposition between the public life of busy achievement and the private life of spiritual cultivation'[9] is somewhat resolved in Meg's personality from the very start. She does not suffer from a bloated conscience and is able to enjoy herself. The dilemma is further resolved in the face of self-knowledge although it comes to her in stages as it did in Gerald Middleton's case. Wilson gives us a clue as to what to expect when he shows how her remarkable success as a socialite is intermittently nagged by her sense of inadequacy for emotional independence. Meg is saddened by her inner condition but is able to revive an escapist kind of happiness when she reads the well-charted worlds of Jane Austen, George Eliot, Trollope and Henry James. However, this is a very temporary kind of release and Meg's inner horror is reflected when she looks down upon the desert below on a night-flight to the Middle East. The 'frightening sadness of dead anonymous nature' grips her being to the core. No attempt to fictionalize her experience comes to her rescue. It is just no good – the Sahara below symbolically externalizes the 'Horror in Between.' Even Bill's scientific explanation of the desert does not pacify her acute discomfiture. She feels as solitary as Alexander Selkirk; once again she identifies herself with Lily Dale and others;

'only that born in a later century, she had avoided their defeats; but their high spirits and their hopes were hers exactly' (*ME* 81).

Meg's husband, Bill, is shot to death. With her husband's sudden death, Meg's patterned life dissolves into hopeless chaos and she enters a phase where the chaos of her mind matches her external condition. In Meg's case there is an extra dimension of pain experienced by the liberal's unobtrusive moral choices and the honest adjustment to oneself. It is on her return to England that Meg is really thrown into the job of reconstructing her new existence. In England she is united with her brother whom she has referred to as living in the 'ghastly Downs' at her farewell party. David possesses a Quietist philosophy of life. Non-interference is his first policy and his shut-out Nursery embedded in the remotest corners of the Sussex country evidences his philosophy of life.

Meg's new life with Bill puts her into a situation where she faces the displacement of values, the peril to self-identity, and the burden of guilt for failing in close personal relationships. *Anglo Saxon Attitudes* points out that insight alone is not enough and cannot be a goal in itself. In the *Middle Age of Mrs Eliot*, Meg Eliot must undergo a series of encounters that bring forth the difficulties of living within the limitations of society and, in particular, within the still narrower limitations of one's own being. Meg is a liberal of sorts but she firmly believes in social interaction and meaningful interference. It is for this reason that, despite its temptations, she finally decides to leave Andredaswood eventually. David and his homosexual friend, Gordon, have withdrawn themselves into an area of security where there are minimal chances of interference.

The differences in the personalities of David, Gordon, and Meg are beautifully depicted by Wilson. While Meg is recovering at Andredaswood from the shock in the initial months of her widowhood, David is also preparing himself for Gordon's medical report, which he knew would finally confirm his impending death. David feels that what is true of his own mental condition at this critical juncture is true of Meg's too. Meg goes back to London in an attempt to restart and reorganize her life once again but no amount of 'intelligent realism' makes people behave any better than they do. Although Meg's endeavours are rewarded with meaningful achievements, the road to recovery is not as easy as she would have wished. Her inner life is bogged with visions of old age and of menacing loneliness. The news of Gordon's death brings about a metamorphosis in Meg's personality. No longer did the coal-fire conjure up images that promised a falsely secure future:

> Gazing into the jutting, craggy landscape of the fire that flickered and glowed each instant, she was carried back to the thousand times she had peopled with her thoughts these burning caves and mountains snow-topped with wood-ash – Alice-like, drying her hair, or like Maggie Tulliver her book fallen to the floor (*ME* 278).

Meg's reunion with David in Book Three is rather forced but this brings about the last phase of Meg's intense metamorphosis. Initially, Meg and David are able to slide back into their childhood days with a shared bond of kindred grief. They also return to fiction for solace. On their trips to Brighton David talks about sex and his life with Gordon. Life is rather cosy with the beauty of Andredaswood to enhance everything. The kind of close, dependent relationship that Meg and David share has not escaped the notice of critics who have pointed out the awkwardness of such an association.[3] Meg too sees the futility and sinfulness of a 'cosy' relationship like this one. Meg's decision to leave is abrupt and is prompted by a guilty feeling that she is warping David's 'real living peace' into mere 'negetable ease' and 'creeping lethargy.' In Paul Bailey's words Meg's epiphanic moment comes when she chooses to 'opt out of the literary enterprise (which Meg and David) have got involved in – an enterprise, she sees with sudden clarity, as sterile and as cosy as her existence' (Bailey, 221). Meg's return to the London scene is not joyless. She still misses Bill but the desperation is gone – the ghosts of the past have fled and the reader has every reason to believe that Meg has a satisfactory life ahead of her.

The heroine of *Late Call* Sylvia Calvert is an apparently contented hotel manageress, and like Meg Eliot, she too has been well established in her profession. She and her husband Arthur are on the verge of retirement and their shifting to the New Town, Carshall, is full of apprehensions and unknown fears. The place as well as the prospect of living with their son's family makes them uneasy, to say the least. The Prologue constitutes a very significant part of the novel because it sets before us the theme of the story which in fact, revolves round the psychological world of Sylvia Calvert. In the Prologue Sylvia, the eldest Tuffield girl, is scolded and humiliated by Mrs. Longmore, a smart Chelsea lady of aesthetic and liberated outlook. However, in her honeyed utterances underlie the hostilities of the pre-Great War class system. The Chelsea lady's urban sensibilities are affronted and she indignantly chides the rustic "Tuffield" girl with epithets such as 'wicked' and 'dreadful' (106). Immediate recognition of Sylvia Calvert as the 'eldest Tuffield girl' is impossible in the first chapter and it is true that different readers established the identity link at different speeds. Mrs. Longmore has done enough harm and one finds that Sylvia has learnt the harsh lessons of childhood only too well. She has learnt that to "give" is the only philosophy of life. Self-fulfillment to her is criminal; in fact, her tragedy is born of having, what Wilson calls, a Calvinist conscience. She is wary and embarrassed, diametrically opposite to her irrepressible 'raffish old sport' type husband, Arthur. Sylvia has learnt from her mother: 'We're not important people' – and this is her retort to her husband's angry reaction over their callously mis-spelt surname, 'Culver' for "Calvert". During her farewell she feels uneasy and distrusts the praise showered on her by the residents of Palmeira Court. Such feelings have their roots in Mrs Longmore's rejection of her as a child. However, for Wilson, as for Arthur Miller in *Death of a Salesman*, 'attention must be paid to such a person.' And so, the ordinary woman's journey from winter to summer, from nobody to somebody, is traced with unusual empathy.

Sylvia Calvert is a person who is evasive of sentimentalism – she is like Bernard and Gerald in that she chooses to dwell upon more temporary issues. Like Meg she resorts to the characters of soap operas and tele-serials. And, although habitual fictional dependence is far from good, the value of myth to cope with life's problems cannot be denied outright.[3] In Sylvia's case however, although fiction helps her to cope with day-to day minor flaws it does not help her in any way to spark off any kind of self-worth.

The couple's arrival at their son, Harold's home, 'The Sycamores', is a big change and Sylvia, who has been used to "serving" others all her life is embarrassed by the physical gestures of kindness showered upon her by her grandchildren. The absence of any kind of living physical communication during childhood and Mrs Longmore's last minute reversal in attitude have cased in her mistrust of human warmth; in fact, this has developed into a mental block. Moreover, the temperature-regulated comfort of "The Sycamores" is not particularly liked by either Arthur or Sylvia nor do they like the other modern comforts. In fact, Sylvia feels all the more "stupid" because she cannot put herself to good use around the house. In the chapter entitled "New Year New Town New Life" Sylvia is seen to be recurrently groping in the dark for something or the other that would lend meaning to her life. She seems to be groping about something that she herself is not sure of. She gazes at the Midlands. 'The challenge of the Midlands is akin to that of the desert in Mrs Eliot, and Sylvia's gradual mastery of it, like Meg's, is a progress which parallels the loosening of the grip of obsessive images of her mind' (Shaw 100). Initially, Sylvia goes around Carshall looking for something to do but is not 'allowed' by Arthur or Harold. So, she continues to build her life around make-believe characters but her visits to town only provide temporary diversion from the more permanent issues of her existence. Moreover, whereas Sylvia has been over-taught in the lessons of loving others, she is unable to love herself. Like little Dorrit of Dickens' novel she believes in the maxim that 'blessed are the meek.'

The safety of the 'Sycamores' which symbolizes a world of external order is not potent enough to assuage the dark fears that envelop Sylvia. The images of worthlessness are disturbing and incessant. One identifies these mental gropings as a journey from darkness to light in the sense that they are an unconscious attempt made by the protagonist to come to terms with the past. In the beginning Sylvia is not able to understand her condition and her depression reaches near-suicidal proportions on that particular Good Friday: 'On this wet Good Friday Sylvia felt so low that she almost picked up the breadknife and made an end of it' (*LC* 182). Coincidentally, Sylvia's salvation begins on Easter Sunday. The old Scott's Easter Sunday sermon is consoling to Sylvia because it tells of the essential loneliness of human life. Moreover, the Sermon indicates the possibility of Grace as an answer to determinism. In his interview with Jack I. Biles, Wilson stated that religion does not play 'a very large part' in his book. However, he says that it is there in *Late Call* because he believes in the concept of Grace very much like E.M. Forster. But no, the Sermon does not magically lift Sylvia out of her deep depression.

Sylvia's morbid fancies reach a phantasmagoric climax just after she returns from church. In order to organize her feelings Sylvia walks down to the vast stretches of country. It becomes a place where the inner and outer, past and present, fiction and reality get synthesized. Sylvia's wanderings in the countryside take her back to an imaginative journey into the childhood world. Initially there are no magical results and she ends up with tired feet and 'laddered stockings.' However, as in Meg's case here too the 'recovery' takes place in imperceptible stages. Also, moods of epiphanic enlightenment are alternated by moods of self-doubt. The 'epiphanic moment' is very much awaiting her but the processing has to be complete. Sylvia's epiphany comes in a moment of action and not only mental thought.

On one of her walks Sylvia finds herself trapped in a bad storm that kind of objectifies her deepest fears. She is in a great dread of the weather but when she sees a child, Mandy Egan, in a worse fit of fear than her own, she forgets herself and rushes to bring the child to safety. In this very moment of kindness does Sylvia come out of all her apprehensions and deep buried anxieties. The act is symbolic and the associations are far-reaching – finally the protagonist reaches a wholesome state of existence. This is indeed a turning point in the life of Sylvia. Self knowledge is undoubtedly the means to understanding human life.

The epiphanies witnessed so far have had one moment or one-time modes in that there is one turning point from which the lives of the characters take a new turn. However, there are also places in Wilson's novels where he shows a multi-layered mode of perception or, if one could say, a series of epiphanies or 'multiple epiphanies'. Experienced one after the other, they help the protagonist to come full circle and deal with the situation they are in. *No Laughing Matter* (1967) and *As If By Magic* show how layers of perception help to show the right way. The fact that myth and literature can be both a positive and a negative influence on people is nothing new. Each novel of Wilson's has this to show. And, although knowledge of literature as counterfeit is a recurrent theme in many writings of the twentieth century, Wilson's treatment of it is far more quintessential.

As If By Magic depicts the spiritual evolution of two protagonists – the first is Hamo Langmuir and the other a twenty one year old female student, Alexandra Grant. A student of English literature, Alexandra imposes an order on life's experiences based on the literature that she has read. She is, in a way, out to redeem the post-war Waste Land with the fertility magic that T.S. Eliot envisaged. The two major literary influences on her life are J.R.R. Tolkien's *Lord of the Rings* and D.H. Lawrence's *Women in Love*. The first book inspires her to look for adventure and achievement and the second drives her to sort out the limitations of a triangular situation in love. Hamo Langmuir is a middle aged plant geneticist who becomes famous on account of a discovery of a rice variety that is called "Magic." He indulges in fictive homosexual fantasy both in his mind and in actuality. Just as Alexandra fantasizes so does Hamo, but his visions of physicality are more graphic and "clinical." Theater, sex, pop music and an interest in fashion were looked upon as magical remedies by people in the nineteen sixties. The technique of role-playing is extended by Alexandra to other areas of life but although there are moments of amusement and exhilaration there are signs of future boredom too. She finally gets weary of her experiments with life and sex in India and wants to return home to England leaving all the squalor and poverty behind.

However, she feels genuinely for the poor and deprived and her basic sanity does not allow her to be cut off from the rest of the world. The pursuit for a magical remedy is easily seen through after a series of disappointing adventures. The epiphanic moments come to her rescue at various instances. For example, while passing through the roads of Goa she observes that the churches, towers and domes of the West were still defying the natural 'disorder' of the tropical jungle. Also, Alexandra shows rare courage when chased by a mob and suddenly realizes that 'A story is a story is a story is a story even a good one like *The Lord of the Rings*' (*ABM* 386).

In a similar manner Hamo also experiences layers of awakening which are based primarily on humanism like they did in Alexandra's case. The sight of struggling farmers and hungry children make him feel inadequate. The magical remedies are sought by him in homosexual fantasy and other professional experimentation but the world at large is too powerful and real. A turning point in Hamo's life comes when Alexandra gives him the field glasses and he looks through them to witness the wonders of nature with which he had lost touch. In this manner Hamo awakens to a universal consciousness fully understanding his role as a responsible human being.

In *No Laughing Matter* we find the family of the six Matthews children grappling with the meaning of modern reality. Jean Sudrann observes that Wilson's characters keep on asking the same question: 'how do we know what is real?' And the novel keeps answering: 'Man makes his reality by self-conscious creation'(132). Once again, fictionality helps to define certain aspects of life. As devised and played out by the six brothers and sisters, "The Game" works at exploring the multiple facets of a single personality – the 'various unrelated persons,' which 'bob like corks inside a single self." It is also a device employed by the author to dramatize the past, offering the reader fresh insights into both the mimickers and the people who are mimicked. Each of the six brothers and sisters has been a victim of their Edwardian parents and are able to come to terms with the harm done only through the fictive mode of play-acting. The theme of fiction as a means to rearrange and reinterpret life's experiences runs through the novel like an organic solution. Each child who grows up comes to realize that neither a fictional representation of reality nor a gross representation of fact can be helpful in the apprehension of a human situation. For the children it is absolutely essential to get rid of the burden of their past but in a positive and wholesome manner. An automatic, new level of understanding is reached by them all. There is a radical change in their attitudes when they play the game for the last time. It becomes, one could say, a 'forced epiphany' but like all epiphanies it is organic and spontaneous nonetheless. In fact, this becomes a superb example where Wilson plays 'art against art' in order to bring about the total truth of a situation.

Wilson's last novel, *Setting the World on Fire* (1980) is an attempt made by the writer to objectify the instinct-intellect dichotomy. The entire narrative revolves round Tothill House and its occupants. Tothill House embodies the world of self-sufficient aristocracy where existential problems of day-to-day life are reduced to a minimum and therefore leaves Wilson with enough space to fully exploit the symbolic mode. Quite a major part of the symbolism revolves round the unique structure of this mansion that is based on two divergent varieties of architecture. One part, or rather the major portion of the house had been designed by Sir Roger Pratt, who based his pattern on regular, classical symmetry. Later on when Sir Francis Tothill inherited the house, it was modified with a Great Hall constructed by Captain John Vanbrugh, a famous playwright. The distinguishing feature of the Hall is that there is a sprawling painting by Verrio depicting Phaeton's chariot ride painted right across the ceiling. The painting shows Phaeton's progress from his taking the reins of the chariot of the sun, to his fall. Although the Phaeton myth is not as pervasive as the Judeo-Christian myth or other myths such as that of Faust or of the Fall, there is no denying that it also has an important place in Western art. Piers Mosson and Tom Mosson, the two heirs of Tothill Estate, are brought into direct parallelism with the two contrasting architectures. The polarity of the brothers lies in the elder brother's espousal of the Phaeton side that reflects the brave irregularity of genius and in the younger brother's espousal of the Pratt sensibility which represents order and proportion. However, Wilson is very clear in rejecting both extremes; he advocates neither unbridled freedom nor protective constraint but proposes a synthetic view.

Piers' identification with Phaeton is akin to the mythical role of all creative geniuses who dare defy even the gods. So inspired is Piers by the brave Phaeton that he dances naked in the Great Hall in a kind of celebration. On the other hand Tom is bewildered over the happy expression on the face of Phaeton even while falling to his death. Whereas Piers is all for variety and change in Tothill House Tom is obsessed with the thought of maintaining stability and order. During his career as a dramatist Piers is only too willing to take up the challenges of theatrical techniques. Tom, on the other hand, panics at the slightest defiance of order be it on the domestic front or on the theatrical one. However, both brothers realize the sanctity of the other in their own moments of epiphanic enlightenment. During a chaotic situation at the theater Tom is quick to locate the points of danger because of his alert and ordered mind. However, Tom loses his life in the bargain and courts the very chaos that had him gripped in terror all his life for the love of his brother, Piers. This is a moment of epiphany for Tom; he realises the significance of courting chaos in order to save his dear brother's life. Tom's undramatic life ends in a bid to save Piers, the heir to Tothill House. His Phaeton-like death resolves the dichotomy for once and for all. Tom may be accredited for his wonderful sacrifice that is born of a necessarily brave and courageous moral fibre, but Wilson himself sees him as an essentially 'passive' person who is 'a supportive force for those who are actually active'. In the ambulance the two brothers have their last snatches of conversation together. Piers promises Tom that he will not allow terrorism to put to rout 'art and shape'. The 'histrionic modern-day Phaeton' vows to protect and preserve the order and tradition that Tom so much revered. As Piers leaves the hospital and walks across the very same bridge that he and Tom had crossed so many times in the past, Piers momentarily assumes his brother's character:

> Every step that he took... seemed to shake the bridge, seemed to shake the world. The water flowing below, the starred sky above him.... What good were his wonderful Vanbrugh inventions in a dead chaotic universe? (*SWF* 296)

This epiphanic moment is one of the saddest moments of Piers' life – a gift from his brother forever.

To conclude, with the insights and perceptions that Angus Wilson's fiction has to offer the concept of 'epiphany' is used in a more secular mode. The original 'religious' connotation is of course at the centre of the experience but it also enables us to connect the ordinary with the sublime so that a direct human experience lends us the insight to probe deeper. The sublime lies at the bottom of all human experience that rejoices at the creation of God and helps us to resolve the dichotomy of human life without the need for us to reject this ultimate truth. It is this faith with which Angus Wilson's novels gently illustrate the belief that a conscious acceptance of the mixed nature of life with an ever-vigilant self-awareness can turn a fragmented existence into an integrated whole.

Notes

Texts referred to in this article have been abbreviated as follows:

The Old Men at the Zoo	OMZ
As If By Mazic	ABM
The Middle Age of Mrs. Eliot	ME
The Wild Garden: On Speaking of Writing	WG
Hemlock and After	HA
Anglo Saxon Attitudes	ASA
Late Call	LC
No Laughing Matter	NLM
Setting then World on Fire	SWF

2. See Wilson's article "Evil in the English Novel."
3. This Aspcet has been elaborated upon by Valeric A Shaw in "*The Middle Age of Mrs. Eliot* and *Late Call:* Angus Wilson's Traditionalism."

References

Bailey, Paul. "Meg and Sylvia." *Twentieth Century Literature* 292 (Summer 1983): 221.

Bergonzi, Bernard. "Between Nostalgia and Nightmare." *Critical Essays On Angus Wilson.* Ed. Jay L. Halio. Beston: G.K. Hall and Co. 1985.

The Oxford Companion to English Literature. Ed. Margaret Drabble 5th Ed. Oxford: Oxford UP, 1985. 750.

Shaw, Valerie A. *"The Middle Age of Mrs. Eliot* and *Late Call:* Angus Wilson's Traditionalism" Critical Essays, Ed. Jay L. Halio, 98-115.

Ludrann, Jean "The Lion and Unicorn: Angus Wilson's Triumphant Tragedy". *Critical Essays.* Ed. Jay L. Halio.

Wilson, Angus. *Anglo Saxon Attitudes.* London: Secker, Warburg, 1956

Wilson, Angus. *Hemlock* and After. Harmondsworth: Penguin, 1956.

Wilson, Angus. *The Middle Age of Mrs Eliot.* London: Secker, Warburg, 1958.

Wilson, Angus. *The Old Men at the Zoo.* London: Secker, Warburg, 1961.

Wilson, Angus. "Evil in the English Novel." *The Listener.* LXVIII. 27 December, 1962: 1079-1080.

Wilson, Angus. *The Wild Garden: On Speaking of Writing.* Berkeley: U of California P, 1965.

Wilson, Angus. *As If By Magic.* Harmondsworth: Penguin, 1976.

Wilson, Angus. *No Laughing Mather.* London: Grafton Books, 1979.

Wilson, Angus. *Setting the Would on Fire.* London: Secker, Warburg, 1980.

Wilson, Angus. *Late Call* London: Canada, 1982.

23 Patriarchal Agency and the Agents of Patriarchy

Re-reading Angela Carter's Feminism

Rajul Bhargava

Despite her two genuinely revisionist novels: *The Passion of New Eve* (1977) and *Nights at the Circus* (1985), both of which aim at enhancing female power and countering the inscription of patriarchy, Angela Carter fears that she herself is an agent in furthering the cause of subversive male hegemony. Such a worry is prompted by her appreciation of the erotic and her sense of the feminine as a cultural construct – she fears that she might be misunderstood if only the preamble is read without linking it to the conclusions she arrives at – which literally deconstruct the social fictions that regulate the lives of women. Robert Clark (1987) is one among those who question to what extent Carter's fictions 'offer their readers a knowledge of patriarchy...' and to what extent they 'fall back into reinforcing patriarchal attitudes' (2). Then Patricia Dunker (1984) is another who finds Carter's inhibited sense of the erotic and her retelling of the traditional fairy tales and folk tales 'a re-production rather than an alternative to the sexist-psychology'(6).

However, these fears are misplaced and the assessments faulty for Carter tries her hardest to shatter women's 'mind-forg'd manacles', and to smash, as Hariet Blodgett (1994) says, 'the tablets of patriarchy to fashion much better new mosaics from their shards' (51). Blodgett further asserts that since at least the seventies Carter's fictions have been actively fashioning new images to bring women to knowledge of their gendering and, increasingly, to a sense of power Carter believes is rightly theirs.

In an interview with Anna Katsovos (1994), Carter emphatically points out that her task as a writer is to find out what 'certain configurations of imagery in our society, in our culture, really stand for, what they mean' underneath the kind of semi-religious coating that the world at large has given them. Carter wants to understand these constructions so that she can undermine their very fallacious constructs. As we all know, to deconstruct a particular ideology and a particular set of conventions, it is necessary to invoke those very ideologies and conventions that one wishes to subvert. What one has to do then, she says, 'is to change the rules and make a new game' – and that is really what her avowed project is all about as a writer.

In *Heroes and Villains* (1969) Carter takes up the game of demythologizing which is part of her permanent critique of patriarchy subsumed under a larger project of 'decolonizing our language and our habits of thought' (1983, 75). But in order to do this she feels that she must find out how women are represented, find out more about what their real existential status is, and even if it means using traditional figures of patriarchically constructed mythology – Circe, Leda, Helen – or using images from men manufactured pornography, these are necessary evils in the enterprise of feminist self-assertion for these stories have to be first told in order that they be re-invented *'in the service of women'*. In her most overt act of literary criticism, a Foucauldian study of pornography, *The Sadeian Woman* (1979), Carter explores the culturally determined nature of 'woman', arguing that 'pornographers are the enemies of women only because contemporary ideology or pornography does not encompass the possibility of change, as if we were slaves of history and not its makers, as if sexual relations were not necessarily an expression of social relations' (3). Carter's texts constantly seek not only to investigate the social and sexual fictions that regulate human lives, but also to provide new fictions, for, as

Beth A. Boehm (1995) also points out, 'by revealing the conventions that rule both human behaviour and literature, Carter posits the possibility of change' (38). Carter has consistently rejected the patriarchal myths, including what Eva Karpinski calls 'the utopian elements of myth and mythic element of utopian thought' for these are but 'social fictions that regulate our lives' and Carter dismisses them as 'consolatory nonsense or 'extraordinary lies designed to make people unfree' (1983, 71). And for the cause of freeing oneself from the patriarchal utopian myths Carter resorts to a dystopian romance in *Heroes and Villains* which also proves to be a suitable vehicle for Carter's didactic allegory of the relationship between the sexes, an allegory, that Karpinksi adds, 'uses the utopian ideas of Jean-Jacques Rousseau in order to rewrite the myth of the Fall as it structures Western representations of the social order and sexual difference' (139).

It is in 'the lumber-room of the Western European imagination' (1983, 72) that Carter finds most of her material – in the master narratives like the Bible, in Freud's Oedipal scenario, in Levi-Strauss's anthropology, Matthew Arnold's *Culture and Anarchy*, Swift's *Gulliver's Travels*, Well's *Time Machine,* Conrad's *Heart of Darkness*, Gothic romances such as *Wuthering Heights* and *Frankenstein*, in the Cupid and Psyche myths, and fairy tales like 'The Beauty and the Beast'. All these texts, she points out, dwell on the destructive forces of control that leads to the domination of the other, and in *Heroes and Villians* this force is seen to dwell within patriarchal discourse which dominates the gendered other.

In *Heroes and Villians* Carter describes the surviving society after a nuclear-war which comprises an elite group – the Professors, a nomadic group, the Barbarians, and those mutilated by radiation, the Out People. Each group is antagonistic to the other and this is based on a fear psychosis. Marianne, the protagonist, a Professor's daughter, gets pregnant with a Barbarian, Jewel, and eventually takes over as the leader of his group – Tiger Lady – thus posing a direct polemic with Rousseau's philosophy wherein he 'naturalizes' women's subordination and entrenches the patriarchal model of the family. In her ironic reversal of Rousseau's fantasy of feminity, Carter puts under scrutiny 'the social utopia of the prelapsarian 'primitive' state of nature and the heterosexual utopia of the patriarchal social contract' (Karpinski, 140). Moreover, Marianne dramatizes self-conscious desire as a force within patriarchal discourse, a colonizing drive locked into the dialectic of sameness and difference. It is this drive that aligns Carter with other utopian feminists who base their fiction on tales of 'disabling and enabling conditions of desire' – disabling since the body, the physical manifestation of desire, is reduced to a surface that can be inscribed, with acts of brutality, rape, abuse; and enabling, because the disabling generates a transgressive desire to change the system and subvert its structure, to challenge patriarchal categories, to refuse to endorse victimization.

In *Nights at the Circus* Carter explores the possibility of a feminist metafictional text which. can constantly interrogate the conventions that regulate literature and human behaviour, and suggests Boehm, 'transforming ourselves into Carter's authorial readers requires that we cross the threshold to the unknown, suspending not our disbelief but rather our attachment to androcentric interpretive strategies' (48). Set at the end of 1899, in anticipation of a new century, Carter parodies that resilient nineteenth-century image of the 'angel in the house': the incredible fiction of a pure, modest, giving, servitor without needs or libido of her own. Virginia Woolf immortalized that phantom in her "Professions for Women" as the great obstacle for the woman writer; Carter instead revitalizes her as an inspiration for all women, in the person of a female who is good to herself. Thus Carter subverts Coventry Patmore's original vision of the angel, and as said earlier, Carter's frequent method is to take male authors' images and use them to feminist ends. Utilizing another favorite technique, Carter literalizes the fantastic male construct. A circus performer reared in a brothel, Carter's 'angel' is the winged Sophie, called Feathers but better known as 'Fevvers, the most famous aerialiste of the day; her slogan, "Is she fact or is she fiction?' 'In Paris they called me l'Ange Anglaise, The English Angel'. In a further tribute to the fiction that is patriarchal mythology, like Helen of Troy, Fevvers was not born but ostensibly 'hatched'; behind her, that is, as she is a female, lies a cultural valorization of rape in Leda's story, a painting of which is prominently displayed in the brothel.

A towering figure – 6 feet 2 – with ample bosom, large and vulgar gestures and appetites, and a generous heart, Fevvers is a powerful female in all respects. In her youth she gets to play the role of a statue in the 'house': Winged Victory, with a sword in hand, a weapon; it anticipates her future role. Her most important weapon as an adult proves to be not the small sword she secretes in her bosom but her faith in herself and her knowledge of her own desires; she is truly an autonomous self.

Fevvers's foster mother, Lizzie, like all the whores in the house is a closet suffragist, who sees in Fevvers' gift of wings a emblem of 'the New Age in which no women will be bound down to the ground', and Fevvers herself, who comes to realize that the free mind is any woman's wings, finally subscribes to a vision of such a glorious new world in which the woman who is 'tied hand and foot with the grisly bonds of ritual, will suffer no more of it; she will tear off her mind forg'd manacles, will rise up and fly away' – Carter's quintessential goal for women. Fevvers envisions the day when her winged self will be 'the female paradigm, no longer an imagined fiction but a plain fact'. Since Carter had set herself to deconstructing patriarchal imagery, throughout this novel she repeatedly recasts male images in female terms, doing what supposedly could not be done without becoming ridiculous but which poses no problem in a fantasy world. Fevvers, for example, can recognize herself becoming 'a female Quixote'. Carter substitutes for images of male identification images of women's strength through community, a value she has not before especially acknowledged. Thus, her whores are not only Shavian intelligent women forced into trade by economic necessity but eminently caring and sympathetic.

This champagne-guzzling, bawdy entrepreneur, a feminist picaro has the ability to survive cruel economic and social conditions. As Carter says with respect of the prostitute in *The Sadeian*

Woman, 'At least the girl who sells herself with her eyes open is not a hypocrite, and, in a world with a cash-sale ideology, that is a positive, even a heroic virtue' (55). Just as revisionary as is the masculine bias of this heroic quest: 'We shall set boldly forth and rescue ourselves' (244), so is Carter's treatment of the love plot. Rachel Blau DuPlessis in *Writing Beyond the Ending* (1985) tells us that the quest for women in a love plot was finite, 'we learn that any plot of self-realization was at the service of the marriage plot and was subordinate to, or covered within the magnetic power of that ending' (6). Although the marriage plot is the subject of a discussion near the ending of *Nights at the Circus*, Fevvers refuses to debate its significance saying 'I'm not in the mood for literary criticism' (244). However, forced to contemplate the power of literary conventions that seek to end women's stories with marriage, Fevvers is further terrified of that eventuality which would tie her to the ground and empty her bank accounts. At the end of the novel, though Carter does unite the lovers, not of course in marriage, she does so in a self conscious, metafictional way that Beth Boehm explains as: 'by drawing explicit connections between marriage as a literary device and marriage as a social convention' (42).

Many critics including Mars-Jones have misread Carter's reference to Yeats' "The Circus Animals' Desertion" when Fevvers describes Madame Schreck's museum of female freaks as 'this lumber room of feminity, this rag-and-bone shop of the heart' as the power of the androcentric. But Linda Hutcheon in *The Politics of the Postmodern* (1989) points out that the parodic echoes of *Pericles*, *Hamlet* and *Gulliver's Travels* along with the quotation from Yeats are all 'ironic feminizations of traditional or canonic male representations of the so-called generic human – 'Man'. This is the kind of politics of representation that parody calls to our attention' (98). Similarly, Fevvers' help to the abused Mignon whom she assumes to be her lover Walser's lover too, is often misunderstood. In feminist and also metafictional terms Mignon is one who has no voice of her own, no history she can ascribe to herself, has no present and a 'future too terrible to contemplate' (140), and the succour that Fevvers gives her is like giving voice to those who exist on the margins of the dominant culture and dominant literary structures. What goes unnoticed is that Carter wants us to re-read *Nights at the Circus* by reversing our androcentric reading strategies and recognize that it is not only the creation of a new Helen, more free, more confident and more creative, but the 'more interesting transformation actually occurs to her male reader the American journalist, the skeptical verifier of facts, whose disguise disguises nothing' (45). He comes to realise that identity 'is constructed through both the fictions we are told and the fictions we tell' (Boehm 45). It is he who is reconstructed at the end of the novel. His earlier version of himself is:

> I am Jack Walser, an American citizen. I joined the circus of Colonel Kearney in order to delight my reading public with accounts of a few nights at the circus and, as a clown, performed before the Tsar of All the Russians, to great applause. (What a story!) I was derailed by brigands in Transbaikalia and lived as a wizard among the natives for a while (God, what a story!) Let me introduce my wife, Mrs. Sophie Walser, who formerly had a successful career on the music-hall stage under the name of –' (293-94).

It undergoes a change as the clock strikes midnight of the first day of the new century:

> Jack, ever an adventurous boy, ran away with the circus for the sake of a bottle blonde in whose hands he was putty since the first moment he saw her... And now, hatched out of the shell of unknowing by a combination of a blow on the head and a sharp spasm of erotic ecstasy, I shall have to start all over again (294).

The earlier stance was a typical nineteenth century patriarchal narrative, and the later of the 'constructed' re-imaging that Carter proposes of 'a new man' (281).

And yet again, in *The Passion of New Eve,* Carter uses antimythic premises in her symbol formation. Thus this novel, even more vividly, enacts the change in her writing, a turn towards an avowed criticism of patriarchal culture. *The Passion* is also a dystopian fantasy that locates her militant women in the chaotic sixties who rationalize: 'Our external symbols must always express the life within us... since that life has generated them...' and 'a critique of these symbols is a critique of our lives' (5). The book explicitly states Carter's stand in refusing to accept the androgynous nature of women which posits reductive gender roles.

The novel literalizes de Beauvoir's classic formulation in *The Second Sex*, 'One is not born, but rather becomes, a woman' (6). So the male English visitor and chauvinist Evelyn is surgically and most psychically refashioned as 'Eve' after her capture by an Amazonian tribe of desert dwellers. The plot turns on the fact that, since adolescence Evelyn has been enamored of the cinematic image of Tristessa de St Ange, '*Our Lady of the Sorrows*', purportedly the world's most beautiful woman and the very emblem of female suffering. The point is obvious enough: the romantic image of suffering may be delightful as a cultural myth for men but proves appalling when, as a woman, Eve is obliged literally to experience it. This gender revision is Carter's way to foreground male means to female ends, a parody of female science-fiction cum fertility myth, seasoned with a dash of Freudian Oedipal myth and Lacanian power symbols as Blodgett points out.

The transformation takes place at the hands of Beulah, the desert dwellers, whose leader is a huge and many-breasted, black great goddess, Mother, a skilled plastic surgeon. From the hands of the antiphallocentric Beulah, Eve escapes only to be captured by another desert cult whose leader is Zero, the macho man incarnate who hates and degrades women. Zero is a sadistic rapist but has turned to be a demigod in the eyes of his seven wives who have chosen to deify his sexuality as their defense from death. Lest she be found out, Eve plays at her gender-role and Carter here points to the moral of the story: 'This intensive study of feminine manners, as well as my everyday work about the homestead, kept me in a state of permanent exhaustion. I was tense and preoccupied; although I was a woman, I was now also passing for a woman, but, then, many women born spend their whole lives in just such imitations' (101). Her point that gender is a meaningless, socially imposed category is made most strikingly, however, through the revelation that Tristessa is really a man, though 'seduced by the notion of a woman's being, which is negativity' (137). No wonder then that she – Tristessa, incarnation of he – Tristessa's aspirations for woman, was so potent as it; she embodied purely an image of male desire. When Zero forces Eve to dress up as a man and marry Tristessa in a grotesque wedding ceremony, 'it was a double wedding – both were the bride, both the groom' (135): a consummation Carter advocates, though custom forbids. Eve's 'passion' is both her suffering and her desire; that she may know both, Tristessa, before Carter kills him off, gratifies Eve with her first experiences of true, erotic love and – in an arid desert rather than the fertile garden of traditional iconography – impregnates her as neither Mother nor Zero was able to do.

Eventually Eve makes a heroic journey through caves and into prehistory in search of the Mother only to find that 'Mother, having borne her,...abandons her daughter forever' (186), because the nurturing mother is a patriarchally constructed myth too. Yet Beulah's teaching that one must reach back to one's sources proves true; and having returned to her uterine origins, Eve, in a 'Speleological apotheosis of Tiresias' (186), finds her self. Therefore the ending leaves the resilient Eve ready to embark from American shores, praying, in the last sentence, 'Ocean, ocean, mother of mysteries bear me to the place of birth' (191). She seeks to return to England, that is, and there give birth but seeks also, says 'mother of mysteries,' to discover what else the unconscious waters can generate. For the New Eve, it finally becomes apparent, is not only Evelyn transformed but Carter herself: the androgynous symbol-maker. The reader has experienced her metamorphosis from a writer trained in male paradigms and reveling in male fantasies to a feminist who has learned to live and respond as a female without losing her insight into maleness.

Since 'female plots and plausibilities assume that women writers cannot or will not obey the rules of fiction' (Nancy Miller

44), Carter's deviations are to be seen as conscious rejections of the 'obvious' androcentric 'truths'. Her fiction falls into the speculative 'what if' genre, that is, a system of continuing inquiry especially into the complicated questions about what we expect from human relationships and what we expect from gender; only she signifies differently by inserting a counter-discourse to the dominant patriarchal ones. And in this way she symbolically rehearses two forms of the possible subversion of patriarchy, both already inscribed – through prohibition and injunction – within the system itself subverting patriarchal agency.

References

Blodgett, Harriet. "Fresh Iconography: Subversive Fantasy by Angela Carter" *The Review of Contemporary Fiction* Vol. 14, 1994: 49-56.

Boehm, A Beth. "Feminist Metafiction and Androcentric Reading Strategies; Angela Carter's Reconstructed Reader". *Critique*. Vol. 37, 1995. 35-41.

Carter, Angela. *The Passion of New Eve*. New York: Harcourt Brace Jovanovich, 1977.

Carter, Angela. *The Sadeian Woman and the Ideology of Pornography*. New York: Pantheon Books, 1978

Carter, Angela. *Heroes and Villains*, Harmondsworth: Penguin Books, 1981.

Carter, Angela. "Notes from the Front Line". *On Gender and Writing*. Ed. Micheline Wandor. London: Pandora Press, 1983. 69-76.

Carter, Angela. *Nights at the Circus*, London: Chatto and Windus, 1984.

Clark, Robert. "Angela Carter's Desire Machine." *Women's Studies* 14(1987): 147-156.

Duplessis, Rachel Blau. *Writing Beyond Ending*. Bloomington: Indiana UP, 1985.

Duncker, Patricia. "Re-Imaging The Fairy Tales: Angela Carter's Bloody Chambers." *Literature and History* 10(1984):6.

Hutcheon, Linda. *The Politics of Postmodernism*. London: Routledge, 1989.

Karpinski, Eva C. "Signifying Passion: Angela Carter's *Heroes and Villains* as a Dystopian Romance." *Utopian Studies*. Vol. II, 2000: 137-152.

Katsovos, Anna. "An Interview with Angela Carter." *Review of Contemporary Fiction* 14. 3 (Fall 1994): 11-17.

Mars-Jones, Adam. "From Wonders to Prodigies." *Times Literary Supplement.* September 28, 1984: 1083.

Miller, Nancy K. "Plots and Plausibilities in Women's Fiction." in *Subject to Change: Reading Feminist Writing.* New York: Columbia, 1988.

Rousseau, Jean-Jacques. *The First and Second Discourses.* Ed. and trans. Victor Gourevitch. New York: Harper and Row, 1990.

Contributors

Jasbir Jain, Director, IRIS is currently engaged in research on Indigenous Traditions of Feminism in India. She has published extensively in a wide range of subjects including drama, feminist thought and diaspora studies. Modern Indian Writing, Postcolonial and Feminist Theories and Contemporary American Drama are her major interests.

Prafulla C. Kar is Convener, Forum on Contemporary Theory, Baroda and Editor of the *Journal of Contemporary Thought*. He was Dy. Director at American Studies Research Center, Hyderabad, and Chairperson, Department of English, M.S. University, Baroda.

Sudha Rai, Professor, Department of English, University of Rajasthan. Rai has worked on Expatriate Sensibility and on teaching material. She is currently working on tracing matrilineages.

R.K. Kaul (1928-2003) was educated at Lahore and Delhi before working for a degree from Oxford. Professor Kaul obtained his doctoral degree from London University. He worked at University College, Hoshiarpur and shifted with the Department to Chandigarh, Panjab. From 1963 till his retirement in 1988, he was at the University of Rajasthan, Jaipur. A distinguished scholar, he was thorough and meticulous in every way. A Visiting Fellow at Yale University in 1971, Emeritus Professor at the University of Rajasthan (1988-89), and Fellow of the IIAS, Shimla, he published several books, among which are *Studies in William Jones: An Interpreter of Oriental Literature, The Augustans* and *Nirad C. Chaudhari*.

Santosh Gupta, Professor, taught at the Department of English, University of Rajasthan. Her major interests are in modern fiction, British, American and Indian. Currently she is working on Modern Prison Narratives.

Shaila Mahan worked on the Poetry of Nissim Ezekiel for her doctoral dissertation. She is posted at the Directorate, Rajasthan College Education. She is engaged in research on Indian Women's Writing.

Charu Mathur teaches English at the Maharani's College, University of Rajasthan. Her doctoral thesis was on Modern American Drama. She is now working on Indian Writing in English.

Preeti Bhatt is on the faculty of English, Sant Jayacharya College, Jaipur. She worked on Muriel Spark for her doctoral degree. She is now engaged in research on Indian Fiction in English.

Nidhi Singh teaches at the Maharani's College, University of Rajasthan. Her doctoral research was on Australian Fiction and Randolph Stow. Her currant interests are in Postcolonial theory and literature.

Sudha Shastri is a faculty member at the school of Humanities and Social Sciences at IIT, Mumbai. Her doctoral research was on 'Intertextuality and Victorian Studies'. Her current areas of interest are postmodernist fiction and theory and Indian Writing in English.

Mini Nanda is Associate Professor, Department of English, University of Rajasthan. She has worked on Spatial metaphors in Graham Greene. Currently she is working on the social and cultural contexts of modern Indian Women's Writing.

Bandana Chakrabarty teaches English at Government College, Kala Dera (Rajasthan). She worked on the short stories of Alice Munero for her doctoral degree.

Urmil Talwar is on the faculty of English at the B.G.D. Government Girls' College, Shahpura (Rajasthan). Her doctoral research was on "The Role of Public Schools in Shaping the Literary Culture of England during the 1920's and 1930's".

Veena Singh, Professor and formerly Chairperson, Department of English, University of Rajasthan. She worked for her Ph.D. on Nineteenth Century Women Writers.

Supriya Agarwal teaches English at Khandelwal Girls' College, Jaipur. Her specialisation is in Nineteenth Century Writing, Currently she is researching on the fiction of Charlotte Perkins Gilman.

Krishna Sharma is posted at the Directorate of Rajasthan Collage Education. Her areas of research are Indian Writing in English.

Madhuri Chatterjee teaches English at Subodh College, Jaipur. Currently she is working on women's autobiographies.

Ila Rathor did her doctoral work on Rape Metaphor in Colonial Encounters. She teaches English at Government College, Bilaspur, Himachal Pradesh.

Vijaya Singh teaches English at the Government College at Chandigarh. She did her doctoral research on the films on E.M. Foster's Novels. Her current interests are in Indian Poetry and Fiction. She also writes Poetry.

Joya Chakravarty, Associate Professor, Department of English, University of Rajasthan. Her doctoral research was on the Fiction of Charles Dickens. She is currently working on Man-Woman Relationships in Modern Indian Writing in English.

Manveen Brar is currently working for her doctoral degree on Female Imagination in the short stories of Jean Rhys, Muriel Spark and Doris Lessing. She is appointed in the Rajasthan State Education Services.

Aruna Pandey is on the faculty at Rajasthan College, University of Rajasthan. She worked for her doctoral degree on the novels of Angus Wilson.

Rajul Bhargava is Professor and Chairperson of the Department of English, University of Rajasthan. Her areas of specialisation are linguistics, Language Teaching and Translation Studies. She is also interested in Indian Writing in English.